ROBIN HOOD

For Margaret, again

ROBIN HOOD

A Complete Study of the English Outlaw

Stephen Knight

BLACKWELL
Oxford UK & Cambridge USA

First published 1994
Reprinted 1995

Blackwell Publishers, the publishing imprint of
Basil Blackwell Ltd
108 Cowley Road
Oxford OX4 1JF, UK

Basil Blackwell Inc.
238 Main Street
Cambridge, Massachusetts 02142
USA

British Library Cataloguing in Publication Data
A CIP catalogue record for this book is available from the British Library.

Library of Congress Cataloging-in-Publication Data
Knight, Stephen.
Robin Hood : a complete study of the English outlaw / Stephen Knight.
p.   cm.
Includes bibliographical references and index.
ISBN 0–631–17219–X. — ISBN 0–631–19486–X (pbk.)
1. Robin Hood (Legendary character)   2. English literature—Middle
English, 1100–1500—History and criticism.   3. English literature—History
and criticism.   4. Ballads, English—History and criticism.   5. Outlaws—
England—Fiction.   6. Outlaws in literature.   I. Title.
PR2129.K58 1994
820.9'351—dc20   94–4008
                                                          CIP

Typeset in 11½ on 13pt Garamond
by Graphicraft Typesetters Ltd, Hong Kong
Printed in Great Britain by Hartnolls Ltd, Bodmin, Cornwall

This book is printed on acid-free paper

Contents

List of Illustrations

Preface

Both common sense and critical theory warn that writers are never separate from what is written, but the process of producing this book has been more involved with its topic than might have been expected.

As a whole the Robin Hood myth is insistently opposed to authority, and the origins of this study were in a form of dissent. After completing a study of the tradition of King Arthur, when teaching a course on the British ballads I was struck by the resemblances between the myths of the outlaw and the king, but stimulated to research on Robin Hood by the fact that his tradition was without readily accessible texts or any serious literary study. Royalty obviously ruled, and the forest figure was a cultural fugitive, deserving some scholarly support.

There proved to be further detailed relations between the topic of this book and the process of its making. Research on this long-lasting, widely-spread outlaw myth has occupied a number of years, and also places of varying appropriateness: Nottingham, York and London all have a direct place in the myth; Sydney and Melbourne breathe their own versions of elusive independence, with living respect for Robin Hood's bushranging descendants. Then came a move to De Montfort University in England's East Midlands, where the pervading presence of the Robin Hood tradition has come curiously close, and not just because Simon de Montfort himself appears in Robin Hood narratives by Anthony Munday and G.P.R. James. More specifically, this book was written in a village that once belonged to no one less than the Earl of Huntingdon and is also adjacent to the old royal forest of Barnsdale, a place identical in name to that in Yorkshire long linked to the hero, but with its own strong connections to the myth (see p. 31). The saying 'Robin Hood in Barnsdale stood' had a disconcerting resonance as this book about the hero grew, on its ghostly screen, within bowshot of a fugitive place bearing just the name of his earliest location.

If the essence and setting of the outlaw myth appeared to permeate its own study, the method of approach also proved intrinsic to a figure whose narratives insist on communality, so much so that the highly personalized form of the novel has found it hard to handle this unindividualistic character. Just as collectivity ensures the security of the outlaw group, there are many hands to be traced in the writing of this book, and while I accept the responsibility of calling them together (as Robin does when in distress) I wish to thank them in the ballads' spirit of culminating festival. First thanks go to Lucy Sussex, scholarly researcher from Melbourne, and then to what can only be called a band of others: my thanks for their expert and generous contributions are due to Marilyn Butler, Philip Carpenter, Helen Cooper, Peter Davison, Michele Field, Douglas Gray, John Hirsh, Paula Jacobs, Alex Jones, Veronica Kelly, Pat Kirkham, Gunther Kress, Alan Love, Andrew McNeillie, Ken Ruthven, Judith Smith, Sir Michael Tippett, A.R. Traylen, Paul Wells and Nicholas Wright. No scholar will be surprised at my warm thanks to the skilful librarians who have helped me trace materials through the thickets of popular literature, especially at Sydney's Fisher Library, Melbourne's Baillieu and State Public Library, in Los Angeles the Huntington (again that name), the Bodleian at Oxford, Cambridge University Library, De Montfort's Kimberlin Library and (an especially rewarding deep forest) the British Library.

Travelling tradesmen and clerics used to provide at arrow-point the finance for Robin Hood's activities; the modern scholar aims at nothing worse than funding applications. Ready sources of what Leigh Hunt called, in a Sherwood context, 'plump new coin' have been the University of Melbourne (a compensation for its first Chancellor's condemning to death Ned Kelly), De Montfort University and, with the most laden mules of all, the Australian Research Council, who funded inquiries for two years.

The project that these agencies have so handsomely assisted intends to be a survey and analysis of all the Robin Hood materials that are still in some way available; the study is 'complete' in the sense that I have examined everything accessible to me. Not all the materials studied are discussed in detail; even a generous publisher's sense of time and literary space might be over-extended by that aspiration. But there is still a very full coverage of the tradition, and the only omissions are elements that seemed to suggest no major or innovative point – examples of such deliberately overlooked material would be the sub-Georgian song series *Robin Hood and the Greenwood Gang* by Philippa Frischmann and Philip Lane (1981), several of the pot-boiling mid-Victorian imitations of Pierce Egan's *Robin Hood and Little John* (1840), or many of the school plays and children's anthologies that flourished early in this century. There is reason to be fully inclusive with the earlier periods, where material is usually both rare and enigmatic, and while the analysis of those parts of the tradition is itself very full, a list of all references to Robin Hood up to 1600, collected by Lucy Sussex, is printed as an appendix.

Just as the outlaw story is always in some way social rather than private or merely aesthetic in direction, the overall aim of this study has been to assess the sociocultural significance of all these Robin Hood phenomena, to see how ideas of authority and resistance to it have been reshaped in and for different times and places over five centuries, up to the immediate present. Robin Hood is still alive in all the genres available to modern consumers; this powerful tradition retains considerable and continuing importance as a way to organize and express ideas about authority. A recent musical asserted that Robin is 'the hero that lives in you all'; modern sociocultural theory would argue that we actually live through such myths and they can direct our behaviour. The Poll Tax rioters broke into Nottingham Council Chamber disguised in hoods of Lincoln green.

In keeping with the wide dissemination of the Robin Hood tradition, I have sought to make this book generally accessible, and have I hope eschewed the sheriff-like tendencies found in some modern critical writing to incarcerate thought in reader-hostile language. For the same reason I have sought to make the referencing of material accessible but not overbearing; the text is not studded with numbers or citational asides, but after an initial reference to author and year, amplified fully in the bibliography, I have given only such references to volume, page or line (if they exist) as will help locate further quotations, and as far as is possible I have referred to reliable editions that are reasonably available, at least in major libraries.

Two interrelated specific objectives are behind the whole book: one is to raise the social meaning of the tradition of Robin Hood for public

discussion; the second is to make widely available for such consideration the materials of the tradition, so that others can continue the
investigation from the point to which my own skills and the assistance
of others have brought that analysis.

Some of those others demand final mention. Like any social bandit,
Robin Hood had no family, though when in the sixteenth century he
was gentrified into being a dispossessed earl he did acquire a lady of
suitable rank. I have enjoyed neither the liberty nor the misery of
domestic isolation; my own family spent a good deal of time in the
Robin Hood forests, and have not always thought it a picnic. Nevertheless, Elizabeth has maintained her usual dialectic of curiosity and
support; David directed video technicalities and was a legitimating
presence at many child-oriented films and plays; Margaret, as the
dedication indicates, has as ever been that enlivening partner needed
by any outlaw, or any writer.

Exton, 1993

The publishers have made every effort to trace all copyright holders,
but if any have been inadvertently overlooked, the publishers will be
pleased to make the necessary arrangement at the just opportunity.

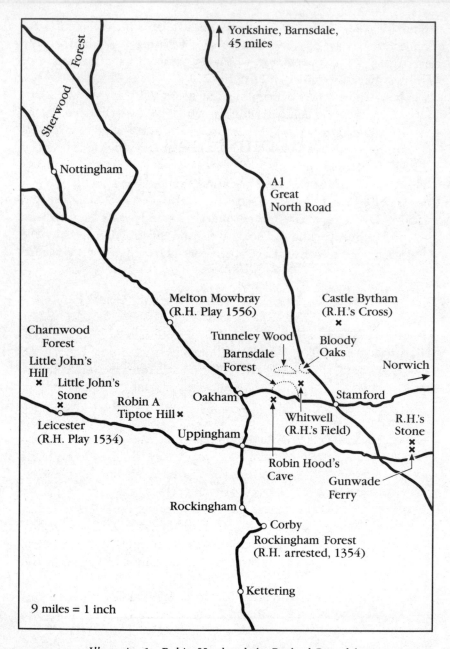

Illustration 1 Robin Hood and the Rutland Barnsdale

1

'Many Men Speak of Robin Hood': Versions of the Hero

1.1   THE STRUCTURES OF THE TRADITION

Robin Hood is the only antique hero to be mythologically alive today. Alexander has faded into classical mists; Arthur is a figure of costume melodrama. The medieval kings celebrated by Shakespeare are now no more than backward-looking references. King Alfred, the most genuinely heroic of all English royalty, is scarcely a name to most twentieth century people.

But they will know about Robin Hood. Hardly a week passes without some journalistic reference to him as a noble thief or a brave opponent of misdirected power; films, television and children's books all keep the ideal outlaw before everybody's eyes, an image of daring response to unfair authority.

Intriguing, inspiring, amusing and invigorating, the figure of Robin Hood represents essentially a higher form of law, a thief who only steals from those who should not possess so much. This concept has power in all periods, and its strength seems only to increase in the present world.

But the hero's own authority has areas of weakness. In terms of 'high culture', the English outlaw is almost invisible. While everyone has heard of Robin Hood, there is no authoritative literary source — very few people know what has been actually written about the hero; no Malory or Tennyson has appeared to provide a transcendental summary of the story at large. While major writers have on a number of

1

occasions dealt with the tradition, the result has either been judged a failure (Tennyson's *The Foresters* is a striking example), or the product has been marginal to their own work (Keats's sprightly verse letter on Robin Hood or Ben Jonson's unfinished masque *The Sad Shepherd*), or the work has been deliberately removed from the Robin Hood world – Shakespeare's *As You Like it* is a consciously non-Robin Hood play, Scott's *Ivanhoe* reduces the radical rebel to a non-commissioned officer in a nationalistic saga.

A sense that the tradition was never shaped for literary grandiosity strengthens in the face of the fact that of some forty novels that draw directly on the Robin Hood tradition, very few have ever been reprinted – Pierce Egan the Younger's Victorian assemblage of the ballad tradition, in its modest newspaper column mode, went through several editions in some twenty years after 1840, and Nicholas Chase's *Locksley* of 1983 made it into Penguin, but was never reprinted. Even *The Prince of Thieves*, attributed to Alexandre Dumas the Elder and published in 1872, was not translated into English until 1903 and lay long unheard of until Hollywood borrowed it as a subtitle in 1990 – and then the famous author was forgotten.

This flamboyantly popular tradition has never inspired general literary enthusiasm, nor has it been artificially sustained through the education industry. There is no 'Robin Hood Reader' for undergraduates, no readily available collection of the ballads, poems and short plays which do, in literary terms, bear the record of the tradition. Nor is there apparently likely to be one: in 1988 both Penguin and Everyman, when invited to publish such an anthology, had no interest in the idea. The only book of this kind, Dobson and Taylor's *Rymes of Robin Hood* (1976), was long unavailable and has only recently been reproduced by a small company to stock the heritage bookshelves in Sherwood and Nottingham. Hardly in print, in one way or another unreadable, the Robin Hood tradition nevertheless thrives in this high cultural silence, and other features of the tradition suggest that its generic thrust is not what is usually regarded as literary at all.

Everybody knows Robin Hood, but not as an intriguing figure of novel-like complexity; he possesses no depths in which readers can see reflected their own wished-for subtlety; the stories reveal no internal niceties of character on which we can critically ruminate. Unlike Sir Lancelot, Robin never considered adultery; contrary to Hamlet, he never had a doubt. The tormented self of our literary reflections finds no place here, nor do the complexities of viewpoint, morality, inter-relationship and self-expression that weave the many-figured carpets of subjectivity which dominate recent literary fiction.

In the Robin Hood tradition the major characters do not change positions, moods and personalities. They may disagree at times, and even fight each other when they first meet (including Robin and Marian in one ballad), but that only binds them closer after the brawl. Sexuality itself is not overt in the tradition and is completely absent as a source of problems – no doubt one of the reasons it has flourished among children's publishers. But then again, perhaps that aspect is not completely without a suggested presence. Robin is always played by a conspicuously handsome man, from the dash of Douglas Fairbanks Senior, through Richard Greene's winsome plumpness to the stirringly stone-faced Kevin Costner. A Freudian code apparently lurks in arrow, hood and greenwood activities.

If there might be certain depths in some of the material, so there is generic strength outside the precincts of conventional prose fiction. Among the many references up to 1600 (see appendix) are over a hundred mentions of Robin Hood 'plays and games'. These may well not have been scripted, may basically be elaborate forms of charity collection, but they were very widespread; drama remained a major genre through the highly elaborate Elizabethan five-act drama, Covent Garden opera of the eighteenth century and Victorian pantomime, while modern performance media have fully recognized the hero's force.

It is evident that dramatic interaction, a conflict performed, is the centre of most of the ballads and plays, and theatre is close to the core of the whole tradition. Actors love playing Robin Hood not only because they can wear green tights and do the Basil Rathbone sword-fight, but because there are almost no lines to learn. A tradition of this centrally dramatic and active nature does not respond well to the modes of the lyric poem and the novel, respondent as those forms are to internalized depth and nuanced representation of feeling. The tech-niques and attitudes of 'high culture' writing seem hostile to the essence of a flexible, popular, immediate and dramatic tradition.

But to find drama central is not to resolve the generic complexity of the tradition. It would be an error worthy of the sheriff to turn what seems like a set of puzzles from a literary viewpoint to a simple structure seen from another generic position. The texts are not simply classifiable as popular and oral. The Robin Hood ballads – and they provide the best set of early texts among the whole of the English language ballad corpus – have almost no tunes; this is no lilting chorus of popular voices humming its way onto the page. Robin Hood materials are in fact real texts; for all their dramatic basis they all belong, in some difficult way, to the world of reading. There are fifteenth-century manuscripts of these ballads, and printed texts appear by the very early sixteenth century. Very few of the other ballads in Child's great collection of *The English and Scottish Popular Ballads* have their origins in such early recorded form. The first Robin Hood story of all is preserved in Latin, in a chronicle of clerical origin with a firmly Christian implication (see p. 35). Similarly, we know so much about the plays and games because they were of interest, at times negatively so, to at least some of the literate, and because they were financially supported by local authorities so that their records survive right across Britain, especially in the sixteenth century.

There are ways, that is, in which the Robin Hood tradition is not fugitive, not to be fantasized as elusive rebellion. It is true that the tradition is sometimes sternly anti-authoritarian: when Robin Hood beheads Guy of Gisborne, he out-guerrillas any sixties idol, and since the young Robin becomes an outlaw by shooting fourteen foresters dead the Sicilian bandit Salvatore Giuliano seems comparatively feeble. But that ferocity itself is not the constant meaning of the figure – he may contest authority more subtly by dressing up as a priest to marry Alan a Dale to his beloved, or impersonate a hangman to free three young men.

If he is in these ways an occasional reformist, at other times Robin is fully incorporated into a conservative role. As a loyal earl resisting bad King John he is nothing more than a figure for a true aristocrat fulfilling his role in a fixed hierarchical model of society. Other forms of rigidity can develop: the Anglo-Saxon freedom fighter of Sir Walter Scott's reinterpretation resists Norman oppressors in the name of an enthusiastic nationalism that, it has become clear, can present its own invitations to oppression.

Variant as they are, all these political formations focus on the tenure of power. The basis of the agon which is the core of the Robin Hood tradition remains a conflict over authority. Robin fights the sheriff to resist his rapacious exploitations of a delegated royal authority. In a recurring sequence, Robin's own authority is explored as he and an adversary fight, draw, and agree to be friends, and then Robin is consistently accepted as the leader of the band by consensus, not birth or violence. The outlaw's recurrent resistance to sheriff or abbot refuses to accept coercive power as a basis for protecting those who are less than powerful. Such a structure can well be represented as radical (Richard Carpenter's long-haired 'Robin of Sherwood' was modelled as a student protest leader, see p. 240), or it can be more generally egalitarian: Richard Greene of the fifties ATV series was a decent officer leading a team of sterling chaps. In its usual gentrified form, the story is politically static, stating that authority depends on true lordship, not social justice. When good King Richard is restored (and his goodness is itself one of the major fictions of the tradition), the Earl of Huntingdon assumes his 'natural' authority without any further challenge.

Robin need not only be a brave representative of resistance, whether yeoman or noble. He can also figure structures that are themselves in conflict with other orders of authority. He can stand for the medieval Catholic church or for a reformed version of it; he can symbolize a repentant revolutionary in 1661, or form an anti-mercantile myth of escape for Victorians and Georgians. All of these features will be discussed in the following pages. But his party can also be oppositional in a more disruptive way – the social bandit side of Robin recurs as a model for Jacobean rural dissidents or Tom Paine-ish revolutionism in the 1790s; later it can act as a legitimation of 1930s leftism or in the present (Kendall or Lincoln green brought up to date) a faith in the ecological future.

What Robin does not stand for is anything static. Not all commentators are light-footed enough to accept that view. Modern historians of the middle ages ignore the rich terrain of actual texts in favour of any crevices of fact into which they can thrust their empiricist pitons and so climb towards the peak of their faith, a historical progenitor of the legend. The 'Real Robin Hood' industry is a fully modern form of the tradition, an acceptance of an ethos that is both materialist and individualist. But the prolific flexibility of the tradition outmanoeuvres such simplicity: the hero's name occurs in all kinds of surprising places, from a ritual in Dundee in 1521 to a man in Sussex with the surname Robynhood as early as 1296. The breadth of the hero's fame overawes the attempts of empiricists to pin a place and name on the

tales of Robin Hood, and so to give the myth an identity which would
be both that of the hero and, by extension, the scholar.

To say that a tradition is multiple, mobile, many-layered and variable sounds all very fine: a suitably subtle and elusive position to
assume by way of introduction. But the problem that emerges is how
in the light of that varied reading of the tradition does a commentator
shape the material? No single historical development is visible, and so
to order the texts chronologically would create one perforce – and be a
falsification. Nor is a generic division available; while to take the texts
in order as ballad, play, novel and film, might be a helpful counter to
the usual modern historiographic plod from Simon de Montfort to the
electronic media, it would nevertheless be in its own way even more
inadequate, being an elision of real historical processes, in which genres
overlap, interweave, and refuse to obey the separations of orderly
scholarship. Another possibility might offer itself as an approach. In
other fields, such as King Arthur studies, it is possible to take major
texts and focus on them as archetypal of particular periods and kinds
of representations; but this procedure would also fail to work, as the
Robin Hood tradition does not have such strong nuclei from which to
grow significant elements of a cultural studies culture.

In what follows I have tried to combine the values of all three
methods. The texts and references have been divided into a series of
domains, each of which centres on a particular period, is most strongly
represented in a particular genre, and offers texts which, if not major,
are at least reasonably strong. These texts can sustain some part of the
process of analysis which will itself involve reference forward and back
to related parts of the tradition and occasional summary treatment of
material too marginal or unimportant to find space in what, though
full and inherently complete, is still a study that must recognize some
limits of space.

1.2   THE MATERIALS OF THE TRADITION

With such thoughts this volume will set off, not I hope too heavily
laden with prejudice or prejudgement, on its journey through the
remarkable mass of this largely unknown body of material. Each chapter
will focus on a particular domain and it may be helpful to delineate

first what these domains will be, and what are the main structures of material to be found.

Chapter 1: c.1220–1600. Historical, topographical, quasi-biographical and literary references

Many of the earliest, and for some the most potent, appearances of Robin Hood are brief mysterious comments in ancient records. These testify to the past power of the myth – as when a bandit calls himself Robin Hood, or Friar Tuck or even, after Little John's alias in the *Gest*, Reynald Greenleaf. That fragmentary magic survives still: modern scholars become extraordinarily enthused about the significance of the most minimal data – like Sir John Paston's comment from 1473 that his servant has gone off to play Robin Hood, or that there was, mysteriously, a ship in Aberdeen named the Robin Hood as early as 1438.

Out of such references has been spun a whole saga of historicism in the 'Real Robin Hood' industry; but the references themselves and what has been made of them need to be reconnected and investigated for their significances, past and present.

Chapter 2: c.1450–seventeenth century. Short narratives in ballad form

A substantial number of early literary ballads survive, in manuscript and printed form. In the fuller texts, the settings involve both the forest and the towns which are nearby, though one-scene narratives will usually only be located in the forest. Robin Hood's role is closest to that of a 'social bandit', resisting improper authority, which may be based in state or church and often has some connection with mercantilism – whether town business or church financial dealings. Seven of the ballads survive from before 1600, and twenty-seven from the seventeenth century.

Texts of this kind continue to be preserved and recorded into the nineteenth and twentieth centuries (including in the USA). Most of Child's thirty-eight Robin Hood ballads fall into this category.

Chapter 3: Late fifteenth century to the later eighteenth century. Performances of many kinds celebrating Robin Hood

In the fifteenth and sixteenth centuries Robin Hood plays, games, processions and charitable rituals are almost all linked with early summer – Whit Sunday in particular. Small rural towns are often the locations and the forest is involved either in practice (they come through the woods) or symbolically (they wear green and carry, or are surrounded with, boughs). Carnivalesque reversals are sometimes involved – Robin appears as the Abbot of Unreason in Scotland, for example, and money is often collected, apparently for redistribution through a charity, not at Robin's own disposal. Robin's social position here is unclear, as is his interaction with other characters, but his role overlaps with that of a folk 'authority' like the 'May Lord' or the 'Summer King'. A small number of surviving plays are related to the ballads as narratives, rather than being play-game celebrations of summer.

From the late sixteenth to the later eighteenth century Robin Hood is often more or less gentrified; this process (suggested by some sixteenth-century historians) is mostly found in five-act drama, masque and light opera from this period, though a few ballads belong to this domain. Seven plays are recorded from 1592 to 1600 (two of them lost) and in the following period each generation seems to see a new Robin Hood performance, at a more or less elevated level. Robin is usually the Earl of Huntingdon, Marian almost always plays a role. The theme of wrongful dispossession is central, and the notion of Robin's personal charity to the poor emerges. The setting is fully pastoral – no towns appear. A hierarchical politics is basic. Material from ballads and chronicles occurs rarely, as classical and feudal elements are highlighted by the narrative, while theatrical conventions and resources provide much new incident and attitude.

Chapter 4: Early nineteenth century to the 1930s. Nationalist nostalgia in non-prestigious genres

Nostalgic representations of a national hero, especially in minor forms of poetry and poetic drama, from Keats to the English 'Georgian' poets, but including novels, mostly juvenile. The forest, now usually tamed as 'the greenwood', is the only setting, though towns may be mentioned, if only with distaste. The theme is rural contentment, which can have a left-wing anti-business spirit, but is usually pastoral and conservative. Robin is a group leader whose position appears natural, never questioned or explained; dispossession is the assumed reason for his outlawry. A bland form of nationalism is often included in which Robin represents the Saxons against the arrogant Norman lords. Relationships between men are often emphasized, and children's literature is a common mode, especially for prose manifestations. Sources are usually ballads, collected by editors such as Ritson (1795) and Gutch (1847) and generalized by anthologists like Howard Pyle (1883) as well as re-collected by influential literary figures like Quiller-Couch in his *Oxford Book of Ballads* (1910).

Chapter 5: Twentieth century.
Popular narratives, especially in film

Popular genres of this period may well have parallels and even sources from the past which were never previously recorded. Magazines, comics, pantomime and musical film are now fully available, Some prose fiction attaches to this tradition, especially children's texts and historical novels. Forest and town are both used as settings, but the former is stressed. Robin's position is usually one of gentrified dispossession as in the more serious plays, though there are also 'radical' accounts which revert to a 'social bandit' model deriving basically from the early ballads.

This a highly flexible domain, containing many carnival-like or burlesque elements. Some aspects of social criticism appear, often in mild or humorous form; nationalism is normally present and can become internationally generalized (as in the Errol Flynn film of 1938, see p. 230); gentrification motifs are usually diluted. There are traces of direct continuity from scholarly reprints of ballads, but most of this century's widely-known material depends simply on a re-popularization of the literary texts from the nineteenth century.

In examining these five domains, this will not be a biographically-oriented study, nor will it present an original Robin Hood whose story spreads through time and space. Nor yet will this account be politically predisposed, lamenting how a rebellious hero has been appropriated to genteel silence, nor even how a noble lord has been traduced in the broadsheet gutters and the manipulations of late capitalist communications industry. Gratifying though such prejudices might be, the processes of popular narrative are consistently more complex and dynamic, even dialectic. The story of Robin Hood is many-sided and seems capable of maintaining its contrasting characteristics in vital form without them weakening or contradicting each other. There are many Robin Hoods in any one period, and the ideological formations that cluster around the English outlaw are as various as can be produced by the many versions of social class, spiritual purpose, productive context and audience expectation that, in their mutual operations, produce and consume the tradition.

Like other fugitive, powerful, in some way menacing characters, such as Ned Ludd, Captain Swing, Jesse James, Billy the Kid, Ned Kelly, Joe Hill, even Kilroy and John Doe, Robin Hood can be anywhere there is a call for an image of resistance to some form of undesirable authority. The fact that this function can be noble, crass, tribal, individual, liberationist, oppressive, mystical or simply ludicrous will express only the multiple nature of human needs and the intimate way in which Robin Hood is integrated with the manifold operations of the power of story in human culture.

The proverb goes 'Many men speak of Robin Hood who never drew his bow.' Over six centuries mysterious strength has remained central to the tradition and its fascination for people of all kinds, who find gratification, release and even a sense of power in the elusive hero's many-sided resistance to authority.

2

'Robin Hood in Barnsdale Stood': Images of an Outlaw

2.1 REALITY OR MYTH?

Because Robin Hood is so elusive people always want to pin him down. The first question after a public lecture on the English outlaw is always, 'Did Robin Hood really exist – and if so, when?' The question has its own restrictions, because existence is being imagined only in terms of human biography, time and place, not in terms of a long-existing potent myth.

Perhaps even stranger than that highly limited question is the fact that there will be multiple answers to it, many fragments of alleged fact to be attached to the famous figure. Also at the public lecture will probably be at least one forthright person who possesses a cherished account of a highly particularized Robin Hood, with a place and period attached, and often a rigmarole of folk scholarship to explain various details in the tradition.

For example, he was from Wakefield, but left because of the oppressive sheriff and marched overland with his men to Whitby – hence Robin Hood's Bay. Or he lived in the hills above Derby, crossing to Sherwood in good highway-robbing weather, hence all the caves and wells in the eastern Peak District that bear his name or that of Little John. Both of those quite unrecorded accounts have actually come up in recent public discussions, from people who were enthusiasts of the outlaw's tradition and related him to their own locale.

Especially specific in their conclusions are those outlaw identifiers who have had access to public records, or at least to digests of them. They tend to be professional historians or academics with a strong

11

faith in the alleged reality of empiricism. Recent scholarship on Robin Hood is heavily weighted towards historical biography. R.B. Dobson and J. Taylor's *Rymes of Robin Hood* (1976) is basically a long introduction followed by an anthology. Both editors were historians, and although they deal sensibly with a wide range of literary matters there is an insistent set towards the possible historicity of the material. That broad-based empiricism was made a good deal narrower by J.C. Holt in his *Robin Hood* (1982) which added to the totemic value of fact that other modern ideal, the individual, and stressed the discussion of evidence for the existence of a 'real' Robin Hood. The narrowing scope of Holt's book was confirmed as the dominant mode of Robin Hood studies when J.C. Bellamy, a historian of the later middle ages, published a short but intensely detailed account, *Robin Hood: An Historical Enquiry* (1985), which held its magnifying glass over the records of fourteenth-century crime and disorder in quest of a single identifiable man.

Being in book form, these approaches have dominated the shelves in libraries and even the Robin Hood tourist centres. Few interested people have had the chance to read the sprightly intelligence of J.B. Bessinger Jr (1966) or the sweeping wisdom of Douglas Gray (1984), because scholarly essays tend to remain sequestered in academic collections. Those scholars' sociocultural approach to the topic will be developed throughout this book, but empirical short-sightedness is still widely visible in Robin Hood studies, and not only in the historicist books: Nottingham's 'Tales of Robin Hood' display centre lays stress on tangible mock-ups of life in medieval Sherwood; visitors can gaze at just the sort of long bow or precisely the kind of quarter staff that an outlaw might have handled.

With a similarly concrete, or perhaps fetishized, concept of history, the historicist scholars have cherished fragments of what appears to be reality. Wakefield property records, York assize documents, Sussex personal names, even London street names: all these bear early traces of a figure called Robin or sometimes Robert Hood and each lode of empirical ore has sustained excavation and speculation about a specific biography at the core of the widely disseminated legend.

When scholars call it a legend they imply, according to the usual distinction between legend and myth, that there *is* a figure at the core. Modern academic scholars usually shy away from the idea of myth, partly because it seems so insubstantial, with nothing to get your professional teeth into, partly because earlier treatments handled the notion too fancifully. Surprisingly, the case for a mythic Robin Hood was made most forcefully in that monument of empiricist individualism, the *Dictionary of National Biography*, where the future editor Sir Sidney Lee (a name that could belong in the *Gest of Robin Hood*) reported that 'The arguments in favour of Robin Hood's historical existence, although very voluminous, will not bear scholarly examination' and provided what to many would seem a challenging summary:

> There can be little doubt, however, that, as in the somewhat similar case of Rory o' the Hills in Ireland, the name originally belonged to a mythical forest-elf, who filled a large space in English, and apparently in Scottish, folk-lore, and that it was afterwards applied by English ballad-writers, chiefly of the northern and midland counties, from the twelfth to the fifteenth centuries to any robber-leader who made his home in forests or moors, excelled in archery, defied the oppressive forest laws, and thus attracted popular sympathy. (XXVI, 1891, pp. 258–91)

The widespread nature of this 'mythic' reading of the tradition around the turn of the century led to the essay in the influential eleventh volume of the *Encyclopedia Britannica* (1910) by J.W. Hales and F.J. Snell, which stated 'it is certain that many mythical elements are contained in this story' (p. 420) and repeated the major arguments of Lee's essay. This reading of Robin Hood was part of the strong contemporary interest in the 'anthropological' approach to literature and lore. When literature seemed decreasingly credible as a set of moral instructions, whether Christian or secular, and when the investigations of philologists and source-hunters became increasingly arid (as they were being institutionalized as part of the academy), the mythic approach to texts and practices seemed to offer new ranges of connection and a generalizing and sophisticating approach that ran parallel to the project of modernism in literature.

It is entirely appropriate, then, that Robert Graves, that subtle modernist, gave a strong form of such a reading to Robin Hood in *The White Goddess*; he spoke of him as a 'popular hero' who was 'regarded as the founder of the Robin Hood religion' which was evidently conceived of as a pre-Christian cult (1948, p. 350). Margaret Murray had laid the basis of this notion in her influential book *The God of the Witches* (1931). In her chapter on 'The Horned God' she argued that Robin was 'the god of the Old Religion', justifying this view by reference to his co-outlaws being 'suggestions of a Grand Master and his coven', and in support noting that they wore green, 'the fairies' colour', were focused on May, a fertility period, and were deeply anti-clerical; she also asserted that Robin 'is so common a term for the "Devil" as to be almost a generic name for him.' (1931, pp. 35–6).

This kind of writing is now regarded by most academics with rationalist crucifix in hand. There do indeed seem to be overstatements by the mythicists, yet it is also true that the tradition of Robin Hood has always had the capacity to slip towards myth to a certain degree. When, in the early eighties television series 'Robin of Sherwood' (see p. 239), Robin was initiated in his heroic role by a stag-headed Herne the Hunter, Richard Carpenter, the script writer, was not merely drawing on the late-seventies interest in magic of many kinds; he articulated the mythic undertow of the tradition, which the 1938 Hollywood 'Adventures of Robin Hood', for example, had realized in the famous and much-imitated scene where the great oak tree comes to life with green-clad outlaws.

There is a persistent contact between Robin Hood and sympathetic magic (the hood, the green costume, the woods, caves, streams, springs, stags and arrows are obvious examples), just as there is a relationship with the tradition of the Trickster, the powerful wag who resists conventional authority and leads his people in actions that are not political resistance of any weight, but provide at least a sense of compensation in games, witticisms and such cultural guerrilla practices. The many references to Robin Hood in the late medieval world indicate that he belongs to folklore; he is a figure of authority in proverbs, an identity for springs, caves, and hills – hence the many Robin Hood's Butts which explain and also mythically dignify odd scarps and swellings in the terrain. These features are felt by the empiricist historians to be signs of a blurred popular appropriation of a real figure; but the reverse is possible, and needs to be contemplated.

The power of individualism and empiricism in our world-view, whether generalized through public media or professionalized in the academy, is such that the existence of a single 'real' figure behind the tradition has long seemed natural, the obvious thing to be sought. The other possible structure, a widely disseminated image of general resistance to authority, realized on many occasions in many forms, has seemed both improbable and indefinite, two equal disqualifications. Those who have faith in a kind of knowledge that is certain have been dismissive of such voyages into what they see as uncertainty. But on a range of grounds the notion has become more and more admissible that the Robin Hood tradition may be not so much a set of transformations of an authentic single person, but rather it might be a force-field of variations, of figures and fables which realize in many different and locally functional ways the concept central to the whole myth, which appears to be a resistance to authority.

Such a multiple interpretation might well be supported by that currently dynamic and consciously counter-historical position, usually called post-modernism, a view which exposes and explains the complex nature of a concept or phenomenon, deconstructing any notionally rigid structure. The overlaps and apparent contradictions of meaning to be found in any set of Robin Hood stories will all respond well to a post-modern understanding of the tradition as a discourse which can represent aspects of dissent to established power and yet can also be complicit with such institutions of authority.

However one need not be armed with the quarterstaff of Francophile theory to resist the search for a positive and unitarian source to the tradition. If all the arguments and evidence for a historical Robin Hood are tested both in their own terms and against wider evidence, then it soon becomes clear that there has always been multiplicity right at the alleged core of the tradition of the identity of Robin Hood, as is plainly recognized by Dobson and Taylor. These historians, who are both clear-headed and open-minded, speak of 'a bewildering variety of persons of that name' and decide that 'the discovery of the name Robert or Robin Hood in a medieval English document is not in itself of particular significance.' (1976, pp. 11 and 12). Barbara Hanawalt sees the same situation from another side when (1992, p. 154) she refuses to look for a historical Robin Hood because 'the evidence is insufficient'.

Such flexibility of understanding has usually been more evident among those who have approached the tradition from a literary point of view; F.J. Child made argumentative play with his perception of 'six Robin Hoods . . . in a period of less than forty years' (1965, III, p. 56) and Jess B. Bessinger summed up with wary irony: 'we are so far from agreement, and indeed of knowledge, about the outlaw's origins that we might better concentrate on the growth of his tradition.' (1966, p. 61) He noted that the early figure is 'a remarkable composite' (1966, p. 62) and in his discussion of that multiplicity saw clearly the polymorphous character of the figure in the early texts.

Not all have looked so closely. The argument of those who have sought for a single line of authority in the Robin Hood tradition will be the theme of the rest of this chapter as it scrutinises the ideas, practices and implications of the historicists who, heedless of their theoretical danger, have plodded off, saddlebags jingling with footnotes and quasi-technicalities, into the forests of empirical speculation.

2.2   DISCOVERING AN EARL

The idea of a single, identifiable, locatable Robin Hood goes back a long way, but when in the past the hero was treated as a real person, it was almost always in the context of gentrification: this kind of biography was an outline of a great man's status, not a moral X-ray of a modern sentient subject, as becomes clear from a survey of the older 'biographic' tradition, which is found largely outside the literary texts.

'Robin Hood in Barnsdale stood' was a legal maxim from the late middle ages, exemplifying a statement of well-known fact (see Appendix under 1429, 1520, 1542 and the discussion in Bolland, 1925, p. 107). Yet that should not be taken as ancient support for the 'Real Robin Hood' industry. The earliest references by chroniclers, as is characteristic of medieval thinking, do not make it clear whether history and story are seen as separate categories. They refer to Robin as an outlaw and a hero in fables without needing to draw out any distinction between them as categories. Those earlier chroniclers, properly examined, have considerable light to cast on how the tradition forms, but that process is more appropriately left until the allegedly factual evidence for identity has been thoroughly sifted.

In their own non-biographical way, the early ballads and brief dramas never offer any personal data about the hero: no life narrative is developed. He merely stands in the forest, responds to a crisis, and the fiction ends after a few sharp-edged scenes. The *Gest of Robin Hood* (see pp. 70–81) is longer and does conclude with a hurried account of Robin's ageing and death, but it too lacks the humanist shape and personalized viewpoint of a modern biography. More information is given about the hero when in the sixteenth century he is turned from a free-floating outlaw to a man related to place and time, lands and

history, namely the Earl of Huntingdon who was displaced by enemies
at court but remained loyal to King Richard I. That hierarchical
narrative lies behind the first major 'art' text of the whole tradition,
the pair of plays by Anthony Munday and perhaps Henry Chettle,
The Downfall of Robert Earle of Huntington and *The Death* of the same
aggrandized hero. Yet neither of these plays (from 1598–9) tells in a
deliberate or full way the story of a life. That was first produced for
a large audience by Martin Parker who in 1632 published, in ballad
form, a quite lengthy biography of the English outlaw. Its title indicates a new sense of veracity and identity combined in this 'True Tale
of Robin Hood' and it ends by reporting his alleged epitaph, so completing the 'Life and Deeds' of a man of status:

> Robert Earle of Huntington
> Lies under this little stone. (Child, 1965, III, p. 233)

So Parker was the first to cast the hero in firmly individualistic
mould, like so many of his period giving shape and depth to the
private being. His biography was much better known, simply because
of its ballad character, than a piece which was composed somewhat
earlier, the 'Life of Robin Hood', a short prose account surviving in a
manuscript in the Sloane collection at the British Library (no. 780,
formerly 715) which is itself little more than a rehash of the events in
the *Gest* with some details taken from other ballads, though it greatly
influenced Joseph Ritson, the late-eighteenth-century anthologist and
forceful popularizer of the outlaw's tradition in his anthology of the
texts (1795).

However, while the literary biographers were confining Robin Hood
to the constraints of the page, popular and localized traditions continued and could themselves be condensed into quasi-factual form, as
is indicated by the notes made by Roger Dodsworth, a seventeenth-
century antiquarian:

> Robert Locksley, born in Bradfield parish, in Hallamshire, wounded
> his stepfather to death at plough: fled into the woods, and was relieved
> by his mother till he was discovered. Then he came to Clifton upon
> Calder, and came acquainted with Little John, that kept the kine;
> which said John is buried at Hathershead in Derbyshire, where he hath
> a fair tomb-stone with an inscription. Mr Long saith that Fabyan saith,
> Little John was an earl Huntingdon. After he joined with Much, the
> Miller's son. (Quoted in Holt, 1982, p. 44)

The Pedigree of Robin Hood, Earl of Huntingdon.

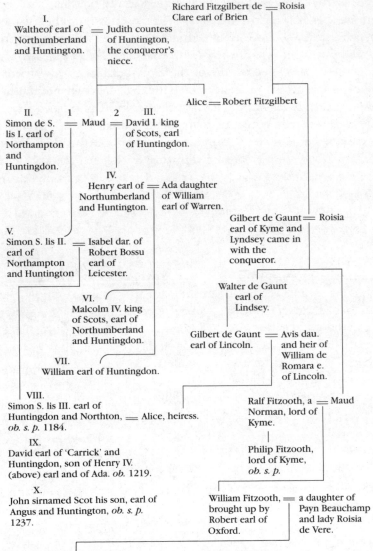

Robert Fitzooth, commonly called Robin Hood, pretended earl
of Huntington, *ob.* 1274 [1247].*

* Stukeley's *Palæographia Britannica*, No. 11. p. 115.

Illustration 2   William Stukeley's Robin Hood pedigree
(From Ritson, 1795 ed.; photo Lensmedia.)

Hallamshire is South Yorkshire, and this story also seems to have strong Derbyshire and Little John influence; the mother motif is very unusual, as is the notion that John held the earldom, which is unique to these notes: Fabian, a sixteenth-century chronicler, does not in fact say that Little John held the Huntingdon title.

It is striking that Holt found it hard to believe Dodsworth was convinced by these 'miscellaneous jottings,' so does not bother to analyse them (1982, p. 44): the modern empiricist is cool about the value of the notes because of their 'popular' tone, yet to be oral and contradictory in this way are characteristics close to the centre of the volatile outlaw myth. A quite different version of the Robin Hood myth is shadowed behind Dodsworth's notes, with an unusual motivation for outlawry and no real sense that Robin was a leader. But that popular and flexible Robin is largely lost in the treatments of other antiquarians, because their mode tends towards a uniform and historicized identity for the hero.

Something distinctly more aristocratic and orderly than the ideas recorded in Dodsworth's jottings is devised by an inventive voice in the tradition of historicization, that of William Stukeley, an eighteenth-century Stamford antiquarian – and also a doctor and parson – who produced a 'pedigree of Robin Hood earl of Huntingdon' which traced his family back on one side to William the Conqueror and on the other to an Anglo-Saxon earl (1746, II. p. 115, see illustration 2). Robert Fitz Ooth, as Stukeley found him to be, was directly descended from the Conqueror's niece Judith and from Earl Waltheof, a noble Saxon survivor. This confirmed him as an earl in the days of bad King John, and was accepted by Ritson in his very influential anthology, and by a surprising number of later commentators, in spite of the inherently improbable nature of the suggestion. It was important, it would seem, for these literary gamekeepers that Robin the apparent poacher should be confirmed as a nobleman in rustic disguise.

The weight of local tradition can itself support the hierarchical positioning of the hero. Such grand figures (as Lord Raglan noted in his analysis of hero-structures, which included Robin Hood, 1949, chap. 4) will tend to have shrines dedicated to them throughout their districts; not only are there Robin Hood place names in plenty by the seventeenth century, but Richard Grafton and William Camden both recorded the existence of a grave to the hero at Kirklees. His name is carved on it, albeit with two other names which no one has, it seems,

Illustration 3   The tomb of Robard Hude and others,
Richard Gough, *Sepulcheal Monument* (permission of the British Library.)

ever even tried to explain – William Goldburh and, simply, Thomas
(Gough, 1786, p. cviii; Grafton, *Chronicle*, 1569, p. 85, see p. 60 below;
Camden, trans. Gough, 1809, vol. 3, p. 38). A drawing was made in
1665 by the scholar Nathaniel Johnston (see illustration 3). Thomas
Gale, the classical scholar and Dean of York till 1702, claimed to have
found a copy of a fuller epitaph:

> Hear underneath this laitl stean
> Lais robert earl of Huntingtun
> Near arcir ver as hei sa geud
> An pipl kauld im robin heud
> sick utlaws as hi an is men
> Wil England nivr si agen. (Quoted by Percy, *Reliques*, 1765, I, p. 74)

Although Holt is convinced of the discovery of those lines (1982, p. 42),
this is obviously a playfully 'antique' version of Parker's own version:

> Robert Earle of Huntington
> Lies under this little stone.

No archer was like him so good:
His wildnesse named him Robbin Hood.
Full thirteene yeares, and something more,
These northerne parts he vexed sore.
Such out-lawes as he and his men
May England never know agen. (Child, III, p. 233)

Away from the studies of the scholars, a heroic biography emerged rather slowly from the more inchoate shape of unconnected deeds. The well-known form of the 'Robin Hood Garland', a frequently published collection of popular ballads in pamphlet form, usually from sixteen to twenty-four in number, only occasionally presents the shape of a hero's life. They include that remarkably aggressive account of how Robin became an outlaw, 'Robin Hood's Progress to Nottingham (Child no. 139), see pp. 64–5, and often end with the 'Death', but these are only a frame for disconnected dramatic episodes.

Even when the later processes of biographical completion occur they still have a strongly centrifugal effect. Mrs Brown of Falkland, the most prolific of ballad-transmitters, apparently became aware that there was no ballad of the birth of Robin Hood, and so turned up with one (see Fowler, 1968, p. 304) which is an obvious pastiche of the art-touched ballads that were so popular among collectors in her time and, equally, has never been within a minstrel's arm's length of any other Robin Hood ballad at all. It is actually recorded by Child as a variant of 'Willie and Earl Richard's Daughter' (Child no. 102A), indicating how Mrs Brown neatly substituted one hero for another in a manoeuvre without any impact on the tradition as a whole.

Some popular forms did shape a hero's life by themselves. For example there is the prose pamphlet grandly entitled *The Noble Birth and Gallant Achievements of That Remarkable Outlaw Robin Hood* which was, its subtitle says, 'Newly collected into One Volume by an Ingenious Antiquary' and which apparently was first published in 1662. That year's new royalism found a parallel in this upmarket titling of what was effectively Martin Parker's story with some gilding, a pseudo-biography which, for all its prose form, links up with the more rhetorical and quasi-courtly of the seventeenth-century ballads, and in its introduction gives the outlaw the improbably honoured and peaceful end of a superannuated squire: '. . . he spent his Old Age in peace, at a house of his own, not far from Nottingham, being generally loved and respected of all.'

This is conventionality rather than biography; any 'real' Robin Hood seems as far away from this flaccid prose as from the least personalized of the ballads. However, one scholar, of considerable influence, did attempt to pull together all the strands of the tradition into a coherent humanist account. Joseph Ritson, himself an austere analyst of texts and others' opinions, wrote a substantial introduction to his 1795 collection of the ballads. It was basically an extended life of the aristocratic outlaw in all its accreted detail, based on his Norman identity as Robert Fitz Ooth and reprinting Stukeley's exotic genealogy. As well as nobility and democratic instincts, a combination of the public man at once conservative and radical, Ritson also spoke for the first time of the hero's 'personal character'. It was hardly an anguished post-Freudian exposé, but it was as close as the period could come to that, and it set the pattern for later biographic representations: '. . . it is sufficiently evident that he was active, brave, prudent, patient; possessed of uncommon bodily strength, and considerable military skill; just, generous, benevolent, faithful and beloved or revered by his followers or adherents for his excellent and amiable qualities. (p. xii)

The biographical scholarship and the popularity of Ritson's edition had a combined impact: it was this apparently authoritative formulation of the displaced, yet also democratic, aristocrat that became the authoritative version of the hero's life, and it underlies most of the versions that appeared after Ritson and right up to the present day.

2.3 ARCHIVES OF AN OUTLAW

Not all were persuaded by the gentrified Robin Hood and some scholars sought in an older past for traces of a more credible character. Thomas Percy, that avid collector of medieval material and himself a keen pursuer of the aristocracy – he went so far as to change his name from Piercy to the Earl of Northumberland's family name (*Dictionary of National Biography*, XLIV, 1895, pp. 437–9) – was scholar enough to suggest that the aristocratic Robin Hood did not appear in the earliest ballads: 'the most ancient poems on Robin Hood make no mention of this earldom.' (1765, p. 104). Later scholars have known quite well that King Richard's loyal thane could not be their man, as the Earl of Huntingdon was not in that period some Robert Fitz Ooth but David, brother to King William of Scotland. In addition, the ballads are much later than that period, the long bow was apparently not then in widespread use, the social relations and contemporary references of the earliest texts are fourteenth century at the earliest. The development of the 1190s as a setting is clearly a product of the sixteenth century (see p. 37).

However, disbelieving the gentrification fantasy was, for empiricist historians of the nineteenth century, only the start of an equally delusory quest. Inherently distrustful, in any case, of literary texts as bearing anything of value, the historians went to the records and there, closing the circle of their expectations, glimpsed just enough of the fugitive figure to energize their reductive speculations.

Joseph Hunter was a Yorkshire scholar and for nearly thirty years an official of the recently established Public Record Office. He brought the new attitude of objective analysis to the Robin Hood tradition: no ballads attracted his interest, gentry fables never detained his attention and fired his speculations. Elizabethan hierarchizations like the Sloane Life or Parker's self-validating truth as a tale-teller cut no ice with the well-surnamed Hunter. He simply, crucially, went searching through the records for a man of the necessary name.

Amazingly, he found one, and in a very telling place and time. The *Gest*, the largest and one of the earliest of the Robin Hood texts, tells how the hero takes service with King Edward on his trip through the north, goes to court, hates it, and leaves for the forest again. Hunter identified an actual Robyn Hode who was paid as a *valet de chambre* for Edward II in 1324 and left his service then 'because he could no longer work'. (1852, pp. 35–9) This happened in York, and the beginning of the *Gest* firmly places Robin in Barnsdale by the River Went, not thirty miles from York itself.

This remarkable discovery has been largely ignored by other scholars; literary commentators like D.C. Fowler (1968) or Douglas Gray (1984) have judged it irrelevant to their concerns; other historians have seemed too keen to realize their own individualism by locating a different individual, though P. Valentine Harris (1972, p. 72) and John Bellamy (1985, pp. 7–10) have both testified to the scholarship and value of Hunter's connection.

Hunter's man had an aura of probability. A date in the early fourteenth century fitted the longbow and, in a general sense, the

social relations of the tradition. More importantly it meshed quite
well with the fact that the first clear reference to the literary tradition
comes in William Langland's long poem *Piers Plowman*, which in its
second version (usually called the B-text) makes an idle priest, who
represents Sloth, say that he knows 'rymes of Robin Hood' (1975,
Passus V. 395, p. 331). This is dated in the 1370s and two generations
might well seem an appropriate period for a real outlaw, who was in
and out of royal favour, to develop a widespread legend.

Hunter's discovery remains in terms of recorded evidence the closest
to the literary terrain – though Edward's servant is not described as
an outlaw or a warrior in any form. Just as the strength of that identification comes out of the records, so do its weaknesses: in part through
Hunter himself, who went on to flesh out the structure with another
Robin Hood whom he believed to be the same, who had property in
Wakefield and who might (the argument grows fainter) have been
involved with the Contrariants, the supporters of Thomas, Earl of
Lancaster, who resisted Edward II and died after Boroughbridge in
1322 (1852, pp. 47–51).

Trying to nail down his identification, Hunter struck too often and
too hard, so scholars have been able to ignore the force of his basic
connection. Had he left the Wakefield material as merely a miasma of
support, the link between Edward's valet and the *Gest* might have
seemed stronger. But the firmest disagreement with Hunter's case
came from extensions by others of his own methodology, tracing other
Robin or Robert Hoods in the records, who come earlier and in some
cases do have some sort of connection with crime.

One of them was a man living in Sussex in 1296 whose surname
was Robynhood; his first name was, less heroically, Gilbert, and the
surname was probably derived from Gilbert's playing Robin in an
annual pageant (Dobson and Taylor, 1976, p. 12). This indicates that
the tradition could not in fact have started with Edward's recalcitrant
servitor in 1324. Two even earlier candidates have emerged from the
cramped writing of thirteenth-century records. The earliest record to
connect someone called R. Hood with being outlawed, if uncertainly,
was published by L.V.D. Owen (1936, p. xxix): he had unearthed a
York assizes record from 1226 which recorded the confiscation of the
goods of one Robert Hod, described as a fugitive. He owed the money
to St Peter's, York, which has a general appropriateness to Robin's
hostility to the established church in that city; less well focused is the

fact that in the margin he is given the nickname Hobbehod, which nowhere appears in all the Robin Hood tradition, though it might link with Hobgoblin and Robin Goodfellow, at least in the eyes of dedicated mythicists. Thin as the connection is with the later tradition, at least this reference makes him an outlaw.

More recently, and for some much more suggestive of an existing myth, came David Crook's discovery of a record from 1262 which links the hero's name to a criminal who is definitely a fugitive (1984). One William, the son of Robert Le Fevre (the smith), was indicted at Reading in 1261 for larceny. In another reference to the case in 1262 his name is given as William Robehod. Crook took this to mean that Robin Hood was already a well-known name for a fugitive criminal and that the father's name Robert in part made the change seem appropriate. It may well be that some doubters might feel that the resemblance to 'Hobbehod' is an influence on the renaming, either accidental or deliberate, and an ever-deeper sceptic might think the second reference, William Robehod, is just a miswritten or misunderstood version of name and patronymic – William Robert would be a common way of recording this man's name at the time. The record is certainly a slender basis on which to assume the outlaw, definitely known by the 1370s, was already notorious over a century before.

Whatever obscure meanings may lie behind these early appearances of the hero's name, later references are indisputably linked to the outlaw myth. By the fifteenth century, his name was clearly being used to characterize disruptive people. A striking record from Tutbury, Staffordshire, in 1439 says that one Piers Venables, of Aston, gentleman: 'gadered and asembled unto hym many misdoers . . . and, in manere of insurrection, wente into the wodes in that contre, like as it hadde be Robyn Hode and his meyne.' (Quoted in Child, 1965, vol. III, p. 41)

A rebel with a 'meyne', or retinue, in the woods, causing disorder to the sober citizens: Robin Hood is the archetype of such a figure by 1439. But there is no secure evidence that he was known as such nearly two centuries before, in spite of the recent historicist excitements. The historians who bring forward these fragments of an archival biography tend to settle on one point as a nugget of truth: for Owen and Crook, as before for Hunter, there is a bright space where their man could be identified, his trace found there in the records. Such limited versions of history lose their force in the face of the other contenders with similar notional validity; as each new candidate joins the line the others merely take one pace back into the obscurity of outdated certainties.

A more powerful form of historicity emerges when the author offers to knit fragments of empirical evidence together into a grander narrative of possibility. This is the mode of J.C. Holt's book, *Robin Hood* published in 1982 and reissued in 1990 with a short afterword to embrace, rather blandly, the new and inherently contradictory thoughts of Crook and Bellamy.

For Holt historical priority is all, so Owen's 'Hobehood' and Crook's distinctly optimistic reliance on the 1262 name-change must indicate an actual figure before Hunter's man. And so a narrative can unfold – the Hobbehod fugitive establishes, somehow, an early spread of the name of Robin Hood: the 1262 reference indicates a growing public knowledge; Gilbert Robynhood of Sussex in 1296 shows how far the story had travelled; and on the basis of this unconnected triangle of flimsy speculation a thirteenth-century reality is established. Hunter's striking Edward II connection is simply questioned because (revealing again the obsession with priority) some evidence is found to place Robin at court just before Hunter's dating – and so trips up a minor part of his argument, that Edward and Robin met in Nottingham in November 1323. No argument, however, is advanced to dispute the remarkable similarity of fact and *Gest* in the context of Edward's valet Robin Hood (Holt, 1982, pp. 48–9).

So in Holt's persuasive hands a tradition is created. The historical method asserts control: all that we know is causatively linked, as if it is all that actually happened. Some historians call this mining and lumping, gathering a few facts together as if they form a necessary sequence, omitting all the other facts and all the absences, and so constructing an allegedly coherent narrative. In the context of Robin Hood such a process sets aside many other occurrences of the hero's name which indicate not a steady spread from one single human source, but a remarkable diaspora of references.

That pattern of inherent variety is already evident in the striking disparity among the locations of the early references, the places to which the outlaws are linked. These indicate a multiplicity of focus which can readily be seen to arise not from some confused dissemination of an originally 'pure' and ancient Robin Hood reality, but rather from the myth's continuous re-adaptation to a set of varying contexts.

2.4   LOCATING ROBIN HOOD

The first chronicler to mention Robin Hood, Andrew of Wyntoun, writing in about 1420, locates him in Inglewood, the royal forest near Carlisle, but also places him in Barnsdale (see p. 32). If in the early fifteenth century he was thought to have been in Inglewood in 1283, there are other early records equally far away from the alleged heartland in Nottingham and South Yorkshire (see Appendix for details of the following references). In 1354 a Robin Hood was recorded as being charged with breaking into the royal forest of Rockingham in northern Northamptonshire. A ship called Robin Hood was registered at Aberdeen in 1438. In other references from the early period the myth is heard of at Exeter (1426–7), Wiltshire (1432), Norfolk (1473), Thame in Oxfordshire (1474), Edinburgh (1492), Henley (1499); a late fifteenth-century manuscript refers to 'kene men of Combur' who know about 'Reynall and Robyn Hood', which seems to indicate the same area as Wyntoun's Cumberland. Other medieval references locate the hero in the better-known central parts, Sherwood (*c*.1400–25), Slephill, near Barnsdale (*c*.1422), Barnsdale itself (1429).

Some other localizations of the name have seemed so strange to commentators that they assume they refer to someone entirely different – which may well be a comfortingly circular process. A man called Robert Hood, a servant of the Abbot of Cirencester, killed Ralph of Cirencester in that town between 1213 and 1216 (Holt, 1982, p. 54). Too early, too out of the way, most scholars seem to think – yet other references, especially dramatic, indicate a western tradition of the hero and it is also, if surprisingly, true that as Bower's story shows (see p. 35) the outlaw can be a friend of the church in this early period. Another curiosity is that David Laing's edition of Andrew of Wyntoun's chronicle (1872) refers in its index to two mentions of Robin Hood. One is the well-known Inglewood and Barnsdale citation, the other a description of how one 'Hwde of Edname' (the place seems unknown) helps Alexander Ramsay take Roxburgh by storm in 1342. Too late, too far away is the scholar's response, or would be if anyone had noticed it. But there clearly is a Scottish Robin Hood tradition, and the Rockingham reference makes it clear aggressive men were using the name in just that period. Both of these citations may be authentic uses of the all-purpose outlaw alias, and suggest greater flexibility and wider dissemination in the myth than has usually been recognized.

The pattern begins to emerge of a figure whose functions are found right through Britain, with local occurrences of no clearly rationalized distribution, and no more than a slight concentration in the North Midlands – the West Country is as prolific very early. That view becomes more emphatic when the plays are taken into account. Whereas the early ballads appear to link with the small towns developing through craft and mercantilism of central and northern England, the plays are recorded as far away as Exeter and Falkirk, all by 1500. David Wiles's research on the plays' distribution highlights river valleys in the south and west (1981, pp. 3–4) and suggests a link between this area and the drama genre, a view that must cast further doubt on the sense of a single, historical, empirically uniform source and structure to this tradition.

The Rockingham reference is especially intriguing. This Robin Hood lay in prison awaiting trial for an offence committed in the forest of Rockingham. If the thirteenth-century references have any meaning, then the name can be an outlaw's alias or *nom de guerrilla* and this may well be another instance of that pattern. Holt dismisses this reference as being too close to the 1370s to stimulate the *Piers Plowman* references, and not 'enjoying the appropriate success' (Holt, 1982, p. 54). Dobson and Taylor take the same view (1976, pp. 12–13), even though a 'Robin in prison' motif is consistently present through the whole tradition. Bellamy does not even mention the Rockingham event, presumably because his early fourteenth-century Robin Hood would by then be a generation too old.

Rockingham also may have been disqualified because the area did not seem to fit into the usual concept of Robin Hood's geography, the Nottingham, Wakefield, Doncaster triangle. But that too may rest on bogus authority, simply because so little evidence has survived, or even been considered. Leicester, a day's walk away to the north-west of Rockingham, had a Robin Hood play in 1534, and in 1556 so did Melton, equally distant to the north. There are less tangible connections to the myth. Rockingham is structurally the same as the other identified locales, being a forest near an emergent craft-oriented town, Corby. For Tardif (1983, pp. 131–2) that is the key to the Robin Hood locales: he argues that the myth is woven out of urban fantasies of rural liberty – as Sherwood is to Nottingham so Inglewood is to

Carlisle, Richmond Park to London and, apparently the earliest widely known location, Barnsdale to Doncaster.

Barnsdale in Yorkshire, though always cited as a Robin Hood terrain, because the *Gest* says so, is actually a good deal less secure than many might think as the real basis of some real Robin Hood. The most locally well-advised of the historical commentators, Dobson and Taylor, say it presents 'a baffling problem' (1976, p. 20). It was never much of a forest, nor was it ever royal, as is clearly the case in the *Gest*; as historians they know this and are doubtful as a result. The *Gest* describes Wentbridge and even a local plantation called 'The Sayles' where the outlaws ambushed travellers on 'Watling Street' – then used as a name for parts of the Great North Road, but more correctly Ermine Street (Dobson and Taylor, 1976, pp. 21–3). The weight of this identification has overridden the historians' doubt; such is the power of an apparent fact. Part of its force was the apparent suggestion by Child that the *Gest* might be very early in date. That itself will be disputed below (see pp. 46–8), and so, stripped of notional priority, and in the light of other doubts, the Yorkshire Barnsdale seems at best an enigmatic part of the tradition.

Considerable interest, therefore, attaches to a signpost in deepest Rutland (not far across the Welland from Rockingham, but some eighty miles from Wentbridge) pointing to the Barnsdale Country Club. The club seems very modern in mode, with time-share cabins beside the sheen of the new reservoir, Rutland Water. But the sign is not misleading: the name has medieval status, and there are more surprises. The royal forest of Barnsdale in fact lay just twenty-five miles south-west of Nottingham and fifteen north of the edge of Rockingham. Deer still run here, in the heart of hunting country. More Robin Hood possibilities reveal themselves: the Great North Road itself passes just three miles away, and in Tunneley Wood to the north of this Barnsdale and in Bloody Oaks, on the main road itself, there are strong local traditions of outlaw activity. Where Barnsdale Forest touches the hamlet of Whitwell is nothing less than Robin Hood's Field (see illustration 4), and on the south-eastern side of the forest, near Hambleton, was a Robin Hood's Cave. Other topographic references in the vicinity are Robin Hood's Cross at Castle Bytham (Camden, 1607, II, p. 249), and some others, including two to Little John in the Leicester and Charnwood area (see illustration 1, p. xii). This siting of Barnsdale would make more sense of the remark by

Illustration 4   Near Robin Hood's Field, Whitwell, Rutland
(Courtesy Rutland Historical Society, photo Lensmedia.)

John Paston in 1473 that his servant has 'gone into Barnsdale' to play Robin Hood – Barnsdale, Rutland, is still on the direct road from Norwich to Nottingham.

None of this detail would have much more than spoiling value – posing awkward questions about what authority the author of the *Gest* had to locate his outlaws in an inherently improbable place – were it not for another remarkable Robin Hood connection from Rutland, itself relating to another significant enigma in the tradition.

If the Yorkshire Barnsdale's unsuitability is a nagging concern at the heart of the usual tradition, there is one bizarrely unexplained phenomenon central to the Robin Hood narrative. When in the sixteenth century the playwright Anthony Munday exploited the implications of the chroniclers and turned Robin Hood, rough-handed outlaw, however inherently honourable, into a man of hierarchical honour, a genteel earl dispossessed by his enemies, why on earth does he name him the 'Earle of Huntington'? The only apparently sensible comment on the matter was made long ago by one D.H. (probably the antiquary Richard Gough) writing in the *Gentleman's Magazine*, who suggested this was simply a verbal play on the notion of the hero as a hunter (1793, p. 226).

Imagine then the greater surprise that emerged after discovering that in just the decade when Munday set his story the lord of this particular Rutland Barnsdale was none other than the Earl of Huntingdon. And who was this lord? The connection seemed striking when he turned out to be in the 1190s David, the younger brother of King William the Lion of Scotland, holding this estate of the King of England. All of a sudden it seems obvious why a Scottish chronicler like Andrew of Wyntoun, of all distant people, was interested in an outlaw legend that he located in part near Carlisle (like that of Adam Bell and Johnie Cock) and also in a place called Barnsdale which would almost certainly mean to him not somewhere on the Yorkshire road to London, but an estate hundreds of miles away that was a lucrative domain of the Scots royal house for many years. There is no evident explanation why Munday might have known that connection of Barnsdale and Huntingdon, though he might have heard of the link through the Christmas visit in 1595 paid by his rival company, the Chamberlain's Men, to Burley on the Hill in Rutland, formerly also a lordship of the earl and itself having a forest contiguous to the local Barnsdale (Ungerer, 1961).

This surprising data no doubt falls short of a secure relocation of the hero's activities. But new scholarly facts are not an ambition here: rather this evidence must more usefully shake the simple empiricism of belief in a single original Robin Hood. The Rutland connection has two morals. One is that the allegedly empirical historians did not actually do their work well enough, never bothering to look up Barnsdale properly; they accepted the possibly opportunistic Yorkshire location of the *Gest*. And secondly, and more importantly, there appears to be a web of Robin Hood references across the face of the country. From Aberdeen to Exeter, including the contradictions of Yorkshire and Rutland, there are many fully localized but separated and self-consistent Robin Hoods. The meaning of the myth is to be found in the elements of power, the resolutions and exposures of conflict that exist through those references in their local operations, not in some idealist and unreal construction of a pan-British Robin Hood tradition.

In the light of this view, it is to the special significance of each

Robin Hood reference in its context that this study will turn, and the
first point of inquiry will be the early chroniclers themselves, whose
comments will bear a good deal more interpretative scrutiny than has
so far been accorded them.

2.5   CHRONICLING A HERO

The chroniclers are usually listed in a neat and linear sequence, making a smooth, steady transition for Robin from rogue to lord. But if
they seem so seamless a sequence for hurrying historians, concerned
only with identity and apparent fact, to the literary critic, inured to
the culture of interpretative pondering, the cool language of the
chronicles can unfold into a web of varied implications about the
multiple hero.

Andrew of Wyntoun wrote 'The Orygynale Chronicle' at the request of his patron Sir John of Wemyss; it is a metrical history of
Scotland in octosyllabic couplets, evidently an account intended to be
widely accessible. Andrew was an Augustinian canon and was known
from the records to have been an active defender of his priory of St
Andrews – he became the prior of one of its daughter houses, St Sers
Inch at Loch Leven.

The chronicle was in some ways the first reliable Scottish record:
the *Dictionary of National Biography* not only said that 'With Wyntoun's
chronicle Scottish history made a good beginning' but also felt that it
was 'for the age in which he wrote, singularly accurate as to dates' (vol.
LXIII, 1900, pp. 266–7).

Under the year 1283 Wyntoun writes:

> Litil Iohun and Robert Hude
> Waythmen war commendit gud;
> In Ingilwode and Bernnysdaile
> Thai oyssit al this tyme thar trawale. (1903–14, V., p. 135, lines
>   25–8)

The language may seem obscure: the second line means 'Were well
praised as forest outlaws' and the last means 'All this time they continued their practices.' Though 'waythemen' has a slightly pejorative
sense, this seems a basically favourable account, but the positive force

of 'gud' may be partly accidental, as it provides a convenient rhyme with 'Hude'.

Importantly, Wyntoun makes no suggestion that these two were figures of fiction; they are real historical outlaws who were widely praised. A context can be found to explain that implicit approbation of English law-breakers. This part of the chronicle is discussing the period of Edward I and it lays great stress on his violence towards the Scots – the massacre at Berwick in 1296 is described with anger, and Edward is often called a 'tyrand', even a 'curseyd' one. There is even some distinct connection between the Scots and these 'waythemen' in that the Scots who fled from the English after Dunbar (1296) and Falkirk (1298) took to the forests themselves, and so a broad resemblance between Wallace and Robin Hood is implied, as Ritson noted (1795, p. ix) and as is suggested in some Scottish texts: Lewis Spence refers to a Latin poem of about 1500 (not 1306 as was formerly thought) that calls Wallace the Scottish Robin Hood (1928, pp. 94 and 95).

The significance of the northern location of Robin in Wyntoun has never been investigated, even though sixteenth-century references make it clear that there was an advanced cult of the outlaw in the towns and cities throughout Scotland, and it seems unlikely to be an accident that the first three chroniclers to mention him were Scottish: after Wyntoun came Walter Bower (in the 1440s) and John Major (writing *c.*1500). The topic has been surveyed generally by Spence (1928), who offers a mildly patriotic assertion of an early Scots presence in the tradition. The early strength of the northern evidence suggests most forcefully not a Scots leadership in the myth but the probability that there are many Robin Hoods, and they were especially well-recorded early in the north. The famous name is a generic description of forms of resistance to authority that can emerge in many places, even simultaneously in the north and the south.

The tendency is evident, even in quasi-historical chroniclers, for the figure of Robin Hood to be flexible and to express the changing ideological position of each of the authors. The second reference in this sequence of Scottish outlaw-watchers is by Walter Bower who in the 1440s was continuing the *Scotichronicon* compiled by John of Fordun some twenty years before (1722, V, p. 744). The anti-English tradition remains: Fordun's foreword indicates that his work is meant to replace the chronicles that were destroyed in Edward I's depredations.

Bower continued the account from the 1380s, where Fordun had ended, and also inserted his own additions for earlier years.

Under 1266 he provided a lengthy discussion and exemplification of the fame of the outlaw hero. This is written in rather difficult Latin, assuming, it would seem, a clerical audience, and the reference itself is in keeping. It speaks of Robin as a *'famosus siccarius'*, a well-known cut-throat rather than a robber, and sums up: Then arose the famous murderer, Robert Hood, as well as Little John, together with their accomplices from among the dispossessed, whom the foolish populace are so inordinately fond of celebrating both in tragedy and comedy (quoted by Dobson and Taylor, 1976, p. 5).

The evaluation is more severe than Wyntoun's; the earlier phrase 'commendit gud' has been both expanded and itself evaluated – these figures are widely celebrated, but this is said to be foolish. Again, there is no doubt that these are real people, however much they are fictionalized for public delight. It is of special interest to note that Bower refers to both tragedy and comedy and to consider what he means. The story of 'Robin Hood's Death' (Child no. 120) is the only element which could be called tragic in the whole tradition; while that ballad is not recorded until Thomas Percy's manuscript of romances and ballads, which is at least early seventeenth century, it does appear to be older in terms of its language, though it could hardly date from Bower's time in its present form, unlike 'Robin Hood and the Monk'.

It may be, though, that Bower does not have ballads or ballad-epic in mind at all as a source or a reference. The notion of comedy and a foolish populace also seems rather sweeping if applied to the ballads he might easily have known. 'Robin Hood and the Monk' (Child no. 119), which is in a manuscript of about 1450, could well have been known to Bower and other early ballads like 'Robin Hood and Guy of Gisborne' (Child no. 118) and 'Robin Hood and the Potter' (Child no. 121), both clearly of fifteenth-century origin, could have been among his information. Yet none of these is really foolish, or indeed very popular – they are quite long, without singing refrains. It would seem that Bower is more likely to be referring to the tradition of plays and games which is recorded on a number of occasions in the fifteenth century: there were plays at Exeter as early as 1426–7, the Paston reference is from 1473. King Henry VII saw Robin Hood pageants at York in 1486 and there were games in Edinburgh in 1492 and Wells about 1498.

Bower's remarks imply that the whole tradition was various and widespread by his period, as would be suggested in any case by the general references that are to be found by then (see Appendix). Much more specific, however, is the story he gives as typical of Robin Hood's popularity, which in spite of his introductory description shows the hero as neither a cut-throat nor in any way the worthless idol of a foolish populace. This narrative, clearly written by the late 1440s, must take precedence as the earliest Robin Hood story of all, because 'Robin Hood and the Monk' cannot be dated earlier than *c*.1450.

Bower's Robin Hood story has been remarkably unknown to commentators even though it is printed in Latin in a footnote in Child's introduction to the Robin Hood ballads. It deserves to be rendered in full because of its antiquity, unusualness and the complex light it casts on the tradition from the very beginning. After his summary introduction of the outlaws' crimes and the people's foolish admiration of them, quoted above, Bower continues in a more positive tone:

About whom also certain praiseworthy things are told, as appears in this – that when once in Barnsdale, avoiding the anger of the king and the threats of the prince, he was according to his custom most devoutly hearing mass and had no wish on any account to interrupt the service – on a certain day, when he was hearing mass, having been discovered in that very secluded place in the woods when the mass was taking place by a certain sheriff [literally, viscount] and servants of the king, who had very often lain in wait for him previously, there came to him those who had found this out from their men to suggest that he should make every effort to flee. This, on account of his reverence for the sacrament in which he was then devoutly involved, he completely refused to do. But, the rest of his men trembling through fear of death, Robert, trusting in the one so great whom he worshipped, with the few who then bravely remained with him, confronted his enemies and easily overcame them, and enriched by the spoils he took from them and their ransom, ever afterwards singled out the servants of the church and the masses to be held in greater respect, bearing in mind what is commonly said: 'God hearkens to him who hears mass frequently.' (Latin text in Child, III, p. 41, footnote. Translation by A.I. Jones.)

In this narrative Robin's innate fidelity to the church is both the effect and the mainspring of his courage; the royal officers are seen as

enemies to his noble spirit. Once again the idea of legitimate rebelliousness is present in the very early tradition, though here it is not
specifically related to the context of an anti-Scottish king, as it implicitly was in Wyntoun. Bower has inserted this material under the year
1266, and suggests that Robin was one of the dissidents who were in
rebellion with Simon de Montfort against Henry II; after Simon's
death at Evesham in 1265 they fought on as the 'disinherited', a term
deliberately employed by Bower.

The opening remarks make it clear that Bower knows Wyntoun's
reference, though he has more to tell and a new timing for the hero.
The only apparent reason for his moving the date – apart from Gutch's
view (1847, I, p. 77), in part supported by Holt (1982, pp. 40 and
97–9), that this was the real date of a historical Robin Hood – seems
to be that the Bower story focuses on a royal prince who is the main
villain. In Wynton's 1283 Edward I's eldest son was only twelve (the
future Edward II was only one) and not known for any form of martial
vigour; in 1266, on the other hand, the future Edward I was already
showing the military skill and ferocity which were to make him so
hated later on among the Scots, though at this time he was operating
in the English midlands and north, not across the border. This suggests that Bower adapted a 'Robin versus the Prince' story (of unknown origin) to a suitable year. He must have added for his own
purposes the almost hagiographical tone, which would have been highly
unlikely in the usually anti-clerical popular tradition.

Bower himself was, like Wyntoun, connected to St Andrew's Priory;
in 1418 he was made Abbot of Incholm in the Firth of Forth. Several
places in the busy south east of Scotland, St Andrews, Edinburgh and
indeed Bower's birthplace, Haddington, all have fairly early records of
Robin Hood plays and games, though none fall in Bower's lifetime.
The chronicler's references appear to defer to those traditions, but also
to innovate: his example indicates the way in which heroes can suddenly be used in the service of quite surprising ideologies. This entry
is not Robin Hood's only service to religion, though that is not a
marked feature of his career. But to note that the whole tradition
starts off with what might well be thought an aberrant narrative, so
unlike the ballads about the anti-clerical outlaw, gives a fair sense of
the multi-centred, highly varied and locally attuned character of this
myth.

The third of the Scottish chroniclers is John Major. The connections with predecessors exist: he went to school in Bower's Haddington, but stepped out into a wider world of renaissance learning at Cambridge and then Paris, where he was a noted professor of theology and even earned a fictional mention in Rabelais' *Gargantua* as the author of a treatise on black puddings.

Major returned to Scotland to teach at Glasgow University in about 1500, but he had, apparently, completed his Latin *Historia Majoris Britanniae* (translated as *History of Greater Britain, as well England and Scotland*, 1892) before he returned, though it was not published until 1521, in Paris. This, like Bower's work, is in Latin, but it has a more modern, humane style, invoking the world of European intellectuals rather than the highly clerical Latin of Bower. Major's text is described by the *Dictionary of National Biography* as being 'the first history of Scotland written in a critical spirit' (XXXV, 1893, pp. 386–8) in the sense of comparing sources and resolving conflicts but it does not assume objectivity as a goal. His editor, the grandly named Aeneas Mackay, indicates that here 'history is important for the practical value of the lessons it contains'. (1892, p. xix)

Major's view of Robin Hood is both less contradictory and more admiring than that of Bower or Wyntoun. He says, speaking of the 1190s, the time of Richard I and Prince John:

> About this time it was, as I conceive, that there flourished those most famous robbers Robert Hood, an Englishman, and Little John, who lay in wait in the woods but spoiled of their goods those only that were wealthy. They took the life of no man, unless he either attacked them or offered resistance in defence of his property. Robert was supported by his plundering one hundred bowmen, ready fighters every one, with whom four hundred of the strongest would not dare to engage in combat. The feats of this Robert are told in song all over Britain. He would allow no woman to suffer injustice, nor would he spoil the poor, but rather enriched them from the plunder taken from abbots. The robberies of this man I condemn, but of all robbers he was the humanest and the chief. (1892, pp. 156–7)

Like his predecessors, Major has no doubt that Robin and John are real people, however much they are figures in song across the country. He is definitely pointing to Robin's military and moral virtues, and the treatment suggests there is every likelihood that he was familiar with the *Gest*. Although he was in Paris at the time of its appearance,

as it was first printed in the Netherlands, a copy might easily have
reached him in France. There is clear reference in Major to the part of
the *Gest* in which (see p. 77) Robin enjoins his men to protect women
and the poor, sets them specifically to plunder abbots, and uses the
motif of the large number of ready bowmen who respond to Robin's
horn-call – though that also appears in several early ballads. But the
summary that Robin was both humane and also lordly is a view suited
only to the *Gest* of the material surviving from Major's period, whereas
Bower's identification of Robin as a famous cut-throat seems much
closer to the bloodier ballads like 'Robin Hood and Guy of Gisborne'
and 'Robin Hood and the Monk'; the latter contradicts Major's *Gest*-
oriented suggestion that Robin only kills in self-defence or protection
of his property.

Just as Major evidently knew the English and secular *Gest*, he also
clearly indicates sympathies which go far beyond the Scottish and
clerical disposition of Wyntoun and Bower. He was in touch with a
development of the tradition more ambitious and more moralizing
than the ballads; Major even seems to develop the elements of gentrification which begin to emerge in part in the *Gest* and which are
implied in his use of the word '*princeps*' for Robin as the 'chief' of
robbers, this '*humanissimus*' of thieves. Bower had defined an enemy
with the word '*princeps*' and Major's history has other more overt
variations from the traditions of his land of origin. He removes the
violence of Edward I at Berwick in 1296 (though the later Scottish
chroniclers, Hector Boece and David Buchanan firmly put it back
again in their own histories) and though he does identify Edward
as using 'inhuman cruelty' in Scotland he also suggests that in his
imposition of union 'he would have respected our ancient liberties'.
This sense that Edward's kingship was not a real threat may well be
a partial reason for Major's own major change in the story, which is
to redate Robin Hood to the year 1196. Without a strong sense of
Scottish outrage to validate the outlaw's rebellion, he needed to look
elsewhere for a justification of a figure he clearly admired.

The right location emerged within the English historical tradition
itself – another sign of Major's own inherently non-Scottish positioning. The relocation to the 1190s enables Major to take Robin Hood
out of a period of dissent against kings who seemed to have rightful
authority and locate his resistance in a period when the line of authority
was much less clear and legitimate, with King Richard notoriously on

crusade, and then King John famous for bringing England under papal interdict. It is a double relocation, moving the myth away from what may seem like political agitation by the outlaw and also away from the pro-Scottish implications of the earlier chroniclers. It is important to note that Major does not develop the idea that Robin Hood resisted 'bad King John'; but he did set the stage for that interpretation to develop a good deal later on. His immediate model might have been an existing story of a misunderstood nobleman who suffered at the hands of John.

Just as Wyntoun and perhaps Bower too had Wallace in the forests as an image in which to shape Robin Hood, so Major may well have known the story of Fulk Fitz Warren, a historical figure in the time of King John who was at odds with the king, was dispossessed, lived as an outlaw, and finally regained his lands. A poem in Norman French about Fulk survives, and an English version once existed. While it was clearly not one of the bestsellers of the thirteenth century, the plot does have clear resemblance to the basic pattern of Major's Robin Hood account. The humane bandit of the *Gest* is relocated and effectively ennobled and Fulk may well have been a partial model, as Prideaux argued (1886, pp. 421–4).

Major set the hero on the path to gentrification, developing strongly a few hints in the *Gest*. Later writers would complete Major's redirection of the myth towards a displaced earl, though the popular rebel and even the religious supporter of the earlier chroniclers will consistently reappear in appropriate institutional contexts right through to the present. However, aristocratizing the hero was a crucial move in redirecting the paths of the myth, and a most significant specific step towards Robin the distressed gentleman was embodied in the next important statement by a chronicler on this matter, in the work of Richard Grafton.

Grafton's *Chronicle at Large* appeared in 1569. Written in English and widely disseminated, this major influence on later historiography shaped the gentrification of Robin Hood in a particular direction. Grafton first gives an explicit résumé of Major's account, omitting the statement that Robin's feats were widely praised in song: in Grafton's account he is only a historical figure. The précis of Major ends with the summary 'that among the number of theeues, he was worthie the name of the most gentle theefe' (1569, p. 84).

'Gentle' here is a skilful elision of the humane characteristics that

Major brings forward from the *Gest* and the notion of actual legal nobility: Leland in his *Collecteana* from the 1530s (1770, I, p. 54) describes the hero as '*nobilis exlex*', a noble outlaw. For Grafton this aura of nobility and gentility was made specifically aristocratic. He continues in the next paragraph:

> But in an olde and auncient Pamphlet I finde this written of the sayd Robert Hood. This man (sayth he) discended of a noble parentage: or rather beyng of a base stocke and linage, was for his manhoode and chiualry aduaunced to the noble dignitie of an Erle, excellyng principally in Archery, or shootyng, his manly courage agreeyng thervnto: But afterwardes he so prodigally exceeded in charges and expences, that he fell into great debt, by reason whereof, so many actions and sutes were commenced against him, wherevnto he aunswered not, that by order of lawe he was outlawed, and then for a lewde shift, as his last refuge, gathered together a companye of Roysters and Cutters, and practised robberyes and spoylyng of the kynges subiects, and occupied and frequentede the Forestes or wilde Countries. The which beyng certefyed to the King, and he beyng greatly offended therewith, caused his proclamation to be made that whosoeuer would bryng him quicke or dead, the king would geue him a great summe of money, as by the recordes in the Exchequer is to be seene: But of this promise, no man enioyed any benefite. For the sayd Robert Hood, beyng afterwardes troubled with sicknesse, came to a certein Nonry in Yorkshire called Bircklies, where desiryng to be let blood, he was betrayed and bled to deth. After whose death the Prioresse of the same place caused him to be buried by the high way side, where he had vsed to rob and spoyle those that passed that way. And vpon his graue the sayde Prioresse did lay a very fayre stone, wherein the names of Robert Hood, William of Goldesborough, and others were grauen. And the cause why she buryed him there, was, for that the common passengers and trauailers knowyng and seeyng him there buryed, might more safely and without feare take their iorneys that way, which they durst not do in the life of the sayd outlawes. And at eyther end of the sayde Tombe was erected a crosse of stone, which is to be seene there at this present. (1569, pp. 84–5)

The first question must be, what was this 'olde and auncient Pamphlet' – and did it exist? Grafton is not in general a fanciful chronicler given to inventing sources; he was a printer by profession, more inclined to collect material and as far as possible rationalize it, as appears to have been his method here. Other evidence does exist for the tombstone, though not of a very persuasive kind (see pp. 19–20). It is quite possible that the 'Pamphlet' (which suggests a printed text) was simply the *Gest*: that could have stimulated the criminal narrative and the betrayal and death at 'Birklies' – in early type or writing an easy error for Kirklees, the usual location.

However, that would leave unsourced the account of Robin's nobility, and the fact that this is the first point derived from the alleged 'Pamphlet' might indeed suggest that Grafton did have something more than Leland's word '*nobilis*' and Major's perhaps misinterpretable '*princeps*' as stimuli for gentrification. It is curious that Grafton in his indirect quotation gives two accounts of Robin's gentrification, one by birth and one by merit. Neither is inherently improbable – aristocrats were as often made as born in the middle ages, even in comparison with our meritocratic times. But the double account suggests that Grafton, or perhaps his source, is reconciling two traditions for Robin's advancement, and that some elements of gentrification had already occurred in an oral or lost written tradition. This notion is quite absent from the surviving earlier tradition: the *Gest* has no narrative about the ennobling of the hero in spite of much approbation of his character. None of the early references indicates an aristocratic outlaw, and had the idea been current it seems highly unlikely that it would not have somehow been touched on: after all, the *Piers Plowman* reference in full is to 'rymes of Robin Hood and Randolf Earl of Chester', so the absence of an earldom in Robin's case seems specifically indicated.

And yet against that early lack of gentrification, Grafton's assertion is specific, he is usually reliable, and there may in the depths of the Robin Hood tradition actually be the trace of an early 'aristocratizing' narrative. The late fourteenth-century poem *Gamelyn* will have later contacts with the ballad and even novel forms of the tradition (see pp. 87, 89, 183 and 188), but relevant here is the fact that this poem is about a disinherited gentleman, of knightly class, who takes to the forest and leads an outlaw band, the structure largely followed by Grafton.

In *Gamelyn* the hero is restored to his rights, not betrayed to death; but then Grafton had at least the *Gest* and Leland before him to provide the tragic ending, and perhaps also a version of 'Robin Hood's Death' earlier than that in Percy's manuscript (see p. 60). He may also have known the romance of Fulk Fitz Warren which, while possibly used by Major to shape his own Robin Hood entry, is a good deal closer as a story to Grafton's extended account of aristocratic brigandry. And lest it seem that possible parallels to an early noble Robin story are being piled up willy nilly, attention should be drawn to the apparent relation of *Gamelyn* and the Fulk narrative through the characters' names; Wrennock is the hero's enemy in the para-Robin Hood ballad 'Robyn and Gandelyn' (Child, 1965, III, no. 115) and the son of Morris of Powys, Fulk's enemy, goes by the same name in the French romance.

That there may be in the *Gamelyn*-Fulk Fitz Warren connection the shadow of an early aristocratizing narrative which was also applied to the best known English outlaw is to a high degree speculative, though W.F. Prideaux has developed a complex argument along those lines (1886). It would be less bold to assume that Grafton's remarks simply point to the existence of an earlier gentrifying text, the view basically held by Nelson in his careful study of the development of the renaissance Robin Hood (1973, pp. 33–5).

That version would almost certainly only have been literary, not oral, since the popular tradition shows no sign of such gentrification – but then Grafton, precise as he usually is, indicates clearly that this is a written source, and in fact unlike the previous chroniclers he has no interest in popular tradition at all. A royal printer, a scholar, a man of the new bureaucratic world and centralizing power, Grafton is the right man in the right place to set Robin Hood in a newly hierarchized situation.

An archetype of such men in the sixteenth century was William Cecil, first Lord Burleigh, and so was his second son Robert. The father was actually the person to whom Grafton dedicated his Chronicle; the son was also involved in the Robin Hood tradition. He sharply identified what he felt to be the threatening nature of the anti-authoritarian Robin Hood when, in a letter, he referred to the Gunpowder plotters as 'Robin Hoods' (Winwood, 1725, II, pp. 132–3; Holt, 1982, p. 151), and he was also the victim of the reflexive power of popular myth. Burleigh itself stands within an easy walk of Rutland's Barnsdale, and little further off is Rockingham, which the Cecils by this time owned. Robert settled further south at Hatfield and his oppressions of local liberties were noted in a jingle both radical and resistant:

Not Robin Goodfellow nor Robin Hood
But Robin the encloser of Hatfield Wood.
(Cecil, 1915, p. 379)

Bureaucrats like the Cecils and the processes of enclosure are dominant features of the new world of the later sixteenth century. Contemporaneously, and with clear sociocultural connections, there developed a new version of the myth of Robin Hood. Grafton set in persuasive and highly influential form a tradition about Robin that was going to be massively popular in its many transformations from Elizabethan drama through to Hollywood's love of a lord. Grafton represented the strength of the early tradition of Robin's banditry, but brought it within a gentrified and tragic frame. The 'waythemen' of Wyntoun and Bower's cut-throat have been transmuted into Major's humane robber and Grafton's rash gentleman, and those transformations indicate social and cultural redispositions of symbolic resistance to authority. A fuller understanding of how those changes occurred and what the particular representations of Robin Hood meant in context will come from a closer study of the large number and considerable variety of the ballad texts.

3

❧

'Chief Governor under the Greenwood Tree': Robin Hood in the Ballads

3.1 MATERIALS AND APPROACHES

Robin Hood appears a fugitive figure partly because the ballad, a major element in the tradition, is the most elusive of all the narrative forms. This genre has an essential insubstantiality, whether it comes from the ballads' oral nature -- which must rely for transmission across time on some literate recorder -- or their production as single sheet broadsides, requiring for preservation either a determined collector like Samuel Pepys or Anthony Wood from the seventeenth century, or sheer chance. Most of the important Robin Hood ballads exist in single copies in small, battered prints and even less impressive manuscripts.

Even if they have the fortune to be recorded, the ballads still retain a certain elusiveness. One of the great treasures of Anglophone culture is F.J. Child's *The English and Scottish Popular Ballads*. His volume III (in the five-volume reprint of 1965; originally volume V of ten) is the classic source for Robin Hood ballads, providing thirty-eight different texts. Though there are some comments to be made about the organization and division of the material, and a few other unimportant texts are found elsewhere, it remains the dominant edition.

Yet this rich and closely annotated material has been studied by relatively few scholars; the ballads enjoy no rigmarole of detailed analysis as do high cultural classics like *The Faerie Queene* or *Lyrical Ballads*; and unlike other aspects of popular culture become respectable, from

Shakespeare to Dickens, there is no wealth of scholarship to canonize these apparently lightweight verse-stories. That is largely because their narratives and their presentation of human character do not fit the requirements of modern literary criticism, failing to mesh with the concepts that drive that discipline and are themselves supported by it. None of the ballads offers morally concerned characters, deep and individual, such as we find in the novel tradition and therefore – we like to think – in ourselves. Nor do any of Child's texts offer the historical and sociological sweep that validates the viewpoints of the nationalist historicism which so much energized the thought of the last century.

Most commentators have found little to say about the Robin Hood ballads except that they have a rude nobility, a vigorous wryness and a disappointing sense of incompletion. But if the texts are read in the context of social attitudes across time they reveal a series of interconnected responses to ambient forces, provide in themselves an index to changing attitudes to authority, and form a set of connected groups as analysed in this chapter, with the *Gest* needing to be treated separately because of its length and special nature.

Several preliminary topics need to be considered. To argue, as the following pages do, that the earliest Robin Hood texts represent the hero as a focus for resisting authority must depend on having a clear and confident idea of which actually are the early texts. Some of the dating is unclear and there is an obvious danger of deciding what is the theme of the early ballads and then dictating earliness on the basis of that idea. However, while avoiding such circularity, and following closely the actual chronology of the texts, it is possible to see a distinct coherence about the themes and dates of the earliest material, some elements of which are represented in later texts.

The fact of recording provides a point by which texts must have been in existence: 'Robin Hood and the Monk' (no. 119) is in a manuscript whose handwriting indicates a date of about 1450; 'Robin Hood and the Potter' (no. 121) was clearly written by about 1500 or perhaps a little earlier. The printed texts of the *Gest of Robin Hood* (no. 117, hereafter called the *Gest*) are not easy to date, or even order, with any precision, but the text is clearly in existence by 1500 – there are no manuscript versions.

Child's numbering is in what he felt to be chronological series and there are some doubtful elements in his decisions; the date of the *Gest* is a matter to be discussed shortly, but he inserted two ballads early, even though their texts are quite late. 'Robin Hood and Guy of Gisborne' (no. 118) only survives in the manuscript which Thomas Percy rescued from being used to light fires and from which he then selected his *Reliques* (omitting seven other Robin Hood texts in the process). The Percy manuscript is usually dated in the early to mid-seventeenth century. The evidence for putting 'Guy of Gisborne' as early as Child does is in part that a manuscript play which deals with some of the same events exists in a handwriting dated about 1475; but Child was also guided by the apparent antiquity of the material to place 'Guy of Gisborne' before 'Robin Hood and the Monk', a much more doubtful decision. Something of the same process occurred with the other early-numbered ballad 'Robin Hood's Death' (no. 120) which follows 'Robin Hood and the Monk'. This too appears in the Percy manuscript, but the story must have been well known by the mid-sixteenth century, as the main events in the ballad are mentioned in Grafton's *Chronicle at Large* and were summarized in the fifteenth century *Gest*. The opening closely resembles that of 'Robin Hood and the Monk', so it must have seemed to Child reasonable to locate it before 'Robin Hood and the Potter'.

Although it would not be hard to have minor quibbles with some of these opinions, none of them is contradicted by the content of the ballads, as will be discussed shortly. A more far-reaching and disputable issue is the opinion Child is thought to have passed on the essential date of the *Gest*, which has become doctrine among many later commentators. All he actually claimed was that there were some 'Middle English forms' of language still in the text printed around 1500. He summarized the possibilities: 'The Gest may have been compiled at a time when such forms had gone out of use, and these may be relics of the ballads from which this little epic was made up; or the whole poem may have been put together as early as 1400, or before. There are no firm grounds on which to base an opinion' (1965, III, p. 40).

In his characteristically meticulous manner Child is basically disagreeing with the confident statement that the *Gest* comes from the time of Chaucer made by Gutch, (1847, I. p. vii) but most have ignored the fine detail. Child's first proposal, that the notionally embedded ballads have carried some earlier linguistic forms with them, bespeaks an older idea that epics were composed from pre-existent lays, which has not survived a better comprehension of how longer poems were actually composed. They were substantially recreated, using the materials, not the words, of earlier texts. So if there are older forms in the *Gest* they would indicate an early date of origin for the text roughly as it is.

The question is whether such evidence exists. Child was referring to cases of final 'e' being pronounced, either on its own or in an '-es' plural. Clawson, in his detailed analysis of the *Gest*'s construction, listed uses of final e and decided the text 'extends back to a period when those forms were in general use among the people; to a period, that is, antedating the year 1400' (1909, pp. 5–6). This scholarly and specific support for Child's apparent suggestion has been enough for most later commentators. Keen even stated that it was 'fourteenth century rather than thirteenth', a notion which had never been in linguistic contention but stemmed from historians' speculations about an early 'real' Robin Hood (1961, p. 34); Maddicott stated 1400 'at the latest' (1978, p. 276) and Dobson and Taylor accepted the by now dominant reading of Child's text as supporting a date around 1400 (1976, p. 8).

It is probably no accident that these are not linguistic scholars. It is not merely the printed form that makes the *Gest* look post-medieval; anyone used to the vagaries of fifteenth-century Middle English will see the *Gest* as being quite late. Gray for example suggests cautiously 'there might not be much against assigning the poem in its present form to the earlier part of the fifteenth century' and he clearly meant this as the earliest possible date (1984, p. 23). Sergio Baldi, a fine scholar of these texts, felt the *Gest* was not recorded till *c*.1500, and would only say it was written somewhat earlier (1949, p. 135). Some recent linguistic analysis suggests that Gutch, Clawson and others were dating the evidence half a century too early. Pearsall speaks in his edition of *The Floure and the Leafe* of several mid-fifteenth century texts 'in which the use of final "e", though rare, is perfectly correct and the verse completely assured' (1962, p. 60), and this is precisely the case in the *Gest*. Even some historians have doubted an early origin. Though Holt repeats the standard dating of *c*.1400 (1982, pp. 15 and 191, n. 2), he also (1982, p. 56) suggests the text feels as if it is contemporary with Malory (which would put it in the 1460s, since *Le Morte Darthur* was finished by 1471), while elsewhere he suggests it is 'nearer to 1450 than 1400' (1982, p. 188).

There seems no good reason to place the text before about 1450; indeed the mention of King Edward, called 'our comely king' (st. 353 and 365) and 'grete above his cole' (st. 372) may well suggest the 1460s would be a better time as that is during the reign of the

notoriously handsome and tall Edward IV, depicted in the National
Portrait Gallery as having a very large head and who himself spent
much time in the north, as does the king of the *Gest*. E.K. Chambers,
in writing the literary history of the later middle ages, felt the poem
represented 'the chaotic condition of England under Edward IV' (1945,
p. 132).

This later dating bears not only on the analysis of meaning in the
early Robin Hood poems which is to follow; it also must cast light on
a second major question, namely how the *Gest* itself is constructed.
Child's comments suggest he thought the poem might be an assemblage based on a number of pre-existing ballads, as in the then dominant theories about epics like the *Iliad* and *Beowulf* arising from heroic
lays. Clawson identified seven different ballads that were embedded in
the structure of the *Gest* (not all of them existing in early forms, 1909,
pp. 125–6) and this view has been widely accepted, but it was never
reconciled clearly with the equally accepted early date of the *Gest*. If
it was from Chaucer's time, as most wanted to think, then the constituent ballads were even earlier, but the *Piers Plowman* reference is
the only record, which seems odd for such a notionally popular tradition at that time. If the ballads being referred to in the fifteenth
century were the basis, then the date of this composite *Gest* is pushed
forward.

The only logical way out of this largely unrecognized dilemma was
taken by a scholar who reversed the usual order, and insisted that the
art-based structure of the *Gest* was in fact the original and that the
ballads were 'cut-down' forms of the extended text. This view was
developed by D.C. Fowler, who argued that the ballads are late decadent versions of literary and elite materials (1968, pp. 79–80), and
so he subverted in a major way the old-fashioned sentimental populism
which had wanted to trace ballads back to a communal production
grouping, happily clapping and singing along to the strains of 'Brown
Robin' or 'Johnie Cock'.

But just as Child's caution was ignored by those who sought antiquity, so Fowler's position over-simplified the issues in order to privilege
the socially higher forms – a position with which J.C. Holt's interest
in a genteel audience basically agrees, though his own familiarity with
written sources prevents him being misled on the date of the *Gest*.
Douglas Gray, who of all the commentators knows the texts the best,
has pointed out that there are many other half-ballad half-romance

forms and that a temporal coexistence of the early ballads and the compilation form found in the *Gest* is what you would expect (1984, p. 23). We also have in existence at the same time Bower's direction of the Robin Hood story into the service of the church in complex Latin (see p. 35), so since multiplicity of forms clearly exists, there is no need to put the compilation and the single ballads in any order of developmental precedence. There is no difficulty in seeing a period in the mid to late-fifteenth century when the Robin Hood stories begin to be recorded and the earlier bare references to them take on narrative flesh. This is the period when the reading audience grows so considerably that scribes cannot keep up with the demand and so the printing press becomes profitable. The Robin Hood texts, it seems, are part of that new flood of recorded literary material, and in the *Gest* they produced their fullest version so far, while the ballads and plays represented the popular end of this widespread cultural phenomenon.

To see the ballads in that light helps to explain another oddity about them that was not unnaturally exploited by Fowler in his attempt to downgrade the popular aspects of the tradition. It is often said that the Robin Hood ballads have few tunes. In B.H. Bronson's collection of *The Traditional Tunes of the Child Ballads* (1959–66), a work almost as massive in scale and scholarship as Child's own enterprise, most of the Child ballads are shown to have a range of tunes available, some entries stretching into many pages. But in the case of Robin Hood, Bronson expressed his profound disappointment at what he could find; there were few tunes, of very limited quality, and in any case most of them belonged to other ballads (1966, III, pp. 13–14). This would seem to mesh with the fact that unlike other Child ballads the Robin Hood texts tend to be in written or printed form very early; some existed or at least are heard of in the fifteenth and sixteenth centuries and the great part of them appeared in the broadsides which flooded the London streets in the seventeenth century; they seem to have been especially popular after the restoration and were gathered into 'Garlands' which thrived for two centuries, effectively chapbooks with between twelve and thirty ballads gathered under a loose title like *The Exploits of Renowned Robin Hood* of 1769 or *The Adventures of Robert, Earl of Huntingdon* of 1777.

This raises the last preliminary issue, that of audience. The lack of tunes would suggest a basically literary audience for the Robin Hood material, quite different from the obviously oral context of the love and marriage ballads that dominate Child's collection or the military and trade ballads strongly represented in de Sola Pinto and Rodway's *The Common Muse* (1957). But the very earliest references (see Appendix) do not support a literary context in an unequivocal way. Langland talks of 'rymes' and while singing is not clearly implied, by 1410 the play *Dives and Pauper* speaks equally critically of those who would 'levir to heryn a tale or a song of Robyn Hode or of sum rubaudry than to heryn messe or matynes' (see Appendix for this and following references). A similar ambiguity seems to emerge later: a manuscript of *The Canterbury Tales* written in the period 1460–80 inserts Robin Hood's name into a series of romance heroes, implying literary standing, but then a Scottish manuscript of the same period includes the line 'the sow sate on hye bank and harpyd on Robyn Hode' and a Lambeth manuscript of the late-fifteenth century also seems to relate the tradition to song by saying:

> He that made this songe ful good
> Came of the northe and of the sotherne blode
> And somewhat kyne to Robin Hode.

The multiple location of the hero is intriguing, but in terms of genre, it may be, as Gray suggests (1984, pp. 8–9), that whether sung or not the essence of the tradition is a performed narrative, using different forms of performance and, sometimes, recording. The early printed and literary tradition certainly exists, and has importance, but is itself a version of the whole Robin Hood tradition, not a breakaway phenomenon.

The same multifariousness may well explain some of the disagreements among scholars about the audience of the early ballads, which are themselves bound up with interpretations of the meaning of the tradition at this time. Early commentators had a vague view of the audience – Joseph Ritson's generalized radical enthusiasm in his 1795 collection spoke of 'the people' who responded to what he saw as a sturdy native democratism, the spirit of Tom Paine before his time. Child and his contemporaries tended to idealize, even mythicize, such popularism into 'the ballad muse' which he saw as the origin of the whole tradition. Fowler proposed a literary elite shaping a tradition that became 'decadent' in popular mouths. A view both more socially specific and politically radical was put forward when Hilton (1958, see

1976 reprint ed.) linked the origin of the ballads with the lower class discontents of the fourteenth century that culminated in the so-called Peasants' Revolt of 1381. This was a sharpened focus for Ritson's vaguely radical reading of Robin Hood, and that clarity elicited a response: J.C. Holt wrote first in *Past and Present* (reprinted in Hilton, 1976) and then in his more recent book his determined view that the ballads, centring on the *Gest*, were produced in and for the context of courtly houses and the precise audience was the 'retainers and dependants' of the 'crown, the aristocracy and the landed gentry' (Holt, 1982, p. 110). He held that the discontent expressed was that of the lower stratum of the gentry, petty landholders who were affected by rising labour costs and other economic changes in the fourteenth century.

The debate turned on the meaning of the word 'yeoman': was this figure a sturdy dissenting peasant such as the leaders of the 1381 revolt, or was he a small proprietor? There was evidence for both. What there was not was any sign at all of any agrarian interest in the ballads, and this observation led to a little-noted but innovative essay by Richard Tardif (1983) which stressed the importance of the town in the ballads, pointing out that the forest was always a zone of imaginary freedom near a town. He argued that the term 'yeoman' can also mean journeymen tradesman, and the ballads have an origin in the creation of a cultural consciousness for a new dispossessed urban artisan class. This view certainly meshes well with the notion of early literacy and printing and does fit some of the action of the ballads, as will be discussed shortly, though it may be no more than a legitimate connection for some of the ballads to a relevant time and place.

All contexts for the ballads appear general rather than specific. It seems clear that any precise relation to the late medieval revolts and other risings is not direct, but that the figure of Robin Hood can be used as a symbolic liberator in such events, like the 1497 riots in Wednesbury or those of 1561 in Edinburgh (see pp. 108–9), or even the criminal guerrilla activities of men like Piers Venables (see p. 25) and political rebels like 'Robin of Holderness' and 'Robin of Redesdale' who led risings against the government in different parts of the north in 1469. But no direct political link with 1381 or any other peasant politics is clear. The action of the ballads does not deal directly with agrarian workers' problems nor seems to treat them symbolically either; but equally it never deals with problems of proprietors except in the case of the *Gest*, where the outlaws are uniquely allied to a knight. Yet he is oppressed not by forces of innovation but by the same enemies as Robin Hood and his men, namely the established church and the forces of state legality.

The causes of distress in these early texts are generalized, not specified, and one of the problems about the audience debate is that (apart from Tardif) the commentators have been historians who have had little idea of the mediations and symbolisms that intervene between audience and material in the normal functioning of literature. Shakespeare never wrote about the Elizabethan age: it was British medieval history, classical distance or Mediterranean displacement that permitted him to realize what Raymond Williams would call a contemporary 'structure of feeling'. Similarly, the world of oppression in the early Robin Hood texts is relevant in a symbolic and displaced way to a multiple audience which no doubt includes and may indeed combine the labourer and the proprietor. Such is often the broad-based power that drives new genres, just as the rising crime fiction of the nineteenth century fictionalized new urban distress through threats to the individual body and so caught the attention of a wide and newly sensitized market. In order to establish the ways in which these early texts did imagine threats through fictional symbolism, it is necessary to look closely at some of the major early narratives and then see how the others both developed and then altered the thrust of what appears to be the founding and in varied ways enduring tradition of the Robin Hood texts, an outlaw who expressed forms of resistance to contemporary authority.

3.2   RESISTING AUTHORITY: THE EARLIEST BALLADS

Like many of the traditional ballads, 'Robin Hood and the Monk' is not immediately easy of access. The spelling and language are unfamiliar to those whose early English goes back no further than Shakespeare and, perhaps, Chaucer; there is a gap in the text between stanzas 30 and 31 where a page appears to have been lost in copying, and there are a few lines missing elsewhere, the sort of eye-skip error that scribes often commited. But in spite of these problems of approach, the essence of the ballad is clear, and an interestingly double story presents itself.

The frame deals with the outlaw band and its composition. At first Little John and Robin argue as they go towards Nottingham where Robin wishes to attend church. They part in anger. Alone, Robin is identified by a 'gret-hedid munke' at St Mary's church and the gap in the text occurs just as he runs into the church, presumably for sanctuary. The story picks up after the break as Robin's men have heard of his betrayal by the monk. John, evidently in charge, says he and Much will find the monk and save Robin.

Pretending to be victims of Robin Hood, they meet the monk, kill him out of hand and take his letters on to the king. John receives a warrant to bring Robin to the king; on their return to Nottingham on this errand they are entertained by the sheriff, but that night they break Robin out of prison and return to Sherwood. John points out to Robin he has done him 'a gode turne for an evuyll' and Robin offers to make John 'maister . . . Off all my men and me', but John declines. The outlaw band regathers, the sheriff is tricked, the king is angry, but finally and ruefully notes that Little John 'is trew to his maister' and 'has begyled vs alle.'

An evident theme in this ballad is the danger Robin faces alone, having broken by his rashness the bond of security with John and his men. Equally, Robin's religious instincts lead him into conflict with a monk, who is allied with that other established force of medieval government, the town authorities, in this case backed up fully by the king. Other ballads will separate the themes of security in solidarity from the danger of the abbots and organized religion, and also from the perils of town law. Here these threats are all combined, and opposed to them is the securely collective world of the forest, imbued with love of the Virgin Mary, innate cunning, immediate vigour and a rough form of justice. That world is outlaw to the domain of oppressive law, and is also presented as fully natural – this ballad opens with as fine a spring setting as any, characteristically brief but evocative:

> In somer, when the shawes be sheyne,
>   And leves be large and long
> Hit is full mery in feyre foreste
>   To here the foulys song:
>
> To se the dere draw to the dale,
>   And leve the hilles hee,
> And shadow hem in the leves grene,
>   Under the grenewode tre. (Child, 1965, III, p. 97, st. 1–2)

At Whitsuntide these adventures take place, as if there is a natural equivalent to the Holy Spirit. But the communal forest life is cut across first by improper squabbling and then by the legal constrictions associated with town, church and royalty. Laws, coins, official appointments (of the sheriff and of Little John as the king's yeoman) all threaten to enmesh the outlaws, yet their mixture of solidarity and fidelity, instrumentalized in speedy and flexible response, brings them through the dangers of the narrative.

Child enjoyed 'Robin Hood and the Monk': he said 'Too much could not be said in praise of this ballad' and it was 'very perfection of its kind' (p. 95), though these judgements were not explained or elaborated. Seen in the context of social meaning, the ballad is richly interwoven, making the danger and rescue itself realize the value and structure of the outlaw band as the embodiment of a natural state opposed to a world of alien, modern, threatening acculturation.

The second of the certainly early texts, 'Robin Hood and the Potter' (no. 121) provides a less wide-ranging but equally well-focused account of resistance to contemporary authorities. The language here is even more difficult than in 'Robin Hood and the Monk', but the poem is complete. Child feels there are lines missing occasionally; however, in all cases but one it appears that the author has written a six-line stanza rather than the usual quatrain, though in one stanza (no. 57) it does seem that a line has been lost.

Here again, the time is early summer, with 'The bloschoms on every bow' and the religious parallel, Robin's 'loffe of owre ladey', is established immediately. Rather than him journeying into adventure, here, as is equally common, adventure comes to the forest.

A 'proud potter' appears who has fought Little John well, and Robin bets on himself against the newcomer. The Potter wins and is paid; then Robin exchanges clothes with him, and goes off to Nottingham in the guise of a potter. Little John is an important bystander during this action, and so, as in the 'Monk', he is effectively the 'despatcher' as folk tales have it, the embodiment of the band which is left behind as Robin goes off alone into danger.

In the town, Robin sells his pots very rapidly because he prices them too low; he gives the last to the sheriff's wife and is invited to dinner. The sheriff's men speak of a shooting match for forty shillings (the amount Robin has just lost to the potter). Robin says if he had a bow, he would shoot; he is given one; he wins, and the sheriff praises him.

The alleged potter says he has a bow in his cart that Robin Hood gave him, and the sheriff says he would give a hundred pound to meet Robin Hood.

Next day they leave; Robin gives the sheriff's wife a gold ring; in the forest Robin says he will blow his horn to see if Robin is about. The outlaws all appear, take away the sheriff's gold and send him home on foot. Robin sends the sheriff's wife a white palfrey, a lady's horse. The wife laughs when she hears the story and tells the sheriff he has paid for the pots Robin gave her. Back in the forest Robin gives the potter the huge sum of ten pounds for his pots and says he will always be welcome in the forest.

The poem ends with an interesting version of the usual 'round-up', detailing briskly the conclusion, the setting and adding a Christian and social message:

> Thes partyd Robyn, the screffe and the potter,
>   Ondernethe the grene-wod tre;
> God haffe mersey on Roben Hodys solle,
>   And saffe all god yemanrey. (p. 113, st. 83)

The issue is – what is meant by 'good yeomanry'? The ballad clearly repeats the values of solidarity and fidelity as in 'Robin Hood and the Monk', but adds to them expertise in fighting with sword and bow, having sporting attitudes to these skills, and also the spiritual value of faith in our lady. The sheriff is still a clear enemy, but there is no mention of the threat of the organized church. Instead Robin recognizes and discounts the mercantile practices of the town and trades: his process of pot-selling is quite unrealistic, but also massively generous. This touches certain important issues in late medieval culture. Generosity is constantly stressed as a virtue of a lord, simply because salaries and contracts did not effectively exist as a dominant mode and the lord's pleasure was the central economic determinant in a culture that was still feudal in consciousness, if increasingly mercantile in reality.

'Robin Hood and the Potter' gives an monetary edge to the restrictions of the town, just as Chaucer's most corrupted members of the church, the Pardoner and the Friar, are the only people in his poetry who speak much about coins – and speak almost obsessively on that topic. Tardif's argument is that this expresses the discontent of the artisans who must now work for wages, an early version of alienated labour; that is evidently one possible impact of the ballad (1983, p. 140). But it also expresses more generally a sense that there is a natural social and economic order, and set against it is a new oppressive formation where people are not grouped collectively, where they count coins rather than show largesse. Legal restrictions and town prisons belong to this new world and are emotionally opposed by the older, and imaginatively freer, summer world embodied in the positive imagery of the Robin Hood tradition as it is shown in these early texts.

One curious feature of 'Robin Hood and the Potter' is that it is very rare, particularly in this early period, in showing Robin having any dealing at all with a woman. There seems to be some distinct if indirect contact with the sheriff's wife through the gift of pots, a ring and a horse; her near-scorn of her husband suggests a certain sexual symbolism lurking around the outlaw figure. Common as that is in modern representations, it is not at all frequent in the early ballads, and indicates another way in which 'Robin Hood and the Potter' is both precise and wide-ranging in its levels of suggestion.

It remained a well-remembered ballad, sharing its theme with a short play (see pp. 102–3) and being the obvious source of 'Robin Hood and the Butcher', a ballad from the Percy manuscript and also in seventeenth-century circulation, which tells the same story in a somewhat simpler form and using a different trade as focus.

Another complex early ballad is 'Robin Hood and Guy of Gisborne' (no. 118). Even though he places this by implication very early in the tradition, Child makes no general comment on it, but it is a stark and dramatic ballad of special interest to those who favour a mythic origin for Robin Hood.

> The opening is full summer and two 'wight yeoman' appear. They must be Robin and John, but then the text appears to break off as one (Robin, presumably) introduces a dream of violence he has had. It is easy enough to follow this ballad, especially if it is sung, and it may be that very little is missing; indeed if one is fully aware of how radical the 'montage' can be in many traditional ballads, it is quite possible that nothing at all is missing which could not have been implied in some way in the type of ballad that Gray has rightly stressed as being essentially a 'performance'.

John and Robin, now named as such, see another 'wight yeoman' who is dressed in horse-hide; but they argue about who will accost him; John leaves angrily, goes to Barnsdale and is taken by the sheriff. Meanwhile Guy and Robin meet, Guy reveals himself as what in the cowboy tradition was called a bounty-hunter, seeking Robin Hood. Robin suggests they share the quest; they stride through the woods amusing themselves with a shooting competition, which Robin wins; then he reveals himself and they fight.

Robin stumbles and is struck in the side, but thinks about 'Our Lady deere' and kills Sir Guy. So much seems honourable, if fierce. But then the ballad grows stronger and stranger. First Robin cuts off Guy's head and 'sticked itt on his bowes end', saying in apparent justification

> Thou hast beene traytor all thy liffe,
> Which thing must haue an ends. (p. 93, st. 41)

But this is not only a greenwood version of mounting a traitor's head on a spear over a city gate; Robin also literally defaces Guy:

> Robin pulled forth an Irish kniffe
> And nicked Sir Guy in the fface,
> That hee was neuer on a woman borne
> Cold tell who Sir Guye was. (p. 93, st. 42)

This seems to have some sort of ancient ferocity about it, a version of the humiliation of the defeated that is part of the epic spirit. And heroic irony certainly follows as Robin changes clothes with the dead Guy:

> If thou haue had the worse stroakes at my hand,
> Thou shall haue the better cloathe. (p. 93, st. 43)

But if there is some mythic antiquity in this passage, there is also functionality. Robin pretends to be Guy as, dressed in his enemy's horse-hide, he blows his own horn. The sheriff assumes it is Guy's horn, then sees his bounty-hunter approaching and asks him what he will have.

The apparent Sir Guy says he will have none of the sheriff's gold but, now he has killed the master — Robin Hood — he will strike the knave, John. With the Irish knife Robin frees John and then gives him Guy's bow. The sheriff runs towards his house in Nottingham but John, using one of Guy's arrows, 'Did cleaue his heart in twinn'.

Opening rather like the Monk, with John and Robin separating, this ballad reverses the action as Robin by his decisive behaviour, murderous success and consequent deception, saves John. There is a difference of emphasis, however, that favours the hero: Robin, though a victim, occupied much of the action in the Monk, while John as victim is mostly offstage here. There is also a difference in that Guy, Robin's opponent, is a much more weighty figure than the Monk whom John tricks and kills.

In his horse-hide and with his skills, Guy seems to represent a false forester, one who acts on his own, seeks money and, through his costume appears to use deception in some way. He is implicitly a false comrade as they walk, shooting, through the woods, a familiar mode of friendly activity in the ballads. Robin, though, represents a world of true value, in green, despising money, rescuing his comrade, praying to our lady, and so personifying a fully natural version of the free hero as he is conceived in these ballads. There are clear continuities with the other two early ballads in the concern with isolation and the value of solidarity, with the dangers of the town, the status of Mary as an object of emotive worship, the value of physical skills, and contempt for financial concerns.

Some historical references show the same kind of resistant community found in the ballads. Gray (1984, p. 37) considers the account of Piers Venables, the rogue gentlemen of Aston, whose actions are described in an indictment of 1439 (see p. 25 above) and shows how the group led by Venables under the name of Robin Hood have a livery to express their coherence and a strong sense of community. That essence of the Venables event is very close to the meaning of the action of the earliest ballads. Roberta Kevelson summarizes the way in which the hero focuses narratives which are opposed to what she calls 'statutory law': 'Metaphorically Robin Hood is equivalent with the concept, or sense of outlawry, alienation, rebellion, and, in general, the appearance of something outside the predictable order of known reality' (1977, pp. 78–9). Gray finally sees a similar generalizing effect of symbolic resistance:

> by the standards of the sheriff of Nottingham the outlaw is a criminal
> — yet the outlaw in an unjust society embodies truly the ideals which
> that society professes. One may suspect distinctly mythopoeic tenden-
> cies in the creation of such a folk-hero and such legends. Even if we do

not wish to find his origins in Woden or wood-spirits, we might admit that there is a mythical quality about him, a curiously deep appeal which goes beyond any single 'significance'. (1984, p. 38)

There is one other source for early evidence on the 'significance' of the Robin Hood myth. The mixture of strength, libertarian comedy and mystery which comes through the early ballads and some at least of the legal references can also be traced in the proverbs which form a major component of the early Robin Hood references. The common-est of the proverbs indicates both Robin Hood's mysterious strength and his popularity, with a clear implication of the folly of those who try to match him or pretend to intimate knowledge: 'Many men speak of Robin Hood who never bent his bow'. This proverb is recorded eleven times before 1600, five of them before 1500. It becomes so common a saying that it is also used metaphorically of other people who have mysterious force and widespread reputation like those of Robin Hood.

The hero can also be criticized from a moralizing viewpoint, as is plain in the early references from *Piers Plowman* and *Dives and Pauper* discussed above (see p. 50); this position presumably gives rise to the recurrent notion that 'Tales of Robin Hood are good for fools', yet the sense of playful, even carnivalesque resistance that commentators like Gray and Kevelson have seen in the ballads, that inclination of Robin Hood towards Robin Goodfellow, may well also be supported by such a set of proverbs.

A sense of a trickster's whimsy, and even mystery, combined with topographical mastery, is indicated by some folk-puzzle proverbs typified by the description of a roundabout journey as 'Going round by Robin Hood's barn' and travelling 'A Robin Hood mile' (a long one). A similar sense of the hero's belonging to the landscape, however difficult or austere, appears to lie behind the intriguing expression 'Robin Hood could bear any wind but a thaw wind.' These references all relate to the elusive and elaborated narratives that accrete round Robin Hood as well as the very many topographical references, but the tone of the 'barn' 'mile' and 'wind' proverbs suggest that he is seen as a 'Trickster' figure, which is also, in a negative sense, the impact of the 'tales for fools' notion.

In the discourse of proverbs, then, that grass roots form of popular evaluation, there is a profile of the hero which is fully consonant with the natural, elusive, courageous, collectively conscious yet also whimsical and playful character who comes across in the very early ballads. The semi-mythic sense of resistance and opposition to 'statutory' forces of state, church and emergent mercantilism seems deeply embedded in these tales and references and they are a major mode of opposing those forces in the cultural consciousness of the late medieval period.

3.3   RESISTING AUTHORITY: THE LATER BALLADS

None of the other ballads can be dated with any confidence in the fifteenth century, but there seems to be a group which shares and in some sense extends the concerns realized in the first three ballads discussed above, supported by early references and proverbs. Although some of them share characteristics with other and later groupings, they are best discussed in the context of the early ballads and before the precise role of the *Gest* is discussed, especially since several of them were held by Clawson and others to be part of the formation of the *Gest*.

Child places 'Robin Hood's Death' (no. 120) very early in his numbering, though it only appears in the Percy manuscript. While this ballad does not have any early play comparisons, it appears to agree with the brief account of the hero's death given in the *Gest*, and judging from Grafton's account in 1569 was well known – he tells its story as part of the material coming from 'an olde and auncient Pamphlet'. There is a sense of 'artistic' repetition about a good deal of 'Robin Hood's Death' that suggests the literary ballads rather than the tone of the early ballads which flank the 'Death' in Child: nevertheless there are clear resonances between them and the 'Death', especially in its opening sequence.

At the start Robin says he must go to Churchlees for bloodletting (much as he insists on visiting St Mary's church alone in the 'Monk', on pretending to be a potter, or on tackling Guy himself). Here it is Will Scarlet, not Little John who leads the objections to this isolationist action, but Robin agrees to take John with him, and they go off shooting (as in other ballads).

In an unusual passage, they meet an old woman, who is cursing

Robin Hood: the next sequence is missing, but when the text restarts
other women are weeping and warn that Robin should not give blood
this day. Rather as in 'Guy', we seem in the presence of older, magical
elements, but a simpler narrative continues. The prioress bleeds Robin
too much; John appears; the text is again damaged but Robin apparently escapes through a window and yet is stabbed by Red Roger.
Robin kills him, but is himself fatally wounded; he stops John taking
vengeance by burning the priory, and tells John to bury him – apparently not in the greenwood.

In the *Gest*, there is a Prioress of Kyrkesly who is 'nye kinne' to
Robin; she loves Sir Roger of Donkeslye or Donkester, and between
them they 'betray' him to death in an unspecified way after he goes
to Kyrkesly to be let blood. That only takes three stanzas out of over
four hundred, but it seems very close to the Percy ballad. Only in an
eighteenth-century ballad does Robin go to Kirklees alone and John
appear at the sound of his horn; that now familiar version removes the
hostile Roger and makes the prioress, still Robin's cousin, the sole
villain; it adds the well-known motif of Robin shooting an arrow to
locate his grave.

Compared to the early ballads already discussed, 'Robin Hood's
Death' shows a shared hostility to the church, and includes a villain
knight like Guy, as well as the similar opening sequence. As there is
no other early 'death' story there is little to compare this with, but
it does fit well with other accounts of the death of heroes, especially in the betrayal by kin and the notion of a shrine, as detailed both
by Raglan about the international hero (1949, Chap. 4) and Hobsbawm
(1985, pp. 41–3) in the category of the 'Social Bandit', to which
Robin seems better suited.

A similar limited resemblance to the early material is found in another fairly early ballad that deals with religion in some way. 'Robin
Hood and the Curtal Friar' (no. 123) also appears in Percy's manuscript,
where it is given the title 'Robin Hood and Frier Tucke'. This is certainly the name given to the friar in what seems to be a second scene
added to the Guy of Gisborne play from *c*.1475, but the action there has
nothing to do with the later ballad – the play merely tells of the sheriff
arresting a fighting friar. The same name is used in the play printed
about 1560, and that does agree with the ballad for its first half, but
then resolves itself in a different type of fight (see pp. 101–2).

Child feels it would be improper to use the name of Friar Tuck for this ballad (p. 122) and points out that while that name is found in the May games, he is associated with May Marian (a rather less genteel figure than appears later in the Robin Hood tradition) and in fact only appears in two distinctly gentrified ballads, and then in connection with Marian, namely 'Robin Hood and Queen Katherine' (no. 145) and 'Robin Hood's Golden Prize' (no. 147).

Yet Friar Tuck is also referred to in the context of outlawry and criminality: as early as 1417 a chaplain of Lindfield in Sussex took up a career of robbery under the alias Friar Tuck and *Magnifycence* (Skelton ed. Neuss, 1980, p. 88, lines 721–2) speaks of being made like 'Friar Tuck, To preach out of the pillory hole, Without an anatheme or a stole'. So it appears that the friar was involved in the anti-authoritarian aspects of the outlaw tradition; a play of 1537 called *Thersites* refers to 'as tall a man as Friar Tuck' in the context of fighting, so it certainly seems as if the action of this ballad was associated with this friar by then.

In many a plump representation on stage and film, Tuck has become synonymous with the 'tuck-shop' of public-school fiction, but the name is more likely to refer to the shorter 'tucked-up' gown of the highly mobile friars – in fact 'curtal', which means 'curtailed' and 'tuck' have the same implication. Child offers Latin 'curtialis' as a source, meaning the keeper of a monastery vegetable garden, but this should refer to monks not friars (p. 122). There is full appropriateness in a treaty between an anti-authoritarian outlaw like Robin Hood and a friar, as both were often at odds with church 'possessioners' like monks, canons and even parish priests, and had their own aspects of the Trickster tradition. 'Robin Hood and the Curtal Friar', however, does not go far into this potent alliance:

> It opens in May (like the other early texts) and Robin takes himself off to see the friar of Fountains Abbey; that seems like the opening of the 'Monk', but in the later version there is an opening much like that of the 'Potter' whereby Robin is egged on, by Will this time, to take on the famous fighter. There follows the well-known interchange of carrying each other across the water, then apparently (there is a gap in this text too) Robin blows his horn and calls up his comrades. The friar in turn calls up his dogs, but instead of fighting, the opponents call a truce and before the ballad breaks off it seems they are intending to join forces. The later version has a real fight involving the dogs in which they catch arrows in their mouths: for the friar to rely on dogs

may suggest the medieval interpretation of Dominicanes (the Latin name of one of the major orders of friars) as Domini Canes, the hounds of god. Whatever they mean, in this later version, some of the dogs are killed before the friar agrees to join the outlaw band, the first time he had ever yielded to another in fight.

This ballad in large part belongs to the genre that Child called 'Robin Hood meets his match,' (III. p. 109) of which more will be said shortly (see p. 82), yet its partial reference to religious institutions and its stress on the natural world through the setting and the animals make it also relate thematically to the fifteenth-century texts discussed above.

The same is true of two ballads which have less claim to be seen as early in origin, but set out rather more solidly concerns that are continuous with those of 'Robin Hood and the Monk' and 'Robin Hood and the Potter'. One of the best known of the ballads in the periods of fullest development of the tradition is that known as 'George a Green' or 'The Pinder of Wakefield', in Child entitled 'The Jolly Pinder of Wakefield' (no. 124). It does not appear in full form until it is collected by Anthony Wood as a broadside, and that would date it to the mid-seventeenth century. But 'A ballet of Wakefylde and a grene' was entered in the Stationers' Register in 1557–8 and the story clearly gives rise to Robert Greene's play *George a Greene, The Pinner of Wakefield*, of 1594 (see pp. 119–21), and it is one of the ballads clearly used in compiling the Sloane life, dated around 1600.

Apart from having a good claim to be at least mid-sixteenth century, the ballad's most interesting feature is its strong relationship with the anti-town feeling of 'Robin Hood and the Potter' and 'Robin Hood and the Monk'.

Robin Hood, Little John and Will Scarlet walk into Wakefield across a cornfield. The Pinder, whose job it is to impound stray animals, especially those damaging crops, and by extension act as a general guard of agricultural property in and around the town, criticizes them, and then fights – apparently only against Robin (Child feels there is a gap in the ballad which obscures this point). Eventually they agree to a draw, the Pinder offers them food, and Robin invites him to join them in the forest where he will have two liveries in a year, one green and one brown (just like the trees, it would seem). The Pinder accepts the offer from Michaelmas when his present employment will end.

This is an intriguing exchange. Neither Robin nor the Pinder speaks of freedom or criminality; they strike at the end a new contract of a distinctly formalized kind. The structure of town work is extending in some sense to the forest and these restrictive urban structures are also being appropriated by the more natural forest order. In one sense this is a reworking of forest freedoms in the direction of the 'statutory'; in another it is a distinctly subversive response to town rule. While this ballad also has a strong element of 'Robin Hood meets his match' that simple pattern seems here subjected by the overarching sense of the repressive character of town rules, and the way in which the Robin Hood spirit can overcome and indeed exploit such regulatory practices.

A recurrent feature of the early Robin Hood texts is the way in which Robin or one of his band will pose as a member of the legal apparatus – Little John as the King's yeoman in the 'Monk', Robin himself as an informant in the 'Potter', Robin as Guy the bounty hunter in 'Guy'. This motif recurs many times elsewhere (see Child's list of disguises, III, p. 109). In 'The Jolly Pinder', rather than infiltration it is a matter of straightforward seduction of a legal official into the band, and this too will recur. The motif has an underlying socio-political force, a sense of carnivalization and reversal of authority that is both very pervasive in the tradition to the present day, and also distinctly radical in its potential.

A more drastic form of opposition, in tune with the more ferocious aspects of 'Robin Hood and the Monk' and 'Robin Hood and Guy of Gisborne' emerges in a ballad which Child places rather later in the tradition than he might have done, 'Robin Hood's Progress to Nottingham' (no. 139). This, like 'The Jolly Pinder of Wakefield' is first found in Wood's mid-seventeenth century collection, but it too was clearly in existence before the Sloane life was assembled. Child regarded it as 'a comparatively late ballad' yet still saw that it 'has not come down to us in its oldest form'. He probably set it so late because he regarded it as too ferocious to be other than 'decadent' (III, pp. 175–6).

Robin is fifteen, on his way to Nottingham for dinner. Fifteen foresters accost him; they have been drinking. They have a shooting match and (as often early in a ballad) this is a source of contention; they bet twenty marks he cannot hit the mark at a hundred rod (five hundred and fifty yards). Robin kills a beast at that distance, they refuse to pay him, and he runs off. Then he turns and the story, like others from the early period, hits home:

> Then Robin Hood hee bent his noble bow,
> And his broad arrows he let flye,
> Till fourteen of these fifteen foresters
> Upon the ground did lye. (p. 176, st. 12)

Robin goads them with their misjudgement of him:

> 'You have found mee an archer', saith Robin Hood,
> 'Which will make your wives for to wring' (p. 176, st. 15)

And when the people of Nottingham run out to take him, he turns on them, and:

> Some lost legs, and some lost arms,
> And some did lose their blood, (p. 177, st. 17)

But Robin withdraws to the greenwood (it is not clear if he came from there or not: this action is probably the cause of his outlawing) and the foresters are buried 'all a row'.

This direct, even brutal story fills the slot in the social bandit saga of how the hero first becomes an outlaw. Other versions, some already in the public domain by the mid-seventeenth century, will tell a different story about how and why Robin took to the forest, but here the authority, arrogance and dishonesty of the foresters are the un-avoidable cause. The story has a resonance of Johnie Cock, that fine forest ballad of south-western Scotland which Child, thoughtful as ever, puts at the start of his Robin Hood volume (no. 114), though in most versions Johnie is killed by a second wave of foresters after he has dealt vigorously with an initial onslaught. The comparatively late popularity of 'Robin Hood's Progress to Nottingham' makes it clear that the strongest forms of anti-authoritarian feeling continued in the Robin Hood tradition well after gentrification was firmly established, and the murderous potential of the early outlaws was by no means discarded with their medieval context: some illustrations clearly relished the young Robin's brutal triumph (see illustration 5).

Illustration 5   Robin Hood's body-strewn 'Progress to Nottingham'
(From Ritson, 1795 ed.; photo Lensmedia.)

Three other ballads which have little sign of being genuinely early
should also be mentioned in the context of rejecting authority, because
they all share some of the motifs that are consistently represented
early. These are 'Robin Hood Rescuing Three Squires' (no. 140), 'Robin
Hood and Allen a Dale' (no. 138) and 'The Noble Fisherman, or,
Robin Hood's Preferment' (no. 148).

The ballad that Child entitled 'Robin Hood Rescuing Three Squires'
(no. 140) is a fairly straightforward rescue-from-the-gallows story.

Robin meets a woman who advises him that three young men are
about to be hanged for poaching royal deer, he changes clothes with an
old man, offers himself (in the fuller B version) to the sheriff as the
hangman, blows his horn, his men assemble and the young men are
freed.

There are connections with earlier structures in the motif of infiltration in disguise, in the gathering of the outlaws and in the resistance to royal authority as enacted by the Sheriff of Nottingham. In
date the ballad is not significantly later than those already discussed;
it is in the Percy folio, and as with 'The Jolly Pinder of Wakefield' or
'Robin Hood and the Curtal Friar' there is clear evidence in the drama

of an earlier existence – the plot of the ballad is one of the few popular sources used by Munday in creating *The Downfall of Robert Earle of Huntington* in 1598.

The ballad appears in many garlands – Child lists nine of them – but it has fallen out of the modern collections, probably because the highly popular motif of a rescue from hanging has been transferred to someone much closer to the hero, such as Little John, Will Scarlet or even Robin himself. This gives the plot a much stronger personalizing and emotive impact characteristic of the expressive realism of modern fiction, avoiding the more generalized effect of the outlaw's social service that was apparently attractive and convincing as a mark of heroism in an earlier context.

Apart from that trans-historical variation of the rescue from hanging story, the ballad itself might seem to have a social conflict within its structure. Some of the garland versions use the title that Child gives to his B section, 'Robin Hood Rescuing the Widow's Three Sons', and there appears to be a basic variation – in some versions the woman merely tells Robin about the 'squires' condemned to die and in others she says they are her sons. There is potentially a good deal of social difference here, in that if they are genuinely squires then Robin is serving the knightly class by saving them, whereas if they are the sons of an old widow as the title suggests, then his action is in favour of the peasantry (it is, surprisingly, this version that the gentrifying Munday presents). However, the ballads themselves seem not to make this distinction clearly – in Child's C archetype, for example, they are the sons of an elderly woman but they are still called squires. It appears that this ballad has remarkable social flexibility, offering both a radical and a gentrified form, and the distinctions are not at all clear: what does remain is the sense of the constraint of royal authority and the liberationist force of the immediately responsive Robin, with his remarkable powers of disguise and support.

Another ballad of similar date has the same kind of probable antecedents. 'Robin Hood and Allen a Dale' (no. 138) is not in Percy, but exists in several later seventeenth-century broadsides and is one of the ballads referred to in the Sloane life.

A handsome young man meets the outlaws and instead of fighting with Robin, as is usual, he tells of his blighted love; in return for Robin's help he agrees to serve the outlaw leader. Robin dons the disguise of a harper and goes to the wedding. A wealthy knight is marrying 'a finikin lass' who 'Did shine like glistering gold'.

Robin refers to natural law – 'This is no fit match' and insists the bride 'shall chuse her own dear'. He blows his horn, his men arrive, Alan the first among them. The bishop who is solemnizing the marriage dissents so Robin puts his cope on Little John who performs the wedding in carnival form: the bishop says the new couple have not been 'three times askt', so John, as 'The people began for to laugh' proclaims the banns immediately seven times 'Least three times should not be enough'. And so they all return to the greenwood, 'Amongst the leaves so green', a final natural line repeated as a refrain – this is one of the ballads that is definitely sung.

The ballad is a version of 'a stranger joins the outlaw band' which lacks the fighting sequence and instead focuses like the 'Potter' on a rejection of unnatural practices, itself instrumentalized by disguise and by an imposition of the natural law over the church's attempt to favour an old and inadequate knighthood. This is quite a potent ballad in its social suggestion (it recurs as a medium of satire in eighteenth-century light opera, see p. 150) though it lacks the fierce edge of 'Robin Hood and the Monk,' or 'Robin Hood and Guy of Gisborne'. Yet the drama that is enacted is still in touch with an anti-authoritarian spirit behind the narrative, especially compared with the simplicity of many of the other ballads from the period of the broadsides.

A similar contact with the early tradition, though in a remarkably displaced mode, comes through the ballad called 'The Noble Fisherman, or, Robin Hood's Preferment' (no. 148). This is normally regarded, if noticed at all, as a freak since it tells how Robin is 'weary of the wood-side/And chasing of the fallow deere' (st. 2) and heads off for Scarborough where he has heard the fishermen do well. This may seem an atypical event, though it does presumably refer to the practice of mobility in trade and work which was a marked feature of sixteenth and seventeenth-century life. But the unusual outcome is embedded in a perfectly normal Robin Hood opening, set in 'summer time, when leaves go green' and with Robin announcing to the band his intention to go off alone. But here there is no resistance, and no danger attendant on his isolation; the plot is brisk:

After leaving the forest, Robin arrives at Scarborough under the name of Simon over the Lee (which suggests the *Gest*) and takes service with a widow who owns a ship. Robin is a poor sailor (just as he makes a poor potter and butcher) but when a French pirate ship appears, he shows his quality, shoots every enemy dead and so gains 'Twelve thousand pound of money bright.'

So much has a certain resemblance to the town tradesman ballads, especially the Potter and Butcher where he was an incompetent at business but excellent in conflict; and indeed the end of the ballad seems a specific commentary on those earlier themes and how those anti-mercantile attitudes have to be renegotiated.

Robin, speaking still as Simon, says he will give one half of the prize to 'my dame and children', meaning the widow who has employed him, and one half to 'you that are my fellowes all'. But the master — an interesting title, suggesting both a nautical expert and a craft authority — says 'it shall not be' and states a system of reward quite different from that honourable collectivism:

> For you have won her with your own hand,
> And the owner of it you shall bee. (p. 213, st. 27)

Accepting this, Robin still finds a way to resist the proffered possessive individualism; instead of simple division to those involved in the act of acquisition (as in the laws of nautical prize-taking), he will devote the funds to a generalized charity:

> It shall be so, as I have said;
> And, with this gold, for the opprest
> An habitation I will build
> Where they shall live in peace and rest. (p. 213, st. 28)

Far from being an eccentric and trivial ballad, 'The Noble Fisherman' brings into focus a crucial element of the whole tradition of Robin Hood, the role of charity and the notion of the importance of taking from the rich and giving to the poor.

Although the major early ballads have now been discussed in terms of their social meaning, the concept of an outlaw who taxes the rich to serve the poor has not been raised — because it is never mentioned in the early ballad tradition. As will become clear in discussing the *Gest* and other texts that diverge somewhat from the early anti-authoritarian ballad tradition and tend towards the gentrifying reorganization of the image of the outlaw, taking from the rich and giving to the poor is never a function of the genuinely radical Robin Hood. 'The Noble Fisherman', which in its narrative rejects the greenwood setting and shows Robin seeking a better income, also shows him winning substantial financial rewards through his skill. So it is the first ballad to indicate that the older notions of a collective distribution of wealth to the outlaw's supporters are out of date and the proper mode now lies in the distanced, inherently condescending forms of charity. It may indeed be no accident that the titles of this ballad themselves detach the story from the older, simpler stories of direct conflict and a natural use-economy world: Robin here is either Noble, or gains Preferment.

The shades of the urban, bureaucratic, financial prison-house close around the formerly fully natural outlaw, and this rather complex ballad, again bearing strong relations with the early material and by no means as simple as many of its parallels in the broadsides and garland, also marks a considerable shift in the context and central meaning of the tradition. But such movements are by no means caused by historical development alone; as is evident in Bower's Church-oriented story, the myth is multiple from the very beginning, and clerical condemnation coexists with popular celebration in the very early references. In the same way the remarkably coherent anti-authoritarian thrust of the early ballads coexists in time and to some degree in mode with the longest, most complex and still under-examined text from the early tradition *A Gest of Robin Hood*.

3.4 *A Gest of Robin Hood*

In both its mode of publication and its length the *Gest* (Child no. 117) is different from the other early Robin Hood materials. No manuscript exists, but it was printed at least seven times by the mid-sixteenth century and the surviving versions show clear signs of having been much read. It is written in the ballad metre, or what Bottom called 'eight and six', that is a quatrain that rhymes ABCB with A and C being four-stressed and the B lines three-stressed. A and C occasionally have a half-rhyme but it lacks the internal rhyme in the third line which is characteristic of many of the later, and more obviously song-oriented Robin Hood ballads. More certainly literary is the division into eight 'fyttes'; the opening implies orality, but is less 'song-like' than the other early outlaw texts:

> Lythe and listin, gentilmen
>> That be of frebore blode;
> I shall you tel of a gode yeman,
>> His name was Robyn Hode. (p. 56, st. 1)

The sheer length of the poem puts it in the domain of the literary; four hundred and fifty six four-line stanzas make up a sizable poem, which evidently was in considerable demand among the literate classes, whether aristocratic, mercantile or mixed, who patronized the newly established presses in London and Edinburgh.

Apart from its mode and extent, there are other features in which the *Gest* seems quite different from the ballads. One relates to scope: there is clear effort here to give a narrative that is not only extended but connected. That coherence is not humanist in basis; the final stanzas that briefly relate the circumstances of Robin Hood's death hardly give the overall shape of a biography. The relations made among the parts of the text arise from the way in which one incident will link with another later on. A synopsis of the story will indicate a quite medieval and romance-related process of 'interlacing' the episodes:

Fytte 1

Robin, John, Scarlock and Much are in Barnsdale. Robin says he needs some member of the gentry to pay for his dinner, before which he always hears three masses. He advises his men of their duty to be good to women, ploughmen, yeoman and any knight or squire 'that would be a good felawe', but the higher clergy and the sheriff are regarded as enemies. So Robin sends his men to the Saylis on 'Watling Street' to seek earl, baron, abbot or knight as a lucrative guest.

They meet a wretched knight who dines with them; when asked to pay he says he has only ten shillings and John confirms this. The knight explains he owes St Mary's Abbey, York, £400 because after his son killed a knight and squire, in order to save the boy's life he mortgaged the family lands. Robin lends the knight £400 on the security of St Mary herself, and gives him a 'livery' and a horse: the other outlaws also help equip the knight. Little John goes as the knight's yeoman on his journey to discuss his debt with the abbey.

Fytte 2

The abbot and the high justice are in league to seize the knight's lands; the prior demurs. The knight pretends he has no money and asks for time; this is denied and they offer him money for a release of the land. But to their amazement the knight pays the £400, goes home, praises Robin, and sets himself to save the £400 to return it; he also buys bows and arrows for his hundred men. Finally he leaves to repay Robin but is delayed at a 'wrastelynge' where a yeoman is being denied his rightful victory: the knight and his followers insist on the yeoman's rights and so keep Robin waiting.

Fytte 3

Little John, while the knight's man, wins a shooting contest. The Sheriff of Nottingham sees him, asks for his service and gains it from the knight; John uses the alias 'Reynald Greenleaf'. One day the sheriff is hunting, and John lies in bed. He asks the steward for his dinner and is told he must wait till the lord returns. John beats the butler and seizes food and drink. The cook fights John, but they agree to draw and become friends. They eat and drink well and decide to join Robin Hood, taking with them silver plate and £300. Robin welcomes them, and John thinks of a 'wile'.

He goes to meet the sheriff in the forest and says he has seen a fine green hart with seventy score deer. Seeking these animals, the sheriff is taken by the outlaws, entertained on his own plate, given a green livery, but instead of staying for a year, as Robin wishes, agrees to swear not to harass the outlaws.

Fytte 4

Much, Scarlock and John go back to the Sayles and meet two black 'monks' and their train. Their fifty-two men run off; the monks (canons from St Mary's, York) say they have twenty marks; John finds they actually have £800. Robin praises St Mary as a wonderful security who has returned the money the knight borrowed but has so far failed to repay. The knight now arrives to pay the £400 he owes. Robin says his security has already paid it. The knight gives the bows and arrows to Robin and he in turn gives the knight the extra £400.

Fytte 5

The sheriff arranges an archery contest; all the outlaws go (six to shoot with Robin, the rest to protect them). Robin wins the silver and gold arrow, and the sheriff's men try to seize him; the outlaws escape the ambush; Little John is wounded and asks Robin to kill him to avoid being a prisoner. Much carries him on his back and they fight their way to the knight's castle.

Fytte 6

The sheriff gains help from the king, who promises to come in a fortnight. The sheriff ambushes the knight, the knight's wife tells Robin her husband has been taken to Nottingham. The outlaws enter Nottingham, kill the sheriff and take the knight to the forest, to wait for the king and beg pardon from him.

Fytte 7

The king comes to Nottingham and seizes the knight's lands. He passes through the north and finds no good deer in his forests. The king is in Nottingham for six months while Robin rules in the forest. The king disguises himself as an abbot and five knights as monks, and a forester leads them into the forest. Robin takes them and the king says, truthfully, he has £40 and hands it over; the king, still as the abbot, commends Robin to come to the king, and the outlaws all swear loyalty to him in his absence. The king is impressed by the outlaws' loyalty to Robin. They hold a shooting contest which Robin just fails to win; he invites the king to give him the loser's buffet, the king demurs as an abbot, but then he agrees. They realize it is the king, and beg mercy (including the knight, who is also present). The king invites them to serve him at court and Robin agrees, reserving the right to return to the forest if he dislikes the king's service.

Fytte 8

The king asks for a green livery and they all go to Nottingham, the king and Robin shooting against each other on the way – the loser receives a blow (the game of pluck-buffet). At Nottingham they feast, and the knight's lands are returned. Robin stays with the king, but finds life very expensive and only Little John and Scathlocke (note the name-change – or perhaps this is meant to be a diferent character from Scarlock/Scarlet) remain with him. He misses his former life, and asks the king's permission to visit his chapel of Mary Magdalen in Barnsdale. The king gives him a week's leave. Robin returns to the greenwood, where the birds sing in 'a mery morning'. He kills a 'ful grete harte;' blows his horn, regathers his men and they live there twenty-two years in spite of Edward the king.

Finally he was beguiled by the prioress and Sir Roger and died when he went to Kyrkesly to be let blood. So:

> Cryst have mercy on his soule,
>   That dyed on the rode!
> For he was a good outlawe,
>   And dyde pore men moch god. (p. 78, st. 456)

It is clear that this is an extended plot of some sophistication, belonging more to the medieval romance tradition of interlacing events and adventures than the character-focused, cause and effect based narration of the modern novel. The knight who appears in the first fytte recurs in fyttes two, four and six; Little John's single adventure in fytte three takes its departure from his service of the knight and leads on to the sheriff's revenge in fytte six as well as the archery contest in five which ends which John's wounding and rescue. John and the knight provide alternative foci for the narrative when Robin is not himself central; this is a multiple episode narrative not unlike the constructions that recognize King Arthur or Alexander as of central importance but also enact the values symbolized by the leader through subplots concerning other figures.

There is an element of this kind of structure in 'Robin Hood and the Monk' and a vestige of it in 'Robin Hood and Guy of Gisborne', but the *Gest* stands alone in this formally complex way. The structure has usually been held to be a compilation of pre-existing ballads, and there is good reason for this view. As Clawson showed, there are clear signs of some ballad materials here: he identified the town rescue ('Robin Hood Rescuing Three Squires'), the archery context ('Robin Hood and the Golden Arrow'), the robbery of monks ('Robin Hood's Golden Prize') and the combat with the king ('The King's Disguise and Friendship with Robin Hood') and he saw elements of one of the 'meets his match' ballads in Little John's encounter with the Cook, which, being followed by tricking the sheriff into the forest, makes it seem rather like 'Robin Hood and the Potter' (1909, pp. 125–6).

But it may not be necessary to think of the *Gest* as being a careful compilation of specific ballads so much as a reworking on a larger scale of the known materials of the tradition. Rather than two events being put together as in both the 'Potter' and the 'Monk', many are inter-woven in the medieval style of tapestry-like story telling, as described by Vinaver in *The Rise of Romance* (1971). His evidence is usually French, but it is not necessary to go beyond England and its culture for examples. The *Gest* works in ways familiar enough to those who know, for example, the loosely interwoven narrative of Malory's 'Tale of Sir Tristram' or the equally serial Grail story in that Arthuriad – and to date the *Gest* in the mid-fifteenth century (see p. 47) puts it squarely in this period.

If the *Gest* is, then, a romance-oriented compilation, it is only the romance aspect which is unique in the Robin Hood tradition. Those who have commented on the *Gest* as an unusual structure have not re-cognized the number of compilations in the tradition. Martin Parker's 'True Tale of Robin Hood' (no. 154) is an obvious one, but there are many others like the Sloane life and the prose account of 1662 (both reprinted in Thoms, 1856). The early Douce garland of 1670 is clear-ly organized as a compiled life from 'Progress to Nottingham' to 'Death' and other garlands follow that pattern, like *The English Archer* (Hodges, London, 1750?) or the more ambitious 1777 Glasgow publication by Robertson entitled *The Adventures of Robert, Earl of Huntington, Vulgarly Called Robin Hood*. But some ballads are themselves compilations, a fact hard to trace because editors have disassembled them. Careful study of Child's introductions will reveal that his ballads numbered 128, 129 and 130 were in fact woven together in printed form, though he separates them as 'Robin Hood Newly Revived' (a give-away compendious title), 'Robin Hood and the Prince of Aragon' and 'Robin Hood and the Scotchman', the last just providing a few intervening stanzas for this new and moderately *Gest*-like ensemble. Then Child's no. 145, 'Robin Hood and Queen Katherine' in its original form leads on to 146, 'Robin Hood's Chase', a simple pairing of gentrified episodes. Something more like the *Gest* is the equally concealed aggregation of 'The King's Disguise and Friendship with Robin Hood' (no. 151) and 'Robin Hood and the Valiant Knight' (no. 153), the latter of which has a short and usually unnoticed 'death' sequence partly borrowed from that other compiler Martin Parker.

In ignoring these compilations, Child is not concealing data, but setting aside material of no significance to him. He sought the 'purity' of the ballad as he conceived it and appreciated it most, and in so doing he obscured a tendency for compilation that is long-standing (even including some early plays, see pp. 100–3) and continues in our own day through novels, juvenile anthologies and full-length plays and films. As a compilation, the *Gest* is normal enough, in its somewhat ambitious mode.

However, in keeping with its romance aspiration, there are aspects of its treatment, in terms of both form and content, that seem different from the early ballads which in one way or another the *Gest* tends to compile. There is a specificity about its events that outreaches the symbolized ideality characteristic of the Robin Hood ballads (and indeed all ballads before romantic retouchers like Scott worked on them). There is here an address for the highway robbers: at the Sayles, on Watling Street, above Wentbridge. Naturally, historians like Dobson and Taylor are excited by this empirical detail, and many of their colleagues have treated the *Gest* as gospel as a result of this quasi-precision which they stress beyond its original casual significance, an element that merely functions like the detail in a medieval painting whose mode as a whole remains general or allegorical.

In the same hyper-realistic way, we tend to over-specify the poem by remoulding the title. There is an insistent tendency to call it 'The' *Gest* as a formal title, when in fact its early versions are unanimous in calling it 'A' *Gest*. The position is exactly the same as the recurrent misnaming of Chaucer's prologue to *The Canterbury Tales* as 'The' prologue and all his characters in it as 'the' knight, monk, prioress and so on, when in fact they are either generalized as 'a' knight, or specified for emphasis as 'this' prioress. To call the *Gest* just *A Gest* is to imply it is one of many possible versions; to call it *The* is to make it as single and falsely separate as the imaginary real Robin Hood. It is hard to avoid such specificity in modern English, as to call the poem 'a *Gest*' seems bizarre; but the point is worth remembering.

Such mistitling is no doubt in part provoked by ways in which the *Gest* does have a greater specificity than other early Robin Hood texts. There is notable precision about moral guidance, for example: Robin's opening remarks are quite carefully defined in terms of what the outlaws should do, and who are their natural allies and their legitimate enemies. The established churchmen and the sheriff are always suspect, and earls, barons and knights are expected to be targets as well. That fits with the other ballads though it does spread hostility into the aristocracy, in addition to knights like Sir Guy, Sir Roger and the aged would-be husband of Alan a Dale's beloved. However, the *Gest* also gives much space to a good knight, whom the opening moral instructions would protect because he 'wol be a good felawe'. However, he is not valued in his own right, more through his affiliation with the outlaws. He is a loyal ally after Robin's very generous treatment, and this is unusual. Only in the gentrified forms does Robin move in such elevated circles. Yet Sir Richard is himself severely down on his luck, and shares the same opponents as the outlaw band, so it is not easy to see here the actual beginnings of gentrification or the key to a gentry audience as Fowler would argue (see p. 48). Gray in particular finds no real departure here from the anti-authoritarian message of the ballads in general (1984, pp. 30–2), and while Holt feels this figure is an important basis for his belief that the audience is lower gentry and that the text is linked with 'the knightly romances' (1982, p. 117), the fact that the knight himself makes conscious moves in the direction of plebeian weapons like the bow and arrow and humble sports like wrestling indicates that his attachment is an extension of the band of Robin Hood the popular hero, rather than being a trace of the original gentility of a widely degraded noble outlaw, as a reading like Fowler's or Holt's might suggest.

A striking indication of this relationship is the scene where Robin not only gives the knight money so that he can be relieved of his embarrassment in the fiscal mode of living, but also fulfils the older notions of organic connection by arming him – and this sequence continues through stanzas 70 to 78 so that each of the outlaws plays a part in equipping the knight and at least one sees the process in communal terms: Little John does it 'To praye for all this company' (p. 60, st. 78). This model of the vertically integrated community operating together does not appear in the early ballads, but it is not inconsistent with their spirit.

Nor is the relationship with the king. Like the knight, he is not met with in the other early ballads, but here his negotiations with the outlaws dominate the final sequences. As several commentators have noticed, the model appears to be the recurrent late medieval genre called 'The King and the Subject'. There are many ballads where the king, usually travelling or hunting, meets a fairly unpolished charac- ter, often a merchant or tradesmen of some sort. The action indicates that they are well matched in real human terms, and they become friendly, sometimes after the king is humiliated. When his royal status is finally revealed, the subject fears retaliation, but the king shows true royalty by forgiving the upstart and indicating he has himself learnt much – and so of course, his power is revalidated in the changing social circumstances symbolized by the encounter with this disrup- tive subject. Lengthy ballads like 'King Edward IV and a Tanner of Tamworth', 'John the Reeve', 'The King and the Barker', 'The King and the Shepherd' explore the politically-attuned but eventually quiet- ist possibilities of this conflict.

In the *Gest* the encounter follows these lines, except that after the re-establishment of a master-subject relationship, the hero escapes those ties in returning to the forest. So his own value is finally restated, and the *Gest* finally retains the socially interrogative vigour of ballads like 'Robin Hood and the Monk' or 'Robin Hood and the Potter', but it is important to note that it does that through displacing the tradesman or merchant figure and using instead Robin Hood, a less obvious figure of social mobility. If the structure is like the King and the Subject, the outcome is neither as ultimately hierarchical nor yet as supportive of new urban values. This king may be the same as in the King and Subject structure, but he has a very different, inherently much more elusive form of subject to deal with. The tanner and barker appear alone: Robin has, in fantasy at least, a forest to return to and scores of comrades ready to answer his call.

The same pattern of a partial innovation not actually moving far beyond the shape of the early tradition is found in the very ending of the *Gest*. Robin is finally said to be 'a good outlawe' and this is it seems defined by the following line 'And dyde pore men moch god.' One of the continuing questions of the whole Robin Hood myth is whether this actually means that he took from the rich to give to the poor. The *Gest* seems to move in that direction, because the sources of money mentioned at the beginning are potentially not just gold-laden abbots or the sheriff, those milch-cows of the early ballads. The aristocracy is named as a target – yet never shown actually being robbed. New possibilities are offered, but withdrawn.

The recipients of generosity are just as enigmatic. The only person who actually receives anything from Robin Hood here is the knight, who is allowed to keep the £400 he has saved to repay Robin and has it doubled from the takings from the abbey. Donations to the poor are not mentioned as such; 'dyde pore men moch god' does not mean he gave money to the poor, the remark can suggest a whole organic structure of support. The generosity that Robin actually shows in the early ballads and the *Gest* is that he welcomes people to his service, provides them with food, clothing and protection. The model, it is important to note, is essentially feudal and that of a use economy, not that of later aristocratic charity in cash exchange.

Like other social bandits from Ned Kelly to Salvatore Giuliano, the early Robin Hood takes from the rich to give not to some loosely identified poor, but to protect those who are his own affiliates. It is in 'The Noble Fisherman', in the world of a sailor's pay and ship-prizes resolved into cash (see pp. 68–9), that Robin first encounters the formal processes of exchange-economy charity, where money is used to alleviate misery. While the final reference in the *Gest* to the poor can be, and usually has been, read in the light of financial support, this is probably not the way in which it is meant. When food runs on the land or grows from it, when firewood lies on the ground, when clothes are made from wool and leather, when the products of simple specialisms like pottery, tanning and tinkering themselves are both 'natural' in impact and also very long-lasting, then coinage has a limited value, and the real generosity of a lord, whether in legally recognized form or elusive in the forest, is to protect his people from depredations of all kinds, to show strength, organization, quick response and enduring loyalty and generosity. Those are the modes in which the medieval

Robin Hood shows his good lordship to the poor, and the final lines of the *Gest* are not inherently different from that process.

If in form, characters and ending the *Gest* is not ultimately separate from the medieval ballads and their heritage, in other ways it is fully in accord with the patterns that have been seen throughout the early tradition. Religion here is direct and emotive, a matter of Mary rather than the abbey that bears and traduces her name. Robin's own chapel is that of Mary Magdalen, that good outlaw of the New Testament. The orderly nature and inherent solidarity of the forest group is consistent, though the *Gest* does not include those tense moments of conflict found in the earliest ballads which both test and prove solidarity; here even the notion of the equal fight is displaced to Little John and the Cook, as if this epic scale of story does not require the piecemeal assemblage of the band. Only the financial weight of court life is a significant threat to the integrity of the greenwood company, but the town is, as before, a site of danger, though neither the machinations of the sheriff nor the means needed to counter him are as complex as in 'Robin Hood and the Monk' or 'Robin Hood and Guy of Gisborne'.

Nature remains a central feature, consistent with, but much more fully developed than, the early ballads. Much is made of the greenness of the wood to which they return and the livery shared by the king. This goes further in a recurrent notion that Robin is in some way symbolized as a hart: he is the 'master-hart' to whom Little John leads the sheriff and it is the slaying of a 'full grete harte' that is the decisive action of his final return to the forest, indicating his re-entry into a fully natural order, not that alien unnatural world of the court where his noble largesse had ruined him.

In these ways the *Gest*, in its length, its weight of story and its sense of what Gray calls a world outside the forest and the limited townscape of the other ballads (1984, p. 31), projects the myth of Robin Hood onto a larger screen, linking together in one sequence the forces of authority that are held to be oppressive: church, local government, towns and, here at least, their national focus at the royal level in city and court, though not precisely in the person of the king.

Coss (1985, pp. 70–1) finds the *Gest* subversive and in some way related to the events of the Peasants' Revolt, where the rebels retained allegiance to the crown and to the idea of a true religion, however violent their hatred for lawyers, churchmen and other agents of what they felt to be an oppressive state. Those like Holt who see the *Gest* as basically supporting harmless, honest, local, landowners like the knight and attendant yeoman (1982, p. 110) would read it quite differently, yet they seem to project their own conservative interests backwards onto a text which is in fact a good deal more radical and aggressive in form than they would like to think. The *Gest*, after all, advocates massive theft from the church, civic insurrection against and murder of a properly appointed sheriff, breach of legitimate agreement with a king; and it imagines that all these things can lead to a lengthy and happy life, cut short only by infidelity from within the family and treachery close to the person of the hero. It is a message, both in its positive and negative function, found in many other hero stories and one endemic to the social bandit genre. Like them it is also a story with much potency among people who feel various forms of institutionalized oppression and therefore require the relief of fictional forms of dissent.

Seen in terms of its constituent themes, and with its differences from the early ballads carefully considered, the *Gest* is in itself, as Gray has seen most accurately (1984, pp. 30–2), a strongly anti-anthoritarian text in which the fierce satire of texts like *Piers Plowman* and its descendants is given a positive, even utopian, focus in the person of Robin Hood. He is the hero who stands for an alternative and natural form of lordship, one who has the will and the power not only to elude but also resist and if necessary destroy the agents of the world of legalism, of finance and of regulation that was felt by many in the late middle ages to be increasingly oppressive and urgently deserving an egalitarian reaction. That resistance could take real forms of political action, in which the name of Robin Hood was sometimes engaged, and could also exist in fictional forms, in which his myth was a major focus for the idea that oppressive authorities can be resisted; and so through the power of culture they could – for the many poor for whom the hero did indeed do good – be endured.

3.5 Minor Heroic Ballads

The ballads that have been discussed all have a fairly elaborate narrative involving a change of setting and a sequence of interrelated actions; they also often involve a range of symbolic or suggestive meanings and all of them imply a fairly complex set of evaluations. Many of the other Robin Hood ballads, however, are a good deal more simple in structure and meaning. In particular there are two substantial groups which focus on a fight in which Robin Hood is almost always involved, sometimes with support from Little John and usually one other. These fights can have different significance, depending on the outcome and the context.

One remarkably large and consistent group of ballads is that referred to above by Child's description 'Robin Hood meets his match' (1965, III, p. 109). Time after time a ballad opens with Robin alone in the wood; he meets a person who is new to him; they fight; both perform well and eventually they agree to call it a draw; usually the opponent joins the band of outlaws, though on a few occasions he merely promises good wishes and goes on his way.

The pattern is included in some ballads already discussed: this structure appears in part in 'Robin Hood and the Potter'; much closer in form, with an anti-town overlay, is 'The Jolly Pinder of Wakefield', while an equally clear version, with suggestions of hostility to the church added, is the essence of 'Robin Hood and the Curtal Friar'. There are some muted signs of the structure, without the fight, in 'Robin Hood and Allen a Dale', while Little John clearly plays out a version of the combat of equals with the cook in the *Gest*.

While the 'Robin Hood meets his match' pattern is the largest single grouping among those ballads not yet discussed, it is important to note that Child's title is inadequate: throughout them all there is another element of great importance to the myth. It is not only that Robin meets his match: the special point about Robin Hood's drawn fights is that they strengthen his band either directly through a new member or, as in the case of the Potter, by a new source of good will. The structure also indicates that Robin is not leader of his band by simple physical power and skill, but by consensus, as is shown in particular by the conflict with Little John in 'Robin Hood and the Monk' and by the restoration of his authority after near humiliation in a series of these 'meets his match' stories. In fact the examples of this structure seem better described as 'solidarity ballads', since what emerges is the consensual and enduring unity of the outlaw band.

The classic case and the most important example of solidarity is found in 'Robin Hood and Little John' (no. 125). This was presumably in existence by 1594 when a play called 'Robin Hood and Little John',

now lost, was recorded (though as chapter 4 will show, the Elizabethan plays have a far from simple relationship with the ballad tradition, and this identification cannot be taken for granted). There is
no early copy of the ballad and few in the garlands, yet the song and
the idea are well-known, and it was still being sung, if in attenuated
form, during Cecil Sharp's collecting of English folk-song. Child indeed believes that this ballad has the priority to be the one known in
musical form as 'Robin Hood and the Stranger', the most commonly-
cited tune (1965, III, p. 133). The well-known events of this ballad,
irresistible to almost all film-makers, include a fight on a bridge in
which Robin Hood first falls into the water and then manages to
reverse the situation, usually by some form of cunning. In the earliest
surviving version of the ballad Robin's men intend to set upon John,
but Robin intervenes. In any case, they end up firm friends, John joins
the outlaw band and a joke is usually made about his name as con-
trasted with his enormous size.

The existence and apparent importance of this archetypal solidarity
ballad provides the opportunity to make a comment, as apparently no
one else has done, on the status of Little John in the tradition. As is
clear from the chroniclers' references and the surviving reports of the
games, especially the Scottish versions of them, John played a part as
substantial as Robin in the earlier manifestations of the myth. Wyntoun
puts his name first, though perhaps just to find a rhyme on 'Hude' and
'gude'. The earliest ballads all give John a significant part, showing in
'Robin Hood and the Monk' his great importance in securing Robin's
safety, while in 'Robin Hood and Guy of Gisborne' the situation is
reversed. In both cases, Robin without John is in serious danger, and
that notion recurs in 'Robin Hood's Death'. Early on John is a character of importance second only to Robin, and in the *Gest* he has a
separate role of considerable importance. He appears to have had his
own locality, through Derbyshire into Charnwood Forest to Leicester,
see illustration 1.

The presence of such 'helpers' in folklore indicated that a single
hero was not enough to fulfil a mighty task; in an earlier collective
consciousness, isolation was a state of threat, not self-fulfilment, and
Little John in the earlier ballads consistently has the effect of socializing and so protecting the hero. It is therefore no accident that as the
context of the ballads grows increasingly individualized, in a newly
economistic and humanist culture, the role of Little John is reduced

to that of a foil for Robin, someone to reveal by contrast the luminous character of the leader. Little John grows smaller as the hero grows nobler, both in social status and in individualized personality.

Other characters who fight with and then join Robin are usually not recurrent figures. A number of them, like the Pinder, the Potter and his shadow the Butcher, are artisans with urban and partially mercantile skills. In a vigorous and quite early ballad, Robin fights with a Tanner and their friendship is sealed in the blood that runs from their staff-inflicted wounds. Dobson and Taylor have associated the proliferation of fighting artisans, from the Potter on, with the growth in importance and self-consciousness of tradesmen in this period (1976, p. 125), as if each trade sooner or later fits itself into a Robin Hood ballad, or a crowd-pleasing minstrel does it for them. But as Gray argues (1984, p. 18) the creation of these ballads seems less directly targeted than that. It is certainly a matter of some support for Tardif's arguments about the urban and artisan connection of the Robin Hood ballads that so many are craft connected, and there is a Tinker to add to the trades already mentioned (no. 127); but the generation of such materials is more likely to be broadly motivated rather than simply targeted for money. The proper parallel is with the remarkable number of vulgar songs which use the technical jargon of a particular trade with a specific sexual connotation – tinkers prominent among them: a vivid collection is found in de Sola Pinto and Rodway's *The Common Muse* (1957). The evidence suggests that the consciousness of these newly self-aware groupings was itself constructed as masculine and vigorous through such means; and the ability to fight a draw with the spirit of liberty in the Robin Hood ballads seems another part of such an artisan 'structure of feeling' under development, especially in the seventeenth century.

Some of the solidarity ballads do not deal with townsmen with trades, but with figures who might generally be expected to be enemies of the outlaws. In 'Robin Hood and the Ranger' (no. 131) the kind of figure who finished off Johnie Cock and tried to trick the young Robin on his progress to Nottingham becomes a firm friend. In 'The Bold Pedlar and Robin Hood' (no. 132), the sort of person whom a highway robber might often oppose fights well (like a Potter or a Butcher) becomes Robin's friend – and reveals his name as 'Gamblegold', which is either a suggestion of liberality with money or, more likely, that idea used to explain a misremembered version of

Gamwell, a name that skirts the edges of the tradition. Another traditional enemy of the people of the north and the midlands was the marauding Scot, and he too in 'Robin Hood and the Scotchman' (no. 130) is brought, through a fierce fight and friendly relations afterward, into the utopian fellowship of the greenwood band. It might seem that 'Robin Hood and the Beggar' (no. 133) is one of this group where Robin makes peace with potential enemies, but in fact after the fight Robin takes the beggar's clothes, goes into town and releases, with the help of his men, three 'yeomen' from the gallows. He only very briefly absorbs the beggar into his band, and this is basically the Three Young Men's Rescue type introduced through the structure of the solidarity ballad.

These all belong to the seventeenth century, but not all the ballads that use the 'Robin Hood meets his match' structure have so demotic or democratic a purpose; the structure can become involved with other kinds of bonding. In 'Robin Hood Newly Revived' (no. 128) the stranger who fights well is not an artisan but a relative, the enigmatic figure called Gamwell whom Robin realizes is his own cousin. Clearly this structure was created in connection with *Gamelyn* which, unlike the *Gest*, is certainly from the period of Chaucer because it is found among some manuscripts of *The Canterbury Tales* as a spurious second Cook's Tale. It tells about a gentlemanly youngest son who is disinherited, escapes to the forest, becomes leader of the outlaws, and with their moderately violent help regains his property.

Gamelyn is no yeoman, and 'Robin Hood Newly Revived' has clear gentrification elements, as in its original form it was a compilation with added to it the clearly genteel 'Robin Hood and the Prince of Aragon' (no. 129, to be discussed shortly). Another battle of equals with evident social ascent implied is 'The King's Disguise' (no. 151), which seems, as Child observes, 'a loose paraphrase, with omissions, of the seventh and eighth Fyttes of the *Gest*' (1965, III, p. 220). Even more surprising as a combat which leads to a lasting friendship is 'Robin Hood and Maid Marian' (no. 150), where the woman in Robin's life has, it seems, to go through the generic requirements for joining the outlaws. She was in disguise as a page, and meeting Robin himself disguised it came about 'That they prov'd foes and so fell to blows', indeed 'to cutting they went At least an hour or more'. The battle was by no means one-sided or gentle: 'the blood ran apace from bold Robin's face, And Marian was wounded sore.' Soon enough, though,

Illustration 6 The hero under pressure
(from Ritson 1795 ed.; photo Lensmedia.)

there is recognition, 'kind imbraces and jobbing of faces', a banquet, celebrations, and a happy life in the forest where in spite of their presentation as earl and gallant dame, 'they lived by their hands, without any lands' (Child, 1965, III, pp. 218–19).

If the solidarity ballads offer just two related actions – the fight and the resulting agreement – and so seem simple compared with the anti-authority ballads discussed before, there is a kind of Robin Hood ballad that is even less elaborate than that. A number have only one sequence of action, a fight or a series of fights in which Robin, often supported by two of his men, is either victorious or, in some unusual but vivid cases, humiliated; pictures indicate how much this naive action was admired (see illustration 6).

'Robin Hood and the Shepherd' (no. 135) is a naive brawl, enjoyed for itself, while the second beggar narrative, 'Robin Hood and the Beggar II' (no. 134), is a fight where the opponent wins by cunning as well as strength. Even odder as an item in the hero's ballad cycle is 'Robin Hood and the Pedlars' (no. 137), where Robin, John and Will Scarlet are not only beaten severely by three stout travelling salesmen, but Robin is also administered a 'balsam' by one of them as he lies unconscious and this makes him vomit over himself and his companions, all of whom end up 'besmeard' quite 'piteously' (Child, 1965, III, p. 172).

A little more elevated in tone and effect is the fight by which Robin, John and Will engage with three keepers in 'Robin Hood's Delight' (no. 136), where a long day's battle ends with three days' drinking in Nottingham. This ballad has, as Child notes (1965, vol. III, p. 168), some verbal resemblances to 'Robin Hood and the Shepherd' (no. 135) where 'a jolly shepherd' beats Robin and then John into a submission which they accept cheerfully from this 'flower of shepherd swains' (Child, 1965, vol. III, pp. 166–7). Gentrification hovers around the language of that ballad and is much more plainly developed in the lengthy and rather languorous engagement of 'Robin Hood's Birth, Breeding, Valor and Marriage' (no. 149), a distinctly literary production which starts by referring to the Pinder, then to the parallel outlaw ballad of Adam Bell, involves the family of 'noble George Gamwell of Gamwell Hall', has Robin, equipped with 'basket-hilt sword', defeat everybody at gambols and juggling and then meet in Sherwood both his yeomen and Clorinda the queen of the shepherds. They go to Titbury where he wins not only the undescribed fight but Clorinda's hand in marriage, as she sings to him:

> The bumpkins are beaten, put up thy sword, Bob,
> And now let's dance into the town. (p. 217, st. 45)

That highly complicated (but never complex) ballad seems particularly sentimental and urbanized in tone against the naively medieval meaning of 'Robin Hood and the Golden Arrow' (no. 152). This garland ballad of the eighteenth century draws heavily on the *Gest* for a simple story of how Robin won the competition but because he was not detected felt his honour demanded he let the sheriff know he was there, so he shot a letter to that effect back into the town.

If honour in that narrative meant being known to have dared all, in many of these simpler ballads it just meant fighting well and sportingly, facing the odds of an oppressive world in a spirited, ever-ready way. That was an effective enough low-level ideology for the heroic figure to encompass; but there were other forms of honour – or at least honours – associated with higher social status that the medieval Robin Hood had ever attained, strata of society that the early texts had hardly ever discussed except for the passing and unfulfilled reference in the *Gest* to earl or baron. As the discussion of chapter 2 has indicated, Robin Hood did ascend socially and the structure of his myth changed with that repositioning. There are some – though not very many – of the ballads which represent aspects of that process of social elevation for the hero and his myth.

3.6   GENTRIFICATION, SOCIAL AND RELIGIOUS

Robin Hood's gentrification developed in the hands of chroniclers and commentators who acknowledged and respected centralized power and valued an urbanized 'elevated' culture. This process was not primarily a domain of the ballads; the majority of them deal in varying degrees of sophistication with resistance and solidarity at a low social level. But the impact of Elizabethan gentrification was to some degree represented at the street level of the oral and broadside ballads, and the evidence has survived, intermittently, and seeming essentially no more than a contamination of the continuing forms.

The *Gest*, as has been discussed, is not so much a gentrification of Robin Hood as an extending of his umbrella of solidarity over distressed knightly victims of oppression; the only other non-commoners in the early ballads, Guy of Gisborne and Sir Roger of Doncaster are definite villains, even class enemies of the outlaw.

But later texts make Robin Hood's range of acquaintance and social positioning more varied. 'Robin Hood and the Prince of Aragon' (no. 129) is 'a pseudo-chivalrous romance' as Child notes (1965, III, p. 147) and part of a literary compilation, being attached to 'Robin Hood Newly Revived'; although it only appears in a few late garlands, Child prints it fairly early probably because it does open within the frame of an outlaw fight, beginning with the simple words:

> Nowe Robin Hood, Will Scadlock and Little John
> Are walking over the plain, (p. 147, st. 1)

The story goes on to see Robin summon his ranks of yeoman with a blast of the horn as is usual, before he departs alone.

But it is not with jovial artisans or officious foresters that the outlaws will meet; the fact that Robin has just had breakfast with his nephew (apparently Will) suggests the Gamwell-*Gamelyn* connection, and once Robin has introduced the nephew to his men, the story lurches off outside the outlaw genre, as there appears 'a beautiful damsel' as if from the less enthralling pages of Malory, and the narrative continues in that mode: she is to be married to the Prince of Aragon if no one defeats the prince and his twin giants.

The three outlaws don pilgrims' clothing, deal with the 'tyrant Turk' and receive pardon from the king; the dark beauty chooses Robin as her husband and, to complete the gentrified package, the Earl of Maxfield steps forward and identifies Will Scadlock as his long lost heir Young Gamwell. The new features – a wife for Robin Hood and social connections for his outlaws and (if Will *is* his nephew) apparently himself – take the ballad from the social bandit genre, where the hero is young, alone, and dedicated to general political response, and reshape it in connection with the concerns of romance, where people conflict for worthwhile marriages and trace minutely the lines of blood that denote the right to inherit.

A similar re-formation of the tradition, which survives in the Percy manuscript and has seventeenth-century currency, is 'Robin Hood and Queen Katherine' (no. 145, also entitled in some of its broadside and garland appearances 'Renowned Robin Hood'). Clear connections exist with the *Gest*: Robin is known at court, has a friend named Sir Richard Lee, and prefers the greenwood to the royal circle. The action of the ballad is simply a shooting match between the king and the queen, in which she employs the outlaws in disguise; they win under her protection and finally gain that of the king.

This is obviously an 'art' compilation from elements of the *Gest* and other ballads – the Bishop of Hereford, the outlaw's victim in a ballad that couples his name with the hero (no. 144), is at court and ruefully acknowledges that he too knows Robin Hood. There also seems to be clear reference to the recorded Robin Hood pageants in which Henry VIII indulged himself, to be discussed with other plays and games in chapter 4, see pp. 109–10. The major point is that while the *Gest* located Robin at court, it never showed him in courtly action, but here the acculturation of the hero to the circles of highest power is realized — though, in the earliest of the versions of this ballad, he still suggests a possible demurral to the king when he is finally invited to stay at court.

Closely related, indeed beginning with a summary of 'Robin Hood and Queen Katherine', is 'Robin Hood's Chase' (no. 146), an early garland piece. By now the king regrets having pardoned Robin and chases him through the north – another motif from the *Gest*. They hurry anti-clockwise around Britain via Berwick and Chester; the outlaws go to London to the queen and when the king returns, she begs pardon for her favourite. Child liked this ballad, saying it was 'well-conceived, and only needs to be older' (1965, vol. III, p. 206), but it also has depths, seeming to realize the dangers of gentrification: at court you live at the whim of the king, travel the country non-stop and depend entirely on the favour of others. Robin's elevation, it will be noted, has also changed his syntactical role: 'Robin Hood's Chase' does not refer to a hunt enjoyed by the hero, but to having someone hot on his heels. By accepting the role of a subject, Robin becomes the object of royal whim.

If freedom is banished in that ballad, in 'Robin Hood and the Valiant Knight' (no. 153) the title again indicates a shift of power away from the outlaw and towards established authority. A later garland piece, this encloses the hero fully. At the start the king decides the outlaws 'have been too bold' and there is a danger that 'The land would be over-run'. So a knight is chosen to impose order; Sir William marches off and the quality of his bowmen is given the sparkling approval usually reserved for Robin's ranks of loyal outlaws:

> With long yew bows and shining spears
> They marchd in mickle pride, (p. 225, st. 9)

He serves the royal summons on Robin and pitched battle follows. It is long, bloody, and in military terms indecisive, but the outlaw's career is quickly closed with Robin falling ill and being bled to death by a monk. So with a whimper ends the reign of the outlaw who, the opening stanzas tell us, threatened property and royalty. This ballad is not so much the gentrification of Robin Hood as the suppression of him by the gentry. Even the usually apolitical Child is offended and says this ballad was: 'Written, perhaps, because it was thought that authority should in the end be vindicated against outlaws, which may explain why this piece surpasses in platitude everything that has gone before (p. 225).

The 'art-based' character of these gentrification ballads is obvious, and that is the mode of the most important disseminator of the hero's social elevation in the ballad, Martin Parker's 'A True Tale of Robin Hood' (Child no. 154), published in 1632 and often reprinted and cannibalized. Its subtitle immediately asserts the tonal position: 'A briefe touch of the life and death of that Renowned Outlaw, Robert Earle of Huntington, vulgarly called Robbin Hood who lived and died in 1198.' As if not satisfied with that as a forthright statement, the subtitle ends: 'And published for the satisfaction of those who desire to see Truth purged from falsehood' (p. 227).

With some knowledge of Grafton and of Munday's aristocratizing plays, Parker weaves into that gentrified structure a series of ballad narratives including an attack on the church like that in 'Robin Hood and the Bishop', robbery from the king like that in the beginning of 'Robin Hood and Queen Katherine', and some other adventures which may well have come from lost ballads. Having noted above how the mention of charity is a sign of the transitional context of 'The Noble Fisherman' it is intriguing to observe that in this definitely gentrified ballad-assembly, Robin builds eight almshouses for the poor (st. 71).

The 'True Tale' is quite long, with 120 stanzas modelled on the ballad-metre of the *Gest*. A precis shows that the narrative is relatively dense:

The Earl, an outstanding archer, ruined himself by generosity, the agent of his destruction being the malicious abbot of St Mary's. Robin became an outlaw leader, robbing especially the clergy and giving and lending to 'any in distresse'. He attacked the abbot in person, who complained to the king; then the outlaws robbed the king, who set a price of a thousand marks on Robin, alive or dead; Robin escaped, but did offer to return the king's money. Richard went on crusade and the bishop of Ely, the regent, riding with a thousand men, was attacked by the outlaws. Robin thrived, built almshouses, helped the poor, terrified misers. The king returned and set out to control Robin, who shot an arrow into Nottingham with a message offering to swear allegiance. The king would have accepted but some lords disagreed with this as a dangerous precedent. Some of Robin's men fled to Scotland; only forty diehards were left, whom the king meant to pardon, when Robin Hood sickened and died. The cause was his anger at his men's betrayal, which made him feel ill and in need of bleeding, in which process a friar killed him and the prioress (who also hated him) buried him and set a gravestone.

Parker sums up at length, noting the process of time after the hero's days: the prioress who hated Robin also loved his memory, his epitaph is outworn, his followers were pardoned or resettled elsewhere. We, he states, find the story amazing not only because it is in the past, but because of its anarchic nature. Finally Parker has to disavow the vigour of the outlaw. He states that:

> We that live in these latter dayes
>   Of civill government,
> If neede be, have a hundred wayes
>   Such outlawes to prevent. (p. 232, st. 109)

He reviews the 'barbarous' days when guns did not exist and so outlaws could live in security, even in 'mirth and jollity' and a form of 'courtesie'. Yet, with something of a jolt, Parker returns to the present where things are, it is important to believe, different:

> Let us be thankefull for these times
>   Of plenty, truth and peace,
> And leave our great and horrid crimes
>   Least they cause this to cease. (p. 232, st. 116)

And he closes the file, as it were, on the fascinations of the rebellious hero by locating such dangerous activities firmly in the past:

> Such outlawes as he and his men
>   May England never know agen. (p. 233)

One largely innovative feature of the 'True Tale' is that Robin Hood's main enemy here is not the centralized state as it is in 'Robin Hood and The Valiant Knight' and 'Robin Hood's Chase', but the church, quite plainly realized as medieval and Catholic. Abbot, Monk, Friar and Prioress line up as enemies to this outlaw who is so much admired, if ultimately so firmly contained. The hero is noble because he opposes a church now seen as corrupt, yet as a force of disruption he also deserves to be destroyed by that very same church: the royal protestant state is both safe and clean-handed as a result of Parker's skilful redirection of the dangerously exciting lines of the tradition. It is presumably no accident that his next major production, in 1633, was a King and Subject ballad embodying the same sorts of social control as surround Robin Hood in the earlier piece.

Parker exemplifies the new use of anti-clerical material in the service of both protestantism and gentrification. This is a feature of some of the plays, as will be discussed in chapter 4, but here it is more than an anti-Catholic reaction and is best described as a fiscal form of gentrification at the expense of the church – the sort of thing that almost all local landholders actually engaged in during the mid-sixteenth century, and justified in religious terms through cultural processes like these ballads.

When the early ballads pilloried a monk, abbot or a prioress it was on behalf of the solidarity constructed by Robin, John and the massed ranks of bow-carrying yeoman. However, in a small but well-remembered group of later ballads, Robin pillages the church only for personal gain and the pleasure of humiliating the Catholic hierarchy, just like a reformation land-grabber. There is a limited but crucial redirection of the church-robbing motifs in a direction that is fully consonant with social gentrification and was in that period very often its basis.

'Robin Hood and the Bishop' (no. 143), widely circulated in seventeenth-century broadsides, is, as Child notes (1965, III, p. 191) a variant on the theme of the episode in the Gest when the outlaws relieve St Mary's abbey of £800. Yet there are differences. Robin exchanges clothes with an old woman to escape the bishop's men; they take what they think to be Robin, only to be told:

> Why, I am an old woman, thou cuckoldly bishop;
> Lift up my leg and see (p. 192, st. 18)

In a similar burlesque mode, when Robin and John have relieved the bishop of £500 they tie him to a tree, make him sing mass, then send him home mounted backwards.

None of these modes of comic reversal are un-medieval – carnivalization would be a way of describing them and Stallybrass sees this ballad, rather improbably, as exemplifying a distinctly radical form of carnival (1985, p. 119). But the point is that the purpose of the ballad is not the detailed discussion of oppression that leads to church wealth, as in the Gest, but rather merely to humiliate the Catholic establishment.

Exactly the same role is served in the closely related 'Robin Hood and the Bishop of Hereford' (no. 144), a later garland piece where the outlaws, disguised as shepherds, take the bishop, rob him of £300, make him pay for their merriment and, in the final words of the ballad, force him to 'dance in his boots And glad he could so get away' (p. 195, st. 21).

A minor ballad that belongs more closely with this group than any other is 'Little John a Begging' (no. 142). Seriously incomplete in Percy's manuscript, this appears in full form in a seventeenth-century broadside, and its action shows John begging on behalf of the outlaws – a curious deformation of their independent spirit – disguised as a palmer. He meets four beggars, who prove both physically sounder and much richer than they pretend, but after a fight John takes £603 pounds from them. While they are not priests, the idea of corruption in the context of old religion seems the main point of the ballad, which apart from John's almost trickster-like gaining of funds, appears to attack religious hypocrisy in the past, so relating to the priest-robbing stories that were so popular about this time.

Characteristic of this group of ballads is 'Robin Hood's Golden Prize' (no. 147). Here the hero is disguised as a friar, and the story brings out the hostility between friars and established clergy latent in 'Robin Hood and the Curtal Friar'. Robin simply pulls two priests off their horses and orders them to pray for money. As they are 'all in black' they are presumably Benedictine monks or Augustinian canons, and so there are clear relations to the 'miracle' of our lady by which the canons of St Mary's have £800 in their baggage in the *Gest*. With similar irony, Robin returns £50 to each man as they have prayed so successfully, and makes them swear three oaths, to tell the truth, to be sexually pure and show charity to the poor.

It is not only the last motif, the rich-poor feature, that indicates this ballad is relatively late and related to gentrification. While the setting is medieval enough, the modes are effectively later: Robin acts entirely alone, the tone is a reformist Christianity, replaying traditional mockery and satire against the church itself, and the cash he gains is kept for himself. On its own 'Robin Hood's Golden Prize' might pass for a late and thin reprise of a piece of medieval resistance to an oppressive church, and that could be its distant origin, but in its present form it appears to have been produced in 1656 by Lawrence Price (Dobson and Taylor, 1976, p. 48) and in implication it is

entirely consistent with the personalized and gentrified ballads that
follow the patterns developed in the chroniclers and dramatists of
the sixteenth century to reshape Robin Hood away from a collective
and anti-authoritarian rebel into a figure much more consistent with
the centralized, Protestant and money-oriented state, and so contradictory to the presentation of the hero in the late-medieval ballads and
many of their successors.

A different appropriation of Robin Hood for clerical politics came
in the Marprelate controversy of the mid-sixteenth century, when in
a strange piece of allegory (found in Harley manuscript 367), in order
to make a statement against the expropriation of church lands from a
Catholic position Robin represents the bishops, and, as a manuscript
note explains, his enemies include 'the Puritane which is the Wolfe
and the Poletician which is the ffox'. (Gutch, 1847, II, p. 40; see also
the discussion of the poem by Cooper, 1977, pp. 57–8.) Adam Bell,
another famous outlaw, symbolizes the abbots, Henry VIII is the Lion
while, least probable of all, Little John represents the ancient universities of Oxford and Cambridge. The poem ends by lamenting the
changes come over the ancient church in the guise of Robin Hood:

> When the wolves and foxes sawe
> Adam in the lyons pawe,
> Ours is Robyn, streight they cry'de,
> And sett him round one every side. (p. 44)

That religious use of the tradition was general and political; a much
more personal appropriation was made by Francis Peck who developed
his own version, entitled 'Robin Whood Turned Hermit' (1735; see
Holt, 1982, pp. 180–1 for text and discussion). After a full prose
synopsis of the Robin Hood materials, including 'The Noble Fisherman' but based heavily on Parker's 'True Tale', Peck then provides his
own rhapsody on the concept of the forest nay-sayer to authority, who
becomes in these hands a religious, even a pre-romantic hermit, suggesting, it would seem, sources like William Warner and Ben Jonson
(see pp. 134–6 and 139–42).

> To Depe-dale come, most wisely Robin Whood,
> Surveys each Nook and Corner of the Wood
> At length he finds a lonely rocky cell,

And in Devotion there resolves to dwell.
There he grows wise and for his Patron taks
The Thief repentant, and for him thus bespaks
Happy Robin Whood! Happy Robin Whood.

The outlaw tradition could have more socialized forms of later gentrification. One that goes unrecorded completely, including in the British Library catalogue, was a version of 'The Pindar of Wakefield's Legend' written, according to a contemporary manuscript note in one copy, by John Hughes, whose mother was a friend of Scott, and whose son wrote *Tom Brown's Schooldays*. Dated in 1832, this publication apparently celebrated a particular occasion when a group of Oxford friends met at Donnington Priory under the joint hospitality of Earl Craven and Lord Barrington. They held an archery contest, illustrated in the pamphlet, and used the myth to link together in a benign narrative the large group of friends and colleagues as characters from the legend, all identified in the annotated copy, some with suitable names. Robin Hood was the Rev. J.E. Robinson, and Little John was the Rev. John Jowett. Twenty-four of the party are named with, just like Marian, one lone woman, Lady Barrington herself.

The positioning is pastoral-classical:

When birds sing free in bower and tree
    And sports are to the fore
With fiddle and long-bow forth I fare,
    As Phoebus did of yore. (p. 7)

And the imagination is popular-historical:

When bows hang idly on the wall
    And blazed that yule-clog [*sic*] bright, (p. 23)

This curious text suggests how much of the Robin Hood complex has been lost through never being published at all, or being recorded only in ephemeral ways; it also implies how many varied kinds of social and cultural self-realizations found a space in ballad form in this flexible, and capacious myth. But number and variety exist elsewhere in the tradition as well, and while the volume of the ballads alone might make them seem overwhelming as the primary medium for transmission of the tradition of Robin Hood (and for those who sang songs, collected broadsides or gathered antiquarian materials, that was certainly the case), there was nevertheless another whole genre which was at least as dynamic in the development, dissemination and variety of the Robin Hood myth, and that was drama. It was there that gentrification found its most powerful form, and it was there that the essential conflicts of the myth were most vividly and memorably portrayed. The dramatic tradition is still the most vigorous today, as it was, to judge from early references, in the period before 1600 and the spread of printed broadsides. It is to Robin Hood in performance that this study now will turn.

4

'A Brighter Gleam of
True Nobility':
Robin Hood in Performance

4.1 Plays and Games of Robin Hood

Errol Flynn as the most dashing of outlaws in the miracle of tech-nicolour, Michael Praed as a spirited radical of the early eighties, even Richard Greene, squadron-leader Robin Hood from fifties television – they all appear part of our time, not merely in concept but particularly in mode of delivery. Electronic media seem the ultimate in modernity, and the most remarkable thing about Robin Hood is how this antique myth is still retold in absolutely up-to-date forms.

Yet the essential form of that contemporaneity is itself ancient. Performance, in whatever mode is currently popular, has always been close to the centre of the myth, a fact obscured by the consistent stress in scholarly discussions on the text-based genres of the tradition. In a number of ways the performance tradition is the most clearly unbroken one in the whole Robin Hood myth, marked by considerable variation of mode and meaning but also retaining a coherent dramatic identity.

Communal games of the late middle ages often featured Robin Hood in some sort of sylvan setting, either real or represented, and the populace would gather, admire, participate and offer coins. These activities of popular festival survived for a long time. Kilvert's diary of 17 May 1871 records an essentially unvaried instance as he watched some gentlemanlike 'Foresters' process through Chippenham and after the military figures 'in black coats crossed with green scarves' came a wagon carrying sheep, shepherd and shepherdess; then followed: '. . . another green embowered carriage with a buck's head and horns peering through the branches and Robin Hood lying down on the floor with his bow and arrows' (1938, I, p. 334).

In the fifteenth and sixteenth centuries Robin Hood would visit just such small towns; he would be surrounded with forest imagery, bearing bow and arrows, operating in some form of pageant mode, and collecting money for the community. In nineteenth-century Chippenham the notions of martial gentry and pastoral profit have been included, but the old outlaw figure of forest leisure and liberty is still represented. In the same way, ancient dramatic motifs of quarter-staff fighting, disguise, ambush, humbling of the proud and honouring the simple, all in a setting of sylvan value, still have special force in modern modes from pantomime to video.

Looking back at the beginning of Robin Hood performance will help to clarify just how prevalent and pervasive has been the influence and the institution of drama in the outlaw myth. The Middle Ages had many forms of drama. Some descended from a pre-Christian past as public rituals and folk events, usually in seasonal contexts, from blessing the plough to bringing in the Yule log. Others, less fugitive in the records, were directly stimulated by the social outreach of Christian doctrine such as the cycles of plays produced by townsmen on Corpus Christi day or the more literary allegorical plays like *Everyman*. There was also an early element of court theatre, which was close to what is later called masque.

A recurrent element in the popular domain, with some presence in the courtly modes as well, and even having some contact with the church's interest in plays, was the set of performance practices connected with Robin Hood. They are described by David Wiles, the most recent and best-informed commentator, as remarkable for being, as a cultural tradition, 'wholly indigenous, wholly secular' (1981, p. 2). There is an element of both theatre and amusement – play in its two senses – in all the recorded instances, and while most com-mentators have called them 'plays and games' to embrace both ideas, it is in practice impossible to separate the references into those as separate modes, and the best term for these performances is 'Robin Hood play-game'.

Though most commentators speak with some confidence of the 'May Games' in which Robin Hood appears, few seem to have grasped their essential complexity and variety of character, nor how extraordinarily widespread they were. In the database of early Robin Hood references gathered by Lucy Sussex (see Appendix), Robin Hood playgames have a remarkable predominance. Out of a total of two hundred and sixty citations before 1600, including literary, proverbial, topographical and casual references, one hundred and thirty six refer to some form of performance activity. Record-survival must vary according to context, and performances funded by town authorities have a good chance of survival, but even allowing for that factor there is still a striking number of recorded instances: over fifty of them occur by 1537; even more strikingly the same number occur before 1577, as both the survival of records and the popularity of Robin Hood appears to intensify. Then, as pressure is put upon outlaw-related activities by both church and state sources, there is a distinct reduction of references to the hero, and by 1600 only another twenty-five are recorded, which includes Robin Hood productions in the London-based professional theatre.

Very few texts survive from the non-professional tradition. A manuscript written in about 1475 includes a short play which realizes some of the events described in the ballad 'Robin Hood and Guy of Gisborne' (see pp. 56–8) though Robin's opponent is not named; Dobson and Taylor title the play 'Robin Hood and the Sheriff' (1976, pp. 203–7) as the latter is the ultimate enemy, appearing at beginning and end. Twelve couplets, jammed together on a manuscript page, tell a rapid story. A knight and the sheriff decide on a reward for seizing Robin Hood; the knight meets Robin and agrees to sporting combat; Robin wins at archery, stone casting and wrestling; then they agree to fight 'at outrance', to the end. Robin wins again and acts with brisk ferocity (as he does at more leisure and in a more complicated way in the ballad):

Now I have the maystry here/Off I smite this sorry swyre
This knyghtis clothes wolle I were/ And in my hode his hede woll bere.
(p. 205)

The scene changes suddenly, as in a film montage. Two 'fellows' meet and ask about 'gode Robyn'. He is 'with the sheryffe takyn'. They – presumably Little John and Will Scathelock, or perhaps Much, as this is reminiscent of 'Robin Hood and the Monk' – agree to set off

and kill the sheriff. They see Friar Tuck 'shooting well', but are themselves taken by the sheriff's men and are all imprisoned to await
hanging. The tone is brisk;

(*John?*): Now we be bownden alle in same/ ffrere Tuke this is no game
(*Sheriff?*): Come thou forth thou fals outlawe/ Thou shall be hangyde
and ydrawe
(*Tuck?*): Now allas what shall we doo/ We moste to the prysone goo
(*Sheriff?*): Opyn the yatis faste anon/ And late theis thevys ynne gon

Presumably Robin, having killed the 'knight' and disguised himself in
his clothes, will now rescue his colleagues, as Dobson and Taylor have
suggested in their reconstruction. They think 'the drama breaks off
abruptly at an exciting stage of the action' (1976, p. 204), but this
assumes there must be words for performance to exist. What follows
the end of the verbal text here may simply be heroic action, like the
long final sequences in many films, which usually have no dialogue at
all as Robin rescues friends from a terrible fate and settles scores with
his enemies. What seems a textual silence may indeed be the high
point of performance: the dramatic character of the plays can itself be
suggested by a lack of words.

Two other plays survive in printed form, appearing as addenda after
the *Gest* in William Copland's edition, published in about 1560; they
are reprinted by Dobson and Taylor (1976, pp. 208–19). Copland
represents these on his title page as 'a new playe' and presumably this
is what was entered in the Stationers' Register in 1560 as 'the play of
Robyn Hoode'. The first play, or scene, focuses on a friar; it has been
separately edited (Anon, *c.*1560, ed. Blackstone, 1980) and begins with
Robin's account of meeting a 'stoute frere' who beat and robbed him;
Robin asks for one of the band to bring in the friar. Little John agrees,
but the next scene opens with the boasting friar who has come to
Barnsdale to settle matters with Robin Hood. The hero enters and
they exchange abuse, then blows. Robin sounds his horn, his men
appear; the Friar whistles and his dogs arrive. A fight apparently
ensues, which is presumably drawn. Robin invites the friar to join him
in the usual way, promising 'Thou shalt have both golde and fee', but
more surprisingly says in addition 'And also here is a lady free' whom
he gives to the friar: he makes him 'her chapplyan' in order to, in
double entendre terms, 'serve her for my sake'.

Most interpreters have thought, like Dobson and Taylor that this woman must be the 'Maid Marian of the May game morris dances, in which she almost always partners Friar Tuck' (1976, p. 214. n. 1). However, she is not named in Copland's play, she was never called 'Maid' in the Morris, and to link the Morris and the May Game is itself a doubtful connection (see p. 104 below). The play simply ends with a post-reformation image of the roistering cleric, especially in its rollicking last stanza as the friar celebrates his sexual good fortune:

> Here is an huckle duckle,
> An inch above the buckle.
> She is a trul of trust,
> To serve a frier at his lust,
> A prycker, a prauncer, a terer of shetes,
> A wagger of ballockes when other men slepes. (p. 214)

This lively ending has been omitted from some texts on grounds of decency and, more curiously, 'ballockes' has been misread as 'buttockes'. After this spirited climax, the friar dismisses the outlaws to celebrate the final comic dance which is endemic to the performance tradition, rather than to the Robin Hood myth:

> Go home, ye knaves, and lay crabbes in the fyre
> For my lady and I will daunce in the myre
> For very pure joye. (p. 214)

This vivid piece of performance is followed immediately in the manuscript by another (Dobson and Taylor, 1976, pp. 215–19) – like two episodes from a modern television serial copied onto the same tape. Once again Robin begins by introducing 'an adventure . . . That befell this other daye'. (p. 216) A potter who regularly comes this way has refused to pay 'one peny passage'. Robin seeks someone to extract a toll: as in the previous sequence, Little John agrees to be the band's enforcer.

But, again as before, it is Robin who in the next scene meets the potter's boy and at once begins smashing the pots and abusing the master, who then appears. Appeasingly – and so most unlike the ballad – the potter offers to sell his belongings and split them with Robin, but Robin insists on a toll. The potter chooses to fight, and Robin calls in Little John. The play ends with John's words:

> Be the knave never so stoute,
> I shall rappe hym on the snoute,
> And put hym to flyghte. (p. 219)

Editors assume the play is unfinished, but they have in mind the quite different action of the ballad 'Robin Hood and the Potter' (see pp. 54–5). The length and style of this short dramatic combat with the Potter match the three other Robin Hood sequences that survive in the early plays. They are brisk and depend heavily on action. After a scene-setting opening statement the plays are verbally restricted to a few shouted remarks to set up the conflict which is central to these brisk dramas, and especially their climaxes in combat. Just as Robin's rescue will complete 'Robin Hood and the Sheriff' in the *c.*1475 manuscript, so here an equal battle with the Potter will have the same resolving function, a grand finale of action and celebration.

To interpret the plays in that way as performance pieces is in keeping with Copland's own subtitle, which reads: 'a newe play for to be played in Maye games very plesaunte and ful of pastyme'. The connection with the May Games deserves examination, both as a way of exploring the meaning of those very frequent references in the records to the Robin Hood play-game and also as a way of resolving the question of how these plays relate to the ballads that clearly handle some of the same material.

The references to Robin Hood play-games cover a surprisingly wide range of Britain – 'from Aberdeen to Cornwall' says Wiles, though he also clarifies the more surprising and still unexplained fact that towns and villages in the north of England appear to have no trace of this tradition (1981, pp. 2–4). The play-game also represents a considerable range of activities and purposes, and in order to approach this material it is important to clear up two persistent misconceptions or, rather, misconnections.

One is with May Day. Though these are May Games they are not in any direct way connected with the maypole or the floral dances associated with the first of May, though that error often occurs in general treatments of the topic. The Robin Hood play-games are later in the year than May Day: Warner said the activities came 'ere Pentecost' (*Albion's England*, 1589 ed., chap. 25, p. 121); in 1616 Richard Niccols set them 'When May did clad the woods with lustie greene' (*London's Artillery*, 1616, p. 87); Stow merely said in the 'monethe of May'

(*Annales of England*, 1592, p. 227) but in 1559 Henry Machyn recorded that they took place on 24 June (*Diary*, 1848 ed., p. 201). The well-attested Yeovil events were at Whitsun (Stokes, 1986, p. 5) and this is the date that Wiles, who knows the records well, associates firmly with the event, saying 'there is no basis whatsoever for linking early Robin Hood games with celebrations on May the first' (1981, p. 4). Robin Hood is related to the first phase of full summer, when the hawthorn is white and after the dramatic changes that still overtake the rural landscape so strikingly by the middle of May.

The second confusion is with the Morris dances. Dobson and Taylor give a common view by suggesting they are closely related to the May Games (1976, pp. 40–2, 214, n. 1). This is an oversimplification of the late Elizabethan condensation of the two celebrations, usually by urban writers; Chambers, who is often thought to have connected the two actually gives a more cautious view, suggesting only that the link 'may be literary' (1933, p. 152). It is clear that the 'Morris' dances are late medieval, even sixteenth-century introductions into English festival practices, and the name in the early references is evidently to do with 'Moorish' – it also appears that the figure who became called Marian was originally the 'Murrian' or 'moorish one', and usually had a black face. By the later sixteenth century the festal activities of the May Games had, in rapid social and cultural change, fallen together with Morris dances and were often regarded as interrelated but they are clearly separate in more specifically reminiscent references like Warner's which says in full: 'At Pask began our Morris, and ere Pentecost our May' (*Albions England*, 1589, p. 121).

The other argument that is often raised (see Dobson and Taylor, 1976, pp. 40–2), that the Friar and Marian both transferred to the Robin Hood myth from the Morris dances, is itself not as strong as it might seem. There is a long-lasting connection between Robin and Marian, though not in the context of outlawry. Adam de la Halle's, opera 'Robin et Marion', written in 1280, was being performed in France at Angers regularly around 1392, at Pentecost, or Whitsun. The time of year alone is highly suggestive, and the names remain well known as nature-related lovers, though probably not at a popular level; the learned poet Gower uses them in his French language *Mirour de l'homme* by 1380 and an equally academic writer, Alexander Barclay, speaks in 1513–14 in his version of Virgil's Fourth Eclogue of both figures together:

Yet would I gladly heare nowe some mery fit
Of Maid Marian, or els of Robin Hoode. (ed. White, 1928, p. 166,
lines 721–2)

Barclay may not be thinking of the two figures in the same narrative, though, against such separation, Cooper does note that he often
transposes materials, including French, into English contexts (1977,
pp. 118–19). The Kingston records from 1509 onwards clearly provide costumes for Marian in the context of Robin. It seems, therefore,
that if Robin is conceived of as a lover rather than an outlaw, there is
a name for his partner; the lusty wench of the Morris and the Games
does not need to be the origin of Marian at all, though she may well
be a friar's girlfriend.

Nor need the friar himself come to the myth from that source.
There are many rogue friars in medieval tradition, before the reformation made it religiously correct to relish their misdemeanours. More
to the point, there were outlaws by that name. In 1417, Robert Stafford, chaplain of Lindfield in Sussex, assumed the name of Friar Tuck
when he undertook robberies in the area (where the name of Robin
Hood was also found early, see p. 24). The fighting friar of the 'Robin
Hood and the Sheriff' play is in written form in the *c*.1475 manuscript
before the Morris dances had made any real impact in England. It
looks as if Tuck himself goes back into popular tradition and that an
existing outlaw name becomes attached to the rogue friar who not
unnaturally turns up in the Morris performances.

So if May Day and Morris is what the May Games do not involve,
it is appropriate to examine what and who was part of the Robin Hood
play-game, as is suggested in the records that are found. There was
always a procession of some kind in which Robin, in suitable costume,
usually supported by other named figures like Little John, and leading
a band of people, went to some place to collect money. It might have
been another village or town – there are references to Robin Hood of
Finchhamstead coming to Reading, in 1505, and in the same year
Robin Hood also arrived in Reading from Henley. He was evidently
welcomed with enthusiasm, or something more – in 1571 the people
of Honiton bought a pound of gunpowder for the visit of Robin Hood
from Colyton.

The play-game Robin always has a form of carnivalized authority,
as a King of May, or a Summer Lord, and this power is fully secular,

even though he is usually connected with the church. When the use of the funds collected can be traced, they are deployed for the church or for the parish under the direction of the rector or church wardens, as with buying a new silver censer in Henley in 1499 or attending to the roads in Melton in 1556.

The procession and the fund-raising were only one visible form of activities; others were often, but not necessarily, associated. Plays could be fitted into the games: the four recorded scenes discussed above could very easily be performed in such a context in public, during a pause at a suitable place for performance and collection, as Copland clearly suggests in his subtitle 'very plesaunt to be played in May Games'. The nature of the surviving plays also supports the notion that 'combat' of some kind was a regular part of the Robin Hood procession, and this could be a formal competition as well: in the later sixteenth century references to archery competitions are found, and this is already present in the 'Robin Hood and the Sheriff' play, with the other sports of wrestling and stone casting. Many of the ballads are in fact simply reports of extended dramatic combat, which the play-game could enact.

A different encounter often occurs in the May Games: there is frequent reference to a feast in the later part of the day, and to Robin Hood arriving at certain places and collecting money, or staying to be entertained. This is where the traditional play-game touches the 'Mummer's Play', versions of which exist right across the country. In this framework, with many local variations, a group arrives, usually on a winter's evening, speaks a ritual drama with traditional characters entering and stating their roles. In the Shipton under Wychwood play (Tiddy, 1923) the first to enter and speak is 'Bold rauthra band' a tanner, who enacts his fight with Robin Hood; and then comes in Little John, who is killed, but revived by the Doctor, the next amazing character to appear. Beelzebub rounds up this lively transgressive performance, which obviously has drawn on one of the versions of 'Robin Hood and the Tanner' that names the opponent as Arthur Bland, as in Child's oldest text, no. 126a (1965, vol. III, pp. 137–9).

Whatever performance elements might be fitted into the procession, the basis of the play-game is clearly a public ritual across the border of the natural and the cultural. In the Robin Hood play-game the community celebrates the continued encounter with benign nature, at the season where the renewed promise of summer is clear. This whole process has both social and spiritual aspects. Glynne Wickham has described the basis of all early ritual performance:

> At the moment in time deemed to be special, sacred and thus 'holy', the normal routines of life must be suspended; the community, thus released from its mundane preoccupations, must assemble together; the individual recognised to be endowed with special suitability to conduct the ceremony appropriate to the particular occasion must be correctly attired, and perform the agreed rites, aided by other representatives of the community, also correctly dressed, in choric dance and chant. With these incantatory overtures completed, the time is right for the sacrifice to be made (if any be thought to be demanded); the gifts must then be presented; some manifestation of the god must be consumed; or some other physical action must be executed that is itself indicative of communion with the god. (1981, p. 9)

The Robin Hood performance has, in recorded form, few overt traces of any 'god'. The crucial dynamic is between forest and habitation, and the way in which each community relates itself to the world of wild nature from which it is separated as civilization and on which it depends for its life.

However, although there is something like a recurrent and meaningful set of events in the play-games, which in general match well Wickham's overarching description, the recorded examples are by no means alike, particularly in their social level and their outcome. One common mode, it would seem, is the peaceful, festal, communal self-realization which connects town and country, gathers money and enjoys itself in summery mood as in the detailed Yeovil records surveyed by Stokes. They are 'popular' in that they involve the people of the town, but it is also clear that hierarchy is embedded: the men who wait patiently over the years to play Robin are important figures in the community and have almost always served as churchwarden. This is some way from communal resistance to improper authority: it is rather a means of confirming and exercising inherent authority within the area (Stokes, 1986, p. 6).

Most of the Robin Hood play-game references seem of this uncontroversial kind and were accordingly supported by the powerful and the community at large. Sir John Paston in 1473 wrote in one of the famous family letters that he had for three years kept a man 'to play Robin Hood and St George' (1976, vol. I., p. 461), and though the man absconded, Sir John seemed to feel employing him was a squirely duty, not a contact with rebellion. The carefully funded events at Kingston through the years 1506 to 1529 seem of this socially coherent kind. In Scotland in 1508 Robin Hood is found fitting into a similarly established pattern at Aberdeen when his name and that of Little John are for the first time used to describe the charitable and carnivalesque collectors formerly known as the Abbot and Prior of Bonacord.

However, the play-games can have a less harmonious side; the forms of procession seem to have been used for the purpose of resistance in 1441 when a group of yeomen and labourers blocked the road in Southacre, Norfolk, singing 'We arn Robynhodesmen war war war' and threatening to murder Sir Geoffrey Harsyk (King's Bench, 1441). Sir Piers Venables' rescue of a prisoner and escape to the forest in 1439 did not obviously derive from a May Game, though the trouble-makers were described as behaving like 'Robin Hood and his meyne' (see p. 25). The beginnings of a Robin Hood riot can be clearly traced in 1497, when Roger Marshall of Westbury in Staffordshire defended himself in Star Chamber on the charge of leading a riotous assembly to Willenhall under the name of Robin Hood (Dobson and Taylor, 1976, p. 4).

It began with the arrest in Walsall of two men (from Wednesbury and Dudley) for assault. Marshall and three others, including a priest and a squire, with two hundred followers, assembled in Wednesbury and threatened a rescue. They were forbidden to attend Willenhall fair on Trinity Sunday (the week after Whitsun). But Marshall, now named as Robert, and the priest came with a hundred armed men under the aegis of Robin Hood. Also present were sixty armed men from Wolverhampton led by the 'Abbot of Marram'. They threatened to attack any Walsall men they met at the fair.

In his defence Marshall claimed to be playing the Robin Hood game:

> ... hit hath byn of olde tymes used and accustumed on the said fere day that wyth the inhabitantes of Wolverhampton, Wednesbury and Walsall have comyne to the said fere the capitanns called the Abot of Marham or Robyn Hodys to the intent to gether money with their disportes to the profight of the chirches of the seid lordshipes. (Quoted in Holt, 1982, p. 149)

On this occasion, it seems, nothing worse than threatening behaviour occurred. A more drastic development from this kind of context was shown in the events of 1549 in Wymondham, Norfolk, where the Summer Fair of 8 July turned into an anti-enclosure rebellion under Robert Kett and, as Wiles says, 'the symbolic language of game became the language of rebellion' (1981, p. 55). Kett's main opponent called him 'a captain of fugitives' and the rebels met formally under a great oak tree (Hoare and Hoare, 1985, p. 14). No Robin Hood connection was explicit at Wymondham, but the outlaw's name had been used as a *nom de guerre* in Jack Cade's similar rising of 1450 (Harvey, 1991, p. 65). Riot and the outlaw hero conjoined firmly in Edinburgh in 1561 as reported by no one less than John Knox in his *History*. Apparently apprentices and craftsmen gathered 'efter the auld wikkit maner of Robyn Hoode' and then: 'the rascal Multitude were stirred-up to make a *Robin-Hood*, which enormity was of many years left off and condemned by Statute and Act of Parliament; yet would they not be forbidden, but would disobey and trouble the Town' (Mill, 1927, p. 132).

Walter Scott provides more information in his note on 'Abbot of Unreason' in *The Abbot*; the cause of the riot was apparently the proposed execution of John Guillan for 'playing in Edinburgh with Robin Hood' on 21 June (1892, ed. p. 175). Scott adds that it was in principal the 'craftsmen's servants' who rioted to save him from hanging, and others too, as the mob forced open the Toll-booth jail, smashed a gibbet and imprisoned the magistrates themselves until they published a proclamation pardoning the rioters. This is certainly the strong form of carnival, seen by Stallybrass as being a recurrent possibility in the Robin Hood myth (1985, pp. 115–19), paralleling the representation of Robin Hood as a social bandit in some at least of the early ballads. But this is not a dominant mode – an equal number of references diverge from the blandly communal middle ground in the other political direction and use the figure of the outlaw to celebrate hierarchy in self-validating action.

The loftiest of all the gentrifications of the plays and games occurs quite early – suggesting that the likelihood of recording an event depends on its social status. Hall's chronicle records a kind of royal carnival in 1510 when Henry VIII and eleven nobles broke into the queen's chamber dressed for an elaborate Robin Hood game:

His grace, therles of Essex, Wilshire, and other noble menne, to the
nombre of twelve, came sodainly in a mornyng, into the Quenes Chambre, al appareled in shorte cotes, of Kentish Kendal, with hodes on
their heddes and hosen of the same, every one of them, his bowes and
arrowes, and a sword and a bucklar, like outlawes, or Robin Hoode's
men, wherefor the Quene, the Ladies, and al other there, were abashed
as well for the straunge sight, and also for their sodain comyng, and
after certain daunces and pastime made, thei departed. (1809, p. 515)

The King's second recorded adventure in the myth, in 1515, is also
described by Hall. As the king and queen were passing Shooters Hill
(the name of which may well have suggested the whole performance)
they were confronted by two hundred yeoman in green and invited
into the woods. There a bower and a feast had been prepared – the
king of the outlaws appeared in the form of Robin Hood 'clothed all
in greene', put on a display of archery and invited the King 'into the
grene wood and to se how the outlawes lyve'. Such 'natural' life is
royally acculturated; there was:

> . . . an Arber made of boowes with a hal, and a great chamber and an
> inner chamber very well made and covered with floures and swete
> herbes, which the kyng much praysed. Then said Robyn hood, Sir
> Outlawes brekefastes is venyson, and therefore you must be content
> with such fare as we use. Then the kyng and quene sate doune, and
> were served with venyson and wyne by Robyn hood and his men, to
> their great contentacion. (1809, p. 582)

This enacts the royal feast, a motif found in the *Gest* that has
survived into most modern filmic versions because of its sheer theatricality – and perhaps its conservative politics. Here, as in many later
versions, especially on the stage, the outlaw's role is fully reshaped,
stylized so it has no disruptive force. The same processes could operate
on behalf of town government, turning Robin into a model of armed
citizenship; Richard Robinson's verse memoirs of 1583, *The Ancient
Order of Prince Arthur*, indicate how Robin was a focus for the rural-
izing fancy of the townsmen and also for their own military training.
The May Game, Robinson remembers from his childhood, had become
an occasion

> To traine up young men, stripplings and eche other younger childe
> In shooting, yearly this with solempne feast was by the Guylde

Or Brotherhood of Townsmen done, with sport, with ioy and love
(f. L4v)

An honorific version of such practical urban preparedness can be seen
in Anthony Munday's masque for the Lord Mayor of London, *Metropolis
Coronata* (1615), a version of the play-game that celebrates the urban
gentry to the point of servility.

Varied as the meaning of the Robin Hood figure is through these
quite different versions, some elements recur, however limited in terms
of resistance. He represents youthfulness and physical skill, and he
focuses a natural form of festivity which contrasts with modernity and
realizes a sense of communality. Most important of all, and little
noticed by commentators, he represents locality. He is usually Robin
Hood *of* somewhere, not a country or even a county, but a quite
specific spot. Robin's enemies in the ballads had been those whose
overarching and inorganic authority covered large areas, whether abbot or sheriff, and he preyed especially on those who travelled long
distances with money at hand. Those new forces of the mobile, cash-
related world were the innate enemies of Robin Hood, and the sense
of his local, natural and socially-integrated world persists through the
plays and games, whether they are simply celebratory, like most, fiercely
opposititional, like a few, or idealized into conservatism, like those
involving the king or the town councils of London.

The Robin Hood plays and games were to be strongly attacked
during the later sixteenth century, and both they and the references to
them die out quite rapidly. The reason usually given is the reformation, that a puritan church is against such playful public activities:
Dobson and Taylor talk of 'condemnation of the outlaw cult by sixteenth-century puritans' (1976, p. 43). But it was the Catholic Mary
Queen of Scots who banned Robin Hood in 1562, and she confirmed
a decision taken seven years before by the Protestant Scottish parliament. At Yeovil, where Robin Hood from 1576 on was replaced as the
demiurge of Whitsun entertainment by the vaguely named 'keeper of
the ale', there is no evident religious reason (Stokes, 1986, pp. 6).

In a 1549 sermon Bishop Hugh Latimer referred to a visit he
made some years before (apparently in the 1530s) to a town where
the church stood empty on a Sunday because, he was told, 'it is
Robin Hoodes day. The parishe are gone abroad to gather for Robyn
Hoode.' (1869, pp. 173–4). The outraged Latimer was certainly on

the reforming wing of the church, and died for his beliefs, but the conflict here is not between Catholic and Protestant, but between the authority of a travelling bishop and the practices of the local community – the priest was evidently among Robin Hood's 'meyne' on this particular day of local observance, which Chambers thought was probably in Melton (1903, p. 180, n. 3), a Robin Hood play-location in 1556 and at the centre of the Sherwood, Barnsdale in Rutland, Rockingham belt.

It is clear that figures like Knox and Latimer were against what they saw as unchristian activities, but so had been a devout Catholic like Langland, on equally moralistic grounds; the power of the later moralists to block Robin Hood activities rose from the politically-increased power of the more centralized and nationally organized church, whether Anglican or dissenting.

The forces that foreclosed the local Robin Hood activities were the elements of state authority, powers congruent with those of sheriff and abbot of the older days: they were the forces that the tradition had long targeted as hostile to the spirit of local freedom and authenticity.

Wiles sees this resistance in terms of radical politics – 'Elizabethan authorities, unlike their medieval predecessors, were determined to prevent any institutionalized expression of egalitarian sentiment' (1981, p. 54), but while that repression was sometimes an effect, the cause was more widely based in centralization and regulation than in conservatism for its own sake – indeed the play-game was, in local terms at least, capable of being deeply conservative.

If the reasons for the play-games' repression have been oversimplified, another area of misinterpretation has been the relationship between the four surviving early play-scenes and the ballads. They are clearly linked: what is less clear is the matter of priority. It has usually been assumed that the ballads were the source of the plays; this is Child's view, saying that the play of 'Robin Hood and the Sheriff' is 'founded on' 'Robin Hood and Guy of Gisborne' (1965, III, p. 90); Steadman, in an early essay on the surviving plays, agreed – his title itself is 'The Dramatization of the Robin Hood Ballads' (1919) and recent scholars have seen no reason to vary that opinion (Simeone, 1951, p. 266; Nelson, 1973, pp. 47–51).

But quite different views are possible. One merely reverses the apparent facts. Wiles suggests that 'Robin Hood games did not merely derive from ballads but often inspired the creation of ballads' (1981,

p. 2). Understandable as it is, this inversion of the argument is just as fragile as the earlier assumption. Both views assume the essential difference of the forms, taking the view, as Bessinger summed it up, that the Robin Hood of the play-game 'was only casually related to the ballads, not the outlaw of yeoman origins' (1966, p. 64). But the two are not so easily separable. By putting together all the events and implications that arise from the recorded evidence of the May Games featuring Robin Hood, it is possible to see that in fact they were a performance-based version of the same myth as is presented in the early ballads.

The play-games present a compilation of events and implications: young men, in a collective group, representing a locality; involved in combat for entertainment and, as a feature of their solidarity, led by Robin with others nearly equal; gathering money for communal use by forms of confrontation, which can include threats; in the process of that action disguising themselves and their names; using various reversals of authority as part of their festal play; moving between forest and town; emphasizing a natural economy; having some anti-clerical position especially against distant clergy; resisting distant secular authorities; using liveries or badges as a sign of collectivity; being connected always with early summer; being involved in feasting as a mark of their successful togetherness; relying to some degree on an egalitarian ethic; not involved in direct cash-based charity to the poor.

Remarkably, the events in the ballads all give some narrative form to those play-game features; none of them is missing; no other major issues occur. The ballads, that is, are merely a different mediation of the issues realized in the May Games and, in so far as they are recorded, in the early Robin Hood plays. To state simply that the plays are derived from the ballads is to privilege the written form, and to reverse the order is equally near-sighted. Both views misunderstand the ways in which culture operates in and through a society; it is also a misreading of the plays themselves. The second part of the 'Sheriff' play is a new narrative and not a deformation of 'Robin Hood and Guy of Gisborne'; the Potter play is equally a 'combat' performance, not a cut-down of 'Robin Hood and the Potter'; it may well be that the ballad about the friar and his dogs is itself derived from the Friar play, and the Guy of Gisborne ballad might well be a very fine and contemporary variant of the first part of the 'Sheriff' drama, enriched with literary and mythical force.

If ballad and play-game processions can all be seen as variants of the same set of contemporary forces, then there is no need to trace the May Games in general and Robin Hood in particular back to some ancient pagan figure as John Matthews has recently argued in *Robin Hood: Green Lord of the Wildwood* (1993). Equally, it is simplistic to find too narrow a modern meaning in the figure. For all his detailed scholarship, Wiles opens his account with some political naivety in finding Robin 'the ideal of the free individual, whose true nature must be rescued from an alienating society' (1981, p. 1). This is both to impose a modern ideology and also to import something inherently foreign to the non-individualistic nature of Robin Hood and most other figures from the period. Nor is the outlaw only the figure of radical resistance who is so acceptable to contemporary sociocultural criticism, as Stallybrass has suggested; he sums up his discussion of 'Robin Hood and the Bishop' in which Robin changes places with an old woman to rob the church, as a 'subversion of class and gender hierarchy' and asserts that: 'The symbolic system of carnival is used, then, to legitimate popular justice against the official ideological and legal apparatus which claims to have a monopoly of justice. The outlaw becomes the enforcer of popular law' (1985, p. 119).

This carnivalization, unlike Wiles's 'free individual', does at times genuinely appear in the older tradition, as with the hard-handed outlaw of the social bandit ballads discussed above, and such a concept seems to have participated in the early Robin Hood riots. But that austerely political outlaw is a fugitive and culture-specific figure, hardly visible in the play-game as it has been recorded, nor indeed in the trickster-like comedy of most of the carnivalizing ballads.

Local and communal as he is, Robin Hood has as many versions as there are localities and communities. A figure who is cited so frequently as the Robin Hood of the May games and plays, who is so widely distributed in so many different kinds of social and economic contexts, is not going to be reducible to a narrow set of descriptions. However, it seems clear that he consistently represents the local, the natural, the vigorous, and the unsophisticated. But that particular collection of forces may, depending on occasion and location, please a king or liberate a prisoner; it may provide cultural coherence in a rural town, or focus class identity in emergent urban society. Many figures might find profit in the protecting fictions of Robin Hood, from a sex-starved friar to a timid townsman needing trained archers.

That multiple force has in some sense lasted into the present, but there were also in the sixteenth century pressures acting against the local habitation and even the name of the hero, and they transmuted the Robin Hood myth in a number of ways that are themselves long-lasting, as can be seen in a study of the outlaw as he was newly represented in the professional Elizabethan theatre of the late sixteenth century.

4.2   The Theatre of the Fifteen-Nineties

When the London theatres closed during the plague of 1592, Robin Hood was not part of the professional repertoire. Citations of the hero surviving from that time are restricted to proverbs, continuing attempts to suppress the play-games and general references to the idea of the outlaw hero. But when the theatres reopened, a boom period began, audiences grew and plays were needed for weekdays as well as holidays; the theme of the English outlaw become part of the everyday business of the professional literary theatre of modernizing London.

Why Robin Hood should emerge in this way is a question that cannot be taken separately from the topics of other plays at the time. The taste for English antiquity was strong, already shown in the history plays of Shakespeare and others; but there was also some caution about being too recent and so too political. Robin Hood was not only English and comfortably in the past; his was also a widespread name and the use of highly popular material in a newly conservative context was an elegant manoeuvre for companies eager to please both the lucrative mass audience and also the powerful few who controlled the theatre; a myth with those capacities and also an existing highly theatrical structure was hardly likely to be left untouched in the search for new material.

The hero was mentioned in an increasing number of historical authors and had moved into 'high' poetry with William Warner's *Albion's England* (1589, see pp. 134–6), but a more immediate context to gentrification may have been John Stow's well-known *Annales* of 1592, which restated John Major's ennobling remarks, and stressed the hero's date in the times of Richard I. However, even this did not directly influence the earliest professional representations of the hero, which seem popular in derivation, though not in any coherently connected way. The plays of the 1590s are remarkably independent and eclectic in their materials. Most commentators have focused on the elevation of Robin to an earldom, but that only happens in one playwright, Anthony Munday, influential though the move was to be in general. More striking is the way in which the active vigorous hero of the ballads and play-games is now marginalized, and how little the existing narrative material of the myth is re-used – including the well-known *Gest*. The 1590s plays both reform and in some significant ways deform the Robin Hood myth, largely by making the named hero into a minor figure who is cheerfully subservient to powerful forces and only rarely offers any substantial resistance to authority of any kind.

Seven plays are in question, but there are complications to that folkloric-seeming number. Two have not survived, *Robin Hood and Little John*, listed anonymously in the Stationers' Register for 1594, and *Robin Hood's Penn'orths* listed for 1600–1 and attributed to William Haughton. Two others are best conceived as one; *The Downfall of Robert Hood, Earle of Huntington* and *The Death of Robert Hood, Earle of Huntington* (1598–9) are a closely woven sequence, and appear to have been conceived of originally as one play by Munday, who will be regarded here as the 'author' though it seems clear that Henry Chettle had a significant role in the second play.

The other plays are George Peele's *The Famous Chronicle of Edward I* (by 1593), which has two scenes making full reference to the play-game tradition; *George a Greene* (by 1594, probably by 1592) in which Robin plays a role secondary to that of the Pindar of Wakefield and which is very likely by Robert Greene who died in 1592, though the style is fairly simple for him (Collins, 1905, pp. 160–3); *Looke About You*, a frenetic disguise comedy in which Robin plays a large but secondary part, written by various hands and to be dated in 1599 or perhaps 1600, when it was printed. (For the most recent survey of the plays and their scholarship, see Nelson, 1973, pp. 114–61.)

Taken as a whole the plays show a curious double movement: Robin becomes an increasingly important character as his development into the title shows; but at the same time he has less dynamism as a figure, does less, and is all the more securely contained by the forces of both state hierarchy and dramatic power as realized in the course of the action. Robin Hood's arrival on the London stage is both a process of gentrification and emasculation, as will become clear from a survey of the process and the implications of the texts.

Edward I is the earliest of the London stage plays that refer to Robin Hood tradition. It was printed in 1593 and reprinted in 1599; presumably the main appeal was a national hero imbued with a sense of English grandeur both from the distant past and, by implication, recent times: Edward's achievements are reworked to bear a strong reference to the Spanish wars of the 1580s.

A mixture of chauvinism, bombast and high-handed playmaking, this 'absurd corruption of English history' (Nelson, 1973, p. 88) is of interest still largely because the Robin Hood play-game is woven in as part of the entertainment (Wiles prints a modernized version of the play-game scene, 1981, pp. 82–7). Lluellen, Edward's opponent, is keen on simple amusements, in spite of being a Celtic freedom fighter – or perhaps, the play may be nationalistically suggesting, just because of that. In one of the sudden switches of material through which many playwrights filled out their five acts, the Welsh guerrilla leader decides to play his own Robin Hood game. This has its origin in literary rather than localized and communal practice, as Lluellen indicates:

> weele get the next daie from Brecknocke the booke of *Robin Hood*, the frier he shal instruct vs in his cause and weele even here fair and well since the king hath put us amongst the discarding cards, and as it were turned vs with deuces and traies out of the decke . . . and wander like irregulers vp and down the wilderrnesse, ile be maister of misrule, ile be *Robin Hood* that once, cousin Rice thou shalt be little *John*, and hers Frier *Dauid* as fit as a die for Frier *Tucke*, now my sweet *Nel*, if you will make vp the messe with a good heart for Maide marian and doe well with Lluellen vnder the greene wood trees, with as good a wil as in the good townes, why *plena est curia*. (1593, F4r)

Peele is using the 'forest exile' tradition of Robin Hood from the *Gest* rather than the localized focus of entertainment and ritual found in the May Games: here 'misrule' refers to Edward's displacement of the Welsh prince, rather than a carnivalesque spirit. Yet there is little political bite in the idea of this exile; it has a distinctly idealized character, which comes through in the next scene when the Robin Hood players return and Lluellen celebrates this new way of life. Raymond Williams sees such entertainments as the essence of what he calls 'neo-pastoralism' (1973, pp. 24–33), where rural fictions leave behind the tensions of genuine country life and fantasize about a world recreated for the pleasure of the powerful:

> How well they coucht in forrest greene
> Frolike and liuelie with oaten teen. (1593, Flr)

An indication that Peele did, as Lluellen suggests, draw his material from a book, namely the Copland version of the *Gest*, comes in the sequence where Mortimer, obsessed with the prince's wife, follows them dressed as a potter — which curiously appropriates the heroic 'Robin Hood in disguise' function for the English lord. He joins the band incognito and then, in a new scene, distinctly like the fragmented sequencing of the surviving Robin Hood plays, he fights against the Friar — Peele appears to be condensing into one drama here the plays Copland offers as two in a series.

Next, another of the traditional Robin Hood cards is played: Edward I comes to visit, as the unnumbered Edward did in the *Gest*. The king knows that this 'Robin' is the disguised Welsh prince (a conservative identification of knowledge with hierarchy), but scene 12 follows through a sequence from the *Gest*. 'Robin' demands a toll from the king, namely half every traveller's possession; the king offers to fight for all or nothing. Mortimer rejoins his master, and the two English lords fight a draw against Lluellen and his brother. The scene concludes, as several do in this awkward drama, with the characters simply trooping off the stage, and Peele ends his borrowing of the Robin Hood material as abruptly as it was introduced.

Fragmentary though it is, this use of the myth is essentially consistent with the play-game tradition and the *Gest*. No sense of Robin's gentrification exists, and indeed the aura of rebellion survives, though it has been taken out of English political conflicts into an early colonial context, and securely contained by the death of Lluellen at the end and by the generally well-known nature of Edward's triumph in Wales. Peele is clearly aware of the popular nature of the Robin Hood celebrations, and the presence of Maid Marian and Friar Tuck might be taken as a sign of that connection, as the friar clearly comes through the Copland plays and Marian's possible attachment from an early date has been discussed above. More forward-looking, in terms of the development of the tradition, is Peele's hint of a classical pastoral element: he is to be regarded as the first dramatist to move the forest-dwelling outlaw towards the pastoral gentility that will soon enough be common, but this is a minor and unstressed modernization in what is essentially a backward-looking use of Robin Hood to provide a lively segment of a somewhat plodding exercise in early nationalistic sentimentality.

The next play to appear shifts Robin more determinedly from the centre of the action. *George a Greene*, attributed with some probably unjustified doubt to Robert Greene, focuses on a figure taken from a central text in the Robin Hood tradition, the ballad known to Child as 'The Jolly Pinder of Wakefield' (see pp. 63–4). This was popular in a number of contexts, and George became a hero with his own standing and an early prose history that survives in a 1706 edition but certainly has its origin around the year 1600, probably influenced by this play (Nelson, 1973, pp. 99–100). The growing interest in the Pinder at this time may in part derive from the increasing importance of Wakefield as a market and manufacturing town, but there are political structures involved that dynamize the figure of George a Greene as a representative of the townsman loyal to the crown, not the locally organic anti-state figure of Robin Hood. This play significantly weakens the role of Robin Hood, so that he becomes a minor player, demoted with some difficulty in order to promote the local and also national hero, and so enabling the text to set aside any sense of rebelliousness in a strong man from the lower orders, who is shown to be not only a match for Robin Hood but more politically trustworthy into the bargain.

This play was printed in 1599; it is listed as an 'Enterlude' in the Stationers' Register for 1595 and is referred to in Henslowe's diary for the 29 December 1593. If Greene did, as seems probable, write it, then it must be dated to 1592, the year of his death. Conceivably *Edward I* could have stimulated the play, as in *George a Greene* the king is Edward and both share a strong King and Subject sequence, but both of these could have come separately from the *Gest*. More interesting than speculations about literary sources is a consideration of the politics of the play and how they cause Robin Hood to be displaced.

The ballad sets the free values of the forest outlaws against George's small town proprietorial interest and shows how George chooses to abandon life under a master and share the liberty of the forest. It is clear that George's original standpoint in the ballad, that animals cannot roam free, that corn is sacrosanct – concepts of personal property and enclosure – are features of the modern, constraining and inorganic world that Robin and his band symbolically resist; and gaining the support of the powerful Pinder is a major victory for these forces of communal liberty.

But the play of *George a Greene* abandons that argument entirely and deals with quite different conflicts. It opens much like *Henry IV pt. 1* with a rebellion in the north; here it is led by the Earl of Kendall – an interesting name, since Robin and his outlaws often at this time wear Kendall, not Lincoln, green. There had of course been political risings in the north using the outlaw's first name – Robin of Redesdale and Robin of Holderness were both out for the Lancastrians in 1469 – and it is striking that this story projects the ballad's resistance to town law onto a larger national scale and identifies it with an earl who is not Robin Hood but distinctly like him in some ways – the Pinder in this version of the story, it is relevant to note, confronts the three rebel leaders in a wheatfield, as he did the three outlaws in the ballad.

The fact that resistance has been relocated as rebellion leaves Robin himself with very little to do, and in any case the story is amplified with a range of other elements to fill five acts, especially love, with George himself, Edward IV and even King James of Scotland involved in amatorial activities. Other motifs that flesh out the plot with a more general politics are an ancient noble peasant and son, true Englishmen who capture King James, and a lengthy sequence of King and Subject activity, which takes place in Bradford, where the two kings, now reconciled and involved with the guild of shoemakers, fight against George and Robin Hood.

This brawl is Robin Hood's first major action in the play; he does not appear until IV. 2, and does not meet George until IV. 4, when the narrative of the ballad is briefly enacted. It includes Robin's invitation to George to join his band:

> George, wilt thou forsake Wakefield,
> And go with me?
> Two liueries will I giue thee euerie yeere,
> And fortie crownes shall be thy fee. (987–90)

There are some telling changes from the offer in the ballad, where Robin did not speak of 'forsaking' Wakefield, but said 'wilt thou forsake the pinder his craft', and made no mention of a fee. And even though in the play Robin phrases his question in a townsman's terms, it is never answered: in the ballad George agreed that once he had his fee from his master he would gladly join the more natural world of the outlaws. In the play, George merely welcomes Robin into his house; next they appear disguised in Bradford, fight the two kings and the shoemakers, then George patronizes Robin:

> Here, Robin, sit thou here; for thou art the best man
> At the boord this day. (1078–9)

And Robin finally is bound into royal loyalty as George toasts:

> Robin, heer's a carouse to good King Edwards selfe;
> And they that love him not, I would we had
> The basting of them a litle. (1081–2)

George a Greene is essentially a naive patriotic drama; Robin Hood's complex mixture of value and resistance has been separated out into two simplified forms of political position, the unthinking loyalty of the Pinder, 'True liegeman to the king' (92), and the overt rebellion of the wicked earl. In this nervously nationalistic literature there is no place for the local and libertarian hero.

Though Lluellen was a prince, and Kendall was an earl, neither Peele nor Greene could be said to have involved Robin Hood in direct gentrification. But John Stow, the transmitter of Major's gentrifying ideas into the 1590s was a friend of Anthony Munday, who brought into fictional form the idea that Robin had been an aristocrat embarrassed during the period of Richard I. The plays about the hero's *Downfall* and *Death* have been more often mentioned than carefully examined: they have some surprising features and even more surprising absences. They do not, for example, make Prince John the demon of the story, and they hardly concern themselves at all with any actions by Robin Hood. While the title uses his name forcefully, there are still strong signs of the marginalization of the hero that is a feature of all the professional plays of this period – in the *Death* Robin is gone by the end of Act 1, but the play continues with a protracted siege by Prince John on the virtuous widow, Matilda, now countess in her own right of Huntington.

Munday had already worked for the Admiral's Men with a conventional comedy, *John a Kent and John a Cumber*, based on disguise and popular narrative. He had also produced prose work, including an account of his trip to Rome, and it appears that this was also part of his other activities which included spying and informing against Catholics on behalf of the contemporary authorities. (*Dictionary of National Biography*, XLIX, 1894, pp. 290–7.) This all-purpose man of letters, with demotic tastes, conservative political interests and some knowledge, especially through Stow, of the English past, was commissioned by Henslowe for £5 to produce a Robin Hood play in February 1598; soon after Henry Chettle and Munday shared £5 for the second part and then Chettle drew 10/- for 'mending' the first.

The *Downfall* and *Death*, taken together, have never been claimed as great theatre, and the stress they have received stems in part from the literary orientation of most commentators: here the outlaw's gentrification occurs in a 'big' genre. The idea that Robin was a distressed earl was spread much more widely by Martin Parker and some of the balladeers than by these relatively unsuccessful and little-revived plays. Yet the *Downfall* and *Death* have a special importance outside the simplicities of a merely literary history and beyond a naive account of the genteel hero's fate. They clearly did influence some later literary experiments, including Parker's, and they emphasize moves in the relocating of the hero away from sociopolitical resistance. The difficulty of that enterprise marks the plays heavily through the strains involved in bringing popular material about a localized and communal character into a theatre whose emphases are national and hierarchical.

Complexity is clear from the start. The play opens with an introduction in which the poet Skelton speaks with Sir John Eltham. They are to play parts in this drama, and the framing sequence, which recurs occasionally, will comment on the origin and tone of the materials, distinctly mixed as they all are. As his attitudes indicate, Eltham belongs to the modern world of diplomacy and colonies; Skelton was a figure of the past, by tradition tutor to Henry VIII as well as a humane and humorous poet and personality. But he was also the Trickster hero of a famous joke-book *The Merie Tales of Skelton* (1566), and his deep scholarship was by this time largely forgotten.

The dumb show that outlines the plot in this startling new version reveals Robert Earl of Huntington high in precedence behind King Richard but, as Skelton explains, Warman, his Judas-like steward, is betraying Robin with 'that relentless prior, his uncle Gilbert' (line 93). Robert and Matilda are this day to plight their troth in spite of the passions for them held respectively by Queen Elinor and her son Prince John: but that is a minor threat compared with the 'false guests' who will outlaw the earl at his own betrothal feast.

Much is new here. The hero is earl by right, with no question about his access to the title – Grafton had wondered if it might have been earned by honest merit. This earl is threatened by a new figure, the faithless steward, while an old opponent, the greedy Prior of York, has become a closer danger, as both uncle and owner of the hero's debts. Robin's positioning has become fully aristocratic and so have the threats. No longer an urban sheriff or a punitive church, the enemies to status are very close to home, and disaster strikes from the hands of family and employees. It is a story both realistic enough in the upper echelons, and also celebrated through the fiction of the period from *Le Morte Darthur* to *Othello*.

By comparison the hostility of Prince John and Queen Elinor is only an alarm; royal power is a threat in the personal domain of love, never in the more crucial field of property. The impact of the Elizabethan period's powerful monarchy is evident in the text as the viewpoint accepts royal authority and fears most forcefully those arch-enemies of the hierarchy, the untrustworthy confidante or employee. This is a masterly redirection of the story in terms of the interests of those who ruled the contemporary theatre: it was not for nothing that the companies were owned by lords and state officials, rather than the earlier localized and small-scale control of the Robin Hood play-games. Munday, in this as in his espionage activities, is working close to the interests of the powerful. The fact that he was himself a draper's son, and indeed ended up as something of a poet laureate to the London guilds in no way precludes him from aristocratic service; indeed it makes it all the more likely, especially at such a time of uncertainty and mobility in both politics and profit.

But his plan for the plays is also a major rehandling of the story, and the effort is visible in its effect. Munday is artist enough to realize in the text his own ideologizing of the story: Skelton speaks intriguingly as he describes Robin Hood in the dumb show:

> This youth that leads yon virgin by the hand
> (As doth the Sunne, the morning richly clad)

Is our Earle Robert, or your Robin Hoode,
That in those daies, was Earle of Huntington. (86–9)

The earl, it seems is 'ours', while simple Robin Hood is 'yours'; the
audience is appointed as 'you', and this is clarified a little later on in
the context of a parallel distinction; Skelton ends his account of the
troubled feast and Robert's coming outlawry with: 'The manner and
escape you all shall see'. (108). And when Sir John asks 'Which all,
good Skelton', the interlocutor explains:

Why, all these lookers on:
Whom if wee please, the king will sure be pleas'd. (110–11)

The fiction here is that the play within the play is for Henry VIII
– and reference may well be being made to Henry's taste for Robin
Hood activities, known through Hall's chronicle. But there is also an
evident London audience. Skelton and Munday together are recogniz-
ing the double thrust of this myth: a popular hero belonging to 'you
all' on the floor of the theatre, and also an aristocratized myth revert-
ing to the power structure of this increasingly centralized country.
Local and national elements again conflict, but the strain will be
ignored through a dramatist's sleight of hand.

Specific reference to that process at work comes in the remarkable
sequence that follows. Robert the earl has been told of his outlawing
at his betrothal feast, and as a result he has rushed away from the
table. Little John (also Sir John Eltham, steward in both worlds) is
concerned with this detraction from the earl's 'honourable state' and
'the true noblesse of your worthy house', and in the light of that and
Matilda's evident distress Robert sends back a message that he has
merely been acting as if distressed, and that in reality he was only
disturbed by the failure to arrive of the 'quaint Comedians' who were
to entertain the guests.

Through this double mediation of 'acting', Munday codes into the
process of his text the essence of its new role. For the sake of honour,
Robert plays a noble part and blames the inadequacy of the quaint
comedians; at the same time for the sake of acceptance among the
noble, Munday falsifies into nobility a narrative that formerly has lain
in the hands of just such quaint comedians as are conspicuously absent
from this text, and so can be blamed for its strains.

The topic is resumed overtly later on, when Eltham again chooses 'to speak a word or two beside the play' and notes the rewriting of the tradition:

> Me thinks I see no jeasts of Robin Hoode,
> No merry Morices of Frier Tuck,
> No pleasant skippings up and downe the wodde,
> No hunting songs, no coursing of the Bucke:
> Pray God this Play of ours may haue good lucke,
> And the kings Majestie mislike it not. (2210–15)

Skelton, as Friar Tuck, confirms the absence of the popular material:

> For merry jeasts, they have been showne before
> As how the Frier fell into the Well
> For love of Jinny that faire bonny bell:
> How Greeneleafe robd the Shrieue of Notingham
> And other mirthfull matter, full of game (2221–5)

The story of the Friar and Jinny is told in 'The Friar in the Well' (Child no. 276), mentioned in Skelton's own *Colin Clout*, but has no earlier Robin Hood connection; Greeneleafe, however, comes from the *Gest* as an alias for Little John and was actually used as a real outlaw's name, see Appendix under 1502. By these references Munday is expressing his sense of difference from the popular tradition, and his anxiety about the change appears in the claim of royal approval:

> His Majestie himselfe suruaid the plat,
> And bad me boldly write it, it was good (2219–20)

Sir John is not really right in his judgement; Munday has in fact made use of popular material, but it is transmuted on a royally conservative frame. The prior as an enemy is certainly drawn from the *Gest* and so is the sequence where the sheriff oppresses Little John when he is moving goods about. The forest oath that John issues is a more elaborate and moralized version of the outlaw leader's words to his 'meyne' in the *Gest*, especially 'you never shall the pore man wrong' and never 'use' either 'widow wife or maide' (lines 1314–2, 1354) though both are stipulations beyond the *Gest*, where it was yeomen who were to be protected, and women merely should be treated with respect, not set upon a pedestal of chastity.

A lengthy sequence is drawn from the ballad 'Robin Hood Rescuing Three Young Men' in its 'widow's sons' rather than 'three squires' version; this is bound closer to the plot by making Scarlet and Scathlock themselves her sons – they appear here and often afterwards as two people in spite of the single origin of their names: Munday, like the authors of many earlier romances, rationalizes puzzles in the tradition by 'splitting' a character. Other traces of the ballad tradition occur: towards the end the Pinder is at least mentioned and a mention of Mansfield is also probably from ballad sources.

Yet these connections with the popular literary tradition are outweighed by aristocratic innovations, which Sir John (not to mention Munday) was stressing in his misstatement about the popular sources. The major one is of positioning. This is an earl's story: the 'Downfall' of the title is when he goes from aristocratic honour into the forest. It is not his betrayal to death by a relative, nor his failure to live happily at court, as earlier materials would conceive of the hero's downfall. It is only when Robin is placed at a noble height that this type of fall is significant.

A great deal of material is added, as in *George a Greene*, but here not so much to sideline the hero as to ennoble him. Robin is very much the lord of the forest, and served by John as his steward, who hurries off to pack and move the displaced earl's possessions – far from the John who would not even carry a bow in 'Robin Hood and the Monk'.

In the forest Robin has lordship, not egalitarian participation. He speaks to Marian (Matilda's forest name, though it has, inconsistently, been used before) about Sherwood as an equivalent of a noble house in a particularly fine speech of the kind of 'neo-pastoral' appropriation that Raymond Williams links to courtly house poems (1973, p. 33):

> For the soule-rauishing delicious sound
> Of instrumentall musique, we haue found
> The winged quiristers, with diuers notes,
> Sent from their quaint recording prettie throats,
> On euery braunch that compasseth our bower:
> Without commaund, contenting us each hower.
> For Arras hangings, and rich Tapestrie,
> We haue sweete natures best imbrothery.

For thy steele glasse, wherin thou wontst to looke,
Thy Christall eyes, gaze in a Christall brooke.
At Court, a flower or two did decke thy head:
Now with whole garlands is it circled.
For what in wealth we want, we have in flowers,
And what wee loose in halles, we find in bowers. (1368–81)

Not only are Robin's surroundings seen as a para-stately home; his own behaviour is improbably noble. He forgives the evil prior and the worse Sir Doncaster, as well as the insidious Warman; indeed his ability to forgive is one of the things that Doncaster hates most and it leads to Robin's death in the second play. Exercising such passive virtues is more or less all that Robin does. He is hardly an active hero – in the rescue of Scarlet and Scathlock he does sound his horn for help, but his apparently fierce reference to using a weapon is part of his disguise as the young men's father, not active engagement (984–8). The implication is that the overt possession of power is the only role for an aristocrat, and even in forest exile Robin only enacts that part. He does not even have dramatic vitality; the most vigorous scenes are those involving Prince John in disguise, Warman's grotesque attempts to hang himself, and also the treatment of Ely as a pathetic version of King Lear. Robin is gentrified out of any real activity.

Prince John is quite a positive figure in the play, far from being the villain of later representations. His pursuit of Marian is caused by love, not malice, he defends Little John and vilifies Robin's betrayers. He does have vices, being tempted to take (rather than seize) his brother's power, and is also hot-tempered: he kills Hugh Lacy, a traitor to the state and to Robin, and fights with Marian's father. But after he has been threatened by King Richard for overstepping his authority he, remarkably, behaves himself like a noble outlaw; he takes to the forest in disguise, fights with the friar and is honoured by him as 'a proper man' (2614).

If in this way royal blood is not really bad, the outlaw position that Robin has is itself never drastic: because his enemies are merely personal betrayers, not political enemies, he is easily enough restored to favour when Richard arrives. The *Downfall* ends with a restoration not of Richard but of Robin (as Robert), a fact which marks both the outlaw's new status and also the distance this play has travelled from the real threats to royal and national power which Robin represented in the early ballads. Even the King and Subject theme has been reduced to a good fight between Prince John and the friar; Munday's version of Robin Hood is a remarkable repositioning of the whole story, with many a sign of how difficult this was to achieve, and how much Munday wanted to sideline the surviving force of the older forms of the anti-authoritarian tradition.

One element which was not widely represented in the popular tradition was the death of Robin Hood. Clearly absent from the play-game, the hero's death did end the *Gest* briefly, as a separated coda, and it also inspired a ballad that was probably in circulation by Munday's time (see pp. 60–1). Both of those versions stress betrayal by family and church. That theme is already woven into the *Downfall*; the stronger motive for a substantial representation of Robin's death in the geutrified mode is the need, noted above in the context of versions of historicity in the myth (see p. 60), to have a tomb and funeral to mark the passing and importance of a man of great social and propertied importance.

If the *Downfall* is a play intriguingly marked by the strains of its production, the *Death* is more like a category mistake. Apart from Julius Caesar, few heroes of tragedy can have died sooner; Robin has, for no very clear reason, drunk the poison by line 540, and even his somewhat extended obsequies are finished by line 863. The rest of the play details the new King John's assault on Matilda, herself having the dignity of a countess in her own right, part of King Richard's gift to the dying earl. This draws on Michael Drayton's poem *Matilda the faire and chaste daughter of Lord R. Fitzwater* (1594), which provides a way of finishing off this second Robin Hood play, though in the first, Richard's departure and death in Austria was promised as the big finish (2827–9), which would have elegantly enclosed Robin's death within that of his master, faithful servant that he has become.

The *Death* again opens with Skelton as a voice for uncertainty, here using the jingling poetic style made famous by the real Skelton which operates as a motif of the popular within the ambit of the gentrified play: 'And I like a sot, have wholly forgot The course of our plot' (12–13). But where the *Downfall* opened with conscious artifice and uncertainty, the *Death* plunges without hesitation or subtlety into disaster as Doncaster and Prior vow vengeance on Robin, as much for his noble forgiveness as anything else, and when Warman speaks up for his good master he is murdered by them for his feebleness. A nobler kind of melodrama then follows in an ill-focused scene where it first seems that Robin's poisoned drink will finish the king but then Robin, unexplained, consumes it off stage. Very elaborate death and burial scenes occur, notable for a gloomy pastoral lament: 'Weepe, weepe, ye wod-men waile, Youre hands with sorrow wring' (848–9).

The rest of the *Death* is irrelevant to the Robin Hood tradition, and has been to the theatre in general, though Richard Davenport based *King John and Matilda* on it in 1655, drawing also, as Munday had, on Michael Drayton's poem. The irrelevance of much of Munday's second play to the hero is itself one last mark of strain in this remarkable reformulation of the myth. In return for aristocratic nobility, Robin Hood pays many prices: he loses all humour, all sense of resistance, is bound in service to the crown and its officers; he forgives those who do him most wrong; he has only the most formal of contacts with his lady. Worst of all for a figure of story, he plays no significant part in the action or the imagination of the texts. The Summer Lord of the play-game and ballad has been frozen into inactive actual aristocracy.

The newly conservative political meaning of the play is its own reward for the time-server Munday; he goes on to greater depths of servility with his masque for the London aldermen, *Metropolis Coronata*. Robin returns from the dead to honour the civic gentry as Earl Robert de la Hude 'With these my yeoman tight and tall, Brave Huntsmen and good Archers all.' All notions of conflict are set aside in neo-pastoral banality:

> What life is there like to *Robin Hood*?
> It is so pleasant a thing-a:
> In merry Shirwood he spends his dayes,
> As pleasantly as a king-a. (C3)

This text can be seen as a model both for the enfeebled ballad operas of the next two hundred years and also as a precursor of the 'heritage' representation of Robin Hood, in that the hero is now securely in the past, and can be used consciously to provide consoling mirror images of the politics of the present. That is a general effect which builds on what has been developed in the *Death* and the *Downfall*. In spite of their lack of direct influence, Munday not only shaped in those plays a special new political version of the myth, but also established some features that would long outlive his own reputation and the force of his conservative text, especially as they were transmitted through Ritson's full description and quotation in the introduction to his 1795 collection (see pp. 154–8).

In this new and long-lived structure, Robin Hood is betrayed early in the action by faithless power-figures, usually at a feast; he makes a defiant speech and takes off to the forest, where he provides a state-ment of his values; Marian will be there in some form of disguise; a powerful enemy will lust after her; there will be a gallows rescue; the church is treacherous, except for the populist friar; there will be a scene where Robin blows his horn and gathers his men together; combats will be enjoyed; enemies will be frustrated; the king will visit and give his somewhat equivocal blessing; life in the forest will be happy; after the heroic defeat of enemies the king will resume his power and reprieve Robin.

Many of those elements have been in the tradition before, especially in the *Gest*. But Munday puts them in that order and in spite of all the other extraneous materials he uses, that structure has tended to survive, not so much because of Munday's personal influence, but because this is a new hierarchy-oriented myth in which the elements all mean some specific things in that new ideological context.

There have, however, been other readings of Munday's purpose and effect. Nelson, after all his detailed scholarship, can go no further than suggest that 'escape' is the vanishing point of all this rewriting activ-ity (1973, p. 186). Such an end-of-ideology viewpoint is rejected by David Bevington who reads Tudor drama in general against its specific history and, somewhat remarkably, comes up with the view that Munday's Robin Hood plays are inherently puritan in their ideology. The argument deserves full quotation if only for its unique character:

> . . . the Admiral's men's most ambitious efforts to give sympathetic expression to the Puritan viewpoint are to be found in their popular Robin Hood series . . .
>
> The whole series is an elaborate fable of an oppressive administra-tion and church, which drive all well-intentioned men into outlawry. Robert . . . has previously worked for reform within the political struc-ture; but after the departure of Richard for the Holy Land, the atmo-sphere of the court becomes too poisoned to permit the continued redress of grievances by legal means. This turning point symbolically justifies the retreat from law of well-meaning men in times of unmanageable

oppression and it does so without directly confronting royal authority
. . . In their exile the outcasts form a nearly Utopian society while they
await the return of justice to this earth. (1968, pp. 295–6)

As a description of the play, this seems quite out of touch with its
mixture of aristocratic servility and personalized betrayals, and has no
contact at all with the love plot. However, Bevington does have in
support an argument about the origin of the earl's title; he argues that
Munday refers to: 'the third earl of Huntingdon . . . a candidate for
succession to the throne during the 1560s, the hope of many ardent
Protestants fearful of Elizabeth's untimely death [who] and his brothers had served the Puritan cause in Parliament throughout the reign.
(1968, p. 295)

But the 1560s are a fair way away, the queen is not dead, and this
new outlaw earl seems to have no Puritan tendencies at all except perhaps his insistence on forest chastity. The case is far from made and
Bevington's work is, in its claimed clarity and evident simplicity, no
more than a literary historical equivalent of asking just who was the
real Robin Hood.

The origin of the name is more probably more distant and general.
An Earl of Huntingdon from the 1190s who had differences with the
English authorities would have been familiar enough in the Scottish
royal connection to an amateur archivist like Munday, friend to a
professional one in Stow. Grafton's speculations about Robin Hood
being an earl, Stow's firm location of him in that period and Warner's
more recent assertions about his nobility in forest exile (see pp. 134–
6) may all have guided Munday's thinking that he needed an earl, and
Huntington, in his spelling, was an easy connection for his woodland
lord, whether or not he knew about the Rutland coincidence of that
title and Barnsdale (see p. 3).

In spite of his importance in naming Robin as the hero of two
major plays and his structural organization of the newly ennobled
narrative, in spite of his bringing the outlaw close to a pastoral gentleman who represented a set of tragically lost values, Munday did not
impose immediate mastery on the tradition – quite the opposite is
suggested by the comic chaos of the play with which the Admiral's
Men followed up Munday's work, *Looke About You*, subtitled 'A pleas-
aunt Commodye'. Its authorship remains obscure; candidates include
Antony Wadeson, Chettle and Munday once more, and even Thomas

Dekker: Bevington may well be right to suggest that the play was simply produced by the Admiral's Men's writing team (1968, p. 295).

If so, they must have enjoyed their collaboration. Nelson calls it 'an absurd historical pastiche' with an author 'always ready to sacrifice historical accuracy for entertaining balderdash' (1973, p. 161). Ideas have been developed from the *Downfall* in the context of the fashionable 'disguise' comedy, raising the role-playing characteristic of the tradition into a positive extravaganza of impersonation. The action moves more swiftly and decisively than Munday's plays; the opening voice is that of Skink, a criminal pretending to be a hermit, who has some of the Trickster features of the popular version of Skelton. He is visited by the young Earl of Huntington, on an errand for his master, Richard I, who is wooing Lady Marian Faukenbridge, sister of an enemy of the king – her husband's name presumably comes from *King John*.

So it goes on, a sub-Shakespearean romp, notable for rapid transitions and a series of broad comic scenes. One is based on nothing more subtle than stammering, as practised by a figure called Redcap, a name he finds farcically difficult to pronounce. Another sequence shows how, for obscure reasons, Lady Marian persuades her friend Robin to dress up as herself; he is then pressingly wooed by his own friend and bedfellow, Richard.

Robin Hood is not exactly demeaned in this clowning comedy; he retains youthful vitality at least, and a puppyish kind of nobility. Nevertheless, the austere outlaw of some ballads and the genial supervisor of village delights is hardly to be identified in the stage direction that reads: 'Enter Robin Hood in the Lady Faukenbridge's gowne, night attire on his head' (1913, p. 49).

The play's action lurches between royal politics, Prince John's mischief, and a set of love complications, in all of which Robert plays the role of a glorified messenger boy. He does not become an outlaw, has no followers at all, and suffers nothing worse than mild sexual harassment when in drag. There is a political threat to the king, who is here Henry II, father to Richard and John, but it does not stem directly or with any consistency from Prince John. Robin is nothing more than a sprightly young aristocrat described as 'Huntington's right heyere' (749): the events of Munday's plays seem a stimulus of a sort but the ponderous Robert of those plays is here no more than 'an honorable wag and waggish Erle' (742). He can, it is true, raise two thousand soldiers in an hour (1736) and there is early on some talk of sedition in the north, but reality comes no closer.

In both comedy and reference the play is modern, but this is urban and artificial waggery, not what Bristol has called 'the purposeful contemporaneity of Carnival' (1985, p. 51). As a farcical, apolitical prequel to the Huntington plays, *Looke About You* takes the outlaw figure further down the path of inactivity and bland aristocratized acceptability. This, certainly, is what Nelson calls 'escape', both from theatrical significance and any anti-authoritarian edge to the outlaw myth; it is no more than an attempt to exploit the company's Robin Hood success.

The Chamberlain's Men were rivals to the Admiral's troupe, and it is hardly surprising that their resident playwright Shakespeare produced a forest exile play to answer these Robin Hood activities; it is a moot point whether it was their recent vulgarization of the hero or Shakespeare's own desire for a more exotic form of authority in exile that led him to shape *As You Like It*, where after an early reference to 'Old Robin Hood' as an exile in a 'golden world' (I. 1. 222), the story works through an entirely modern-seeming version of court politics and the difficulties of honorific displacement, set in a deliberately idealized mixture of Italy and the English forest of Arden.

Shakespeare also sought to combine popular comedy and a love narrative with the sense of aristocratic distress, and there is a particular interest in seeing how he went back to a source itself parallel to the Robin Hood materials; Lodge's *Rosalynde* is based on *Gamelyn* (see p. 85) and that enabled Shakespeare to write of the forest life without being involved in the activities of Robin Hood himself, whether as antique rebellion or recent grotesquerie. Thorndike has argued that Shakespeare diverges from Lodge in the direction of Munday in the basic court versus forest situation, in the notion of freedom that is found in the woods, in the spirit of charity that rules both plays, and in the structural use of a fool, a feast and hunting (1902, pp. 68–9). There is sense in these comments and in Thorndike's underlying argument that Shakespeare was responding to the success of Munday's plays, especially the fact that they were performed at court during Christmas. But the decisive fact is that Shakespeare shaped a quite different narrative, producing a gentrified story that had no low-life origins. As a result of his decision, *As You Like It*, (like *Gamelyn* itself, *George a Greene*, as has been argued above and, as will be argued below,

Ivanhoe) is a text that establishes its conservative political meaning by its specific variation from the Robin Hood tradition.

Other versions were to be more influential than Shakespeare's entirely negative contribution to the outlaw myth. The position Munday had shaped for the hero was from a range of sources, and some of those materials appeared in new genres as seventeenth and eighteenth-century writers recreated in their own terms the hero whose career had been so volatile and yet so popular in the extremely varied modes of performance evident throughout the sixteenth century.

4.3   GENTRIFIED PERFORMANCE IN THE SEVENTEENTH AND EIGHTEENTH CENTURIES

The version of Robin Hood developed by the Admiral's Men was both gentrified and constricted, giving the hero no autonomous role and filling out the spaces of the theatrical genre with other materials derived from versions of history, notions of romance and, most notably, recent conventions of professional performance. But there were other resources for both gentrification and theatricality beyond stiff historical politics and the confusions of disguise and these are first seen emerging in some treatments of the Robin Hood theme in a new genre.

The outlaw hero appears in two poems of a new kind; Warner's *Albions England* (1589) and Michael Drayton's *Poly-Olbion* (1622 edition) review the local folklore and traditions of Britain and organize it in a way that is both highly idealized and also inherently supportive of those who own the land and appropriate its wealth. In *Albions England* the voice is that of the mythical Albion, a generalized version of all landowners; in *Poly-Olbion* the speakers of each of the localized sections are rivers, forests and hills, as if the land generated its own wealth and no conflicts were involved in the production of profit. Raymond Williams calls this kind of thing 'the magical invocation of a land that needs no farming' and sees it central to what he calls the process of 'neo-pastoral' (1973, p. 28).

Into this powerfully conservative myth, an early version of the modern heritage culture, Robin Hood is inserted with both a sense of his resistant capacity as an outlaw and also his charm as inoffensive local colour. Like Munday, Warner realizes the contradictory strain of his appropriation of the figure. In book 5 a 'simple northern-man' reflects on the good old days when Robin Hood represented peasant simplicity in relation to festivals of both spring and autumn – distance is lending obscurity to the sight of the figure (1589, p. 108). But this curio from a popular past is not all that Warner has to relate. In chapter 27 a hermit is speaking to the Earl of Lancaster, the 'contrariant' earl who is on the run from Edward II (curiously enough the monarch who at just this time had a chamberlain called Robin Hood, see p. 23). In response to the earl's story of his misfortunes, the hermit introduces Robin Hood as 'a mal content' who in 'first Richard's daies' himself 'liu'd in Woods, as we'.

At first he is reluctant to describe this outlaw, as he did not behave 'deuoutly' (which probably refers to his assaults on clerics, rather than a protestant jibe at Catholicism), but is persuaded because the story involves some 'words worth the note', largely drawn from Grafton:

> Those daies begot some mal-contents, the Principall of whome
> A County was, that with a troope of Yomandry did rome,
> Braue Archers and deliuer men, since nor before so good:
> Those tooke from rich to giue the poore, and manned Robin Hood,
> He fed them well, and lodg'd them safe in plesaunt Caves and bowers
> Oft saying to his merry men 'What iuster life than ours? (p. 132)

These lines combine the rebel and the gentrified traditions in having a malcontent 'county' (the word used for earl in this text, which helps the identification of lordship and land throughout). Warner also provides an early and particularly crisp version of the rich-poor myth and specifies, as sixteenth-century versions tend to do, the importance of archery in the hero's context. He also includes anti-Catholicism, but indirectly – the Robin Hood narrative is interrupted by a traditional joke about the prioress who, rising to chastise a pregnant nun, was seen to have hurriedly donned a canon's underwear instead of her wimple. That pro-Protestant strand would become more closely involved with the Robin Hood story, especially through Parker, as has been discussed above (see pp. 91–3).

But the most innovative element in Warner is the touch of pastoralism: Robin as in some of the ballads feeds his men well, but there has before been no analysis of the 'pleasant' nature of their setting, and the very combination of caves and bowers indicates that a genuinely wild life is here being imaginatively acculturated into something closer to the 'neo-pastoral' leisured image of rural pleasure which is, in the sixteenth century, to be associated with proprietors who visit occasionally and for recreational purposes carefully enclosed and manicured tracts of land, with rural trades presented as aestheticized versions of natural vigour.

That whole new ideology is epitomized in the notion that Robin's men are 'merry', rather than being grim bandits or noble sufferers, as the tradition has before envisaged; 'merry' will remain the touchstone of formal neo-pastoralism. At the same time the satirical purpose of most pastoral is couched in the notion that the outlaws' life is 'juster' than that of others: the serious role of such ruralism is to refocus the vice and folly of urban life as in the satires of Wyatt, Donne and Johnson.

In this brief, and rather hesitantly introduced reference, Warner indicates a new way of thinking about the forest outlaws, one not to be clearly touched by Munday because of the different generic traditions in which he is working, but one that will be particularly dynamic in later theatrical and poetic versions of the myth, through to the present.

Michael Drayton was a much more thorough researcher of material for *Poly-Olbion* (ed. Hebel, 1961), and in his lengthy reference to Robin Hood (in Song 26 in the 1622 edition) he includes a round-up of the traditional material in a basically ungentrified form. Sherwood forest itself speaks in praise of the local hero:

> The merry pranks he playd, would aske an age to tell,
> And the adventures strange that Robin Hood befell,
> When Mansfield many a time for Robin hath bin layd,
> How he hath cosned them, that him would have betrayd;
> How often he hath come to Nottingham disguisd,
> And cunningly escapt, being set to be surprizd. (305–10)

Drayton continues by mentioning familiar characters, Little John, Scarlock, George a Greene, Much and Tuck, and also escapades – 'a hundred valiant men . . . ready at his call', fine archers in Lincoln green who struck the prick at forty-score marks (half a mile), hunters who fed themselves grandly through their skill.

In this rebel Utopia, Robin's deeds are presented as a moralized version of outlawry, with special care for the poor and women and a characteristic hostility to the Catholic church:

> From wealthy Abbots chests, and Churles abundant store,
> What often times he tooke, he shar'd amongst the poore:
> No lordly Bishop came in lusty Robins way,
> To him before he went, but for his Passe must pay:
> The Widdow in distresse he graciously reliev'd,
> And remedied the wrongs of many a Virgin griev'd: (345–50)

This is a spirited and sensually vigorous account of the traditional Robin, with special stress on archery, which seems to have much the standing at a popular level as mounted warfare among the gentry, that is as a martial practice valued for its evaluative force, but at a time when its practical military value was obsolescent – of the eight thousand Londoners who mustered against the invasion of 1588, not one carried a bow.

But Drayton is not merely collecting national traditions, assiduous scholar though he is; he is also setting them in a strongly idealized frame, and it is most striking that this fine survey of the traditional Robin Hood is begun and concluded with new material that crucially redirects the force of the myth.

At the end he moves on from Robin's courtesy to women to his sexuality, such as it is:

> He from the husbands bed no married woman wan,
> But to his Mistris deare, his loved Marian
> Was ever constant knowne, which whersoere shee came,
> Was soveraigne of the Woods, chiefe Lady of the Game:
> Her Clothes tuck'd to the knee, and daintie braided haire,
> With Bow and Quiver arm'd, shee wandred here and there,
> Amongst the forests wild; Diana never knew
> Such pleasures, nor such Harts as Mariana slew. (351–58)

Robin's purity is matched by Marian's transmutation into a figure of myth. That has its own implications for Robin's role which seem to move him far from the heritage prankster of the opening lines, and indeed, Drayton has taken precautions at the very beginning to establish an ennobled frame for his traditional material: the opening words of the description state how Sherwood, herself a fearless authority with

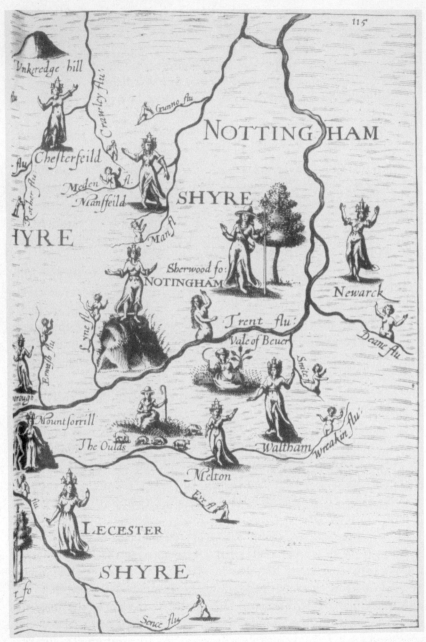

Illustration 7   Drayton's stimulus for Jonson's *Sad Shepherd*
(Courtesy Blackwell; photo Lensmedia.)

'The title of the great'st and bravest of her kind', conceives of her hero in fully hierarchical terms as she:

> . . . determineth to sing
> That lustie Robin Hood, who long time like a King
> To Sherwood still retyr'd, his onely standing Court (299–301)

So Drayton produces a strong neo-pastoral frame for the popular Robin Hood. The hero is firmly elevated, and although his popular persona is noted, as in Munday, no extended narrative of traditional deeds disturbs his gentrified poise. This passivity remains a problem: when Ben Jonson took up the Robin Hood theme, the power of his poetry and the learned force of his imagination could not compensate for the sheer difficulty of finding outlaw-related narrative which was also suitably conservative.

Ben Jonson's *The Sad Shepherd: A Tale of Robin Hood* (ed. Herford and Simpson VI, 1941) has to a marked degree the fugitive character-istics of much of the Robin Hood material. It is unfinished, its date is uncertain, and both structure and themes are distinctly centrifugal – the last point is in itself probably a main reason for the unfinished state of the play rather than the usually offered notion that Jonson died before completing the text.

It was formerly thought that he had worked on this early and abandoned it. In his 1618 discussion with Drummond of Hawthornden he referred to work called 'The May Lord', but it seems very unlikely that this was an early version of *The Sad Shepherd*, as the influence of *Poly-Olbion* and some apparent references in the unfinished play fit better with Jonson's own later attitudes and also the fashion for serious pastoral in the 1630s (Barton, 1984, p. 340; Nelson, 1973, pp. 218–19).

The play exists in two completed acts and the beginning of a third; Jonson also provides three full prose arguments at the beginning of each act. The concept is that Robin Hood, who is the lord of Sher-wood, as in Drayton, has invited a group of genteel shepherds from the Vale of Belvoir to a feast. Their source is evidently the map in *Poly-Olbion*, drawn from Saxton, with a forest figure for Sherwood juxtaposed to a rural person for Belvoir (see illustration 7). Jonson knew the Belvoir area, having written a masque for performance there, and he had travelled in Sherwood recently. In that context he followed both Drayton's map and tone to create an imaginary sequence of action closer to a world of faery than the historical politics or the social banditry of the Robin Hood tradition as it had previously been elaborated at various levels.

However, as happens in fairy tale, disruptions occur. One is itself suggested by the map. A naked nymph is shown in the Trent just between Sherwood and Belvoir; Jonson has interpreted her as drowning, not bathing. Aeglamour, the sad shepherd of the title, mourns the apparent loss in the river of 'Earine the Beautifull'. If all is not well for the pastoral visitors from Belvoir, things are not smooth in Sherwood, where more aggressive problems are involved with a female presence, namely Maudlin the Witch of Papplewick. This is the heart of southern Sherwood's Robin Hood country, which Jonson had visited in the early 1630s: locality is a recurrent force in the myth. Maudlin hates Marian and manages to turn herself into a version of Robin's beloved. Much malevolence stems from this counterfeiting – Jonson is obviously transmuting here the banal disguise-clowning of the Admiral's Men: Robin becomes quite out of sorts after Maudlin/ Marian has proved highly temperamental, and he is quite offensive to the true Marian as a result.

The relationship with Drayton is strong in the detailed realization of Marian the huntress; there is also a discussion of her success and style in killing and 'undoing' deer which is reminiscent of *Sir Gawain and the Green Knight*, or at least the cut-down romance 'The Grene Knight', with a striking parallel in Robin's seizing from the witch her magic girdle (III. 4. 47–8; see Hayes for a comment on this, 1992, p. 181, note 2). The strongest overall relationship with Drayton lies in the idealization of the whole: Robin is here aestheticized as a lord of the forest, and his authority is more or less limited to organizing feasts, welcoming guests and commenting on his men's activities. Though, as Hayes notes (1992, p. 101), he is not an earl, let alone a displaced one, he is more like King Arthur at his most inactive than the spirited outlaw hero of early ballad or recent film.

Robin's marginality is evident in the first 'argument': the opening words name the hero, but his actions are completely passive:

Robin-hood, having invited all the Shep'erds and Shep'erdesses of the Vale of Be'voir to a Feast in the Forrest of Sherwood, and trusting to his Mistris, Maid Marian, with the Wood-men, to kill him Venison against the day: Having left the like charge with Friar Tuck his

Chaplaine, and Steward, to command the rest of his merry men, to see the Bowre made ready, and all things in order for the entertainment; meeting with this Guests at their entrance into the Wood, welcomes and conducts them to his Bowre. (p. 8, 1–10)

Robin is the subject of the verbs but they are all inactive in function. The second 'argument' removes Robin from any role except that of Maudlin's victim and the same is true of the third – in which it seems that Aeglamour's own problems are increasingly being forgotten by Jonson as he himself becomes ensnared by the fascination of rural witchcraft, a topic discussed in some detail by Hayes (1992, pp. 119–33).

A post-Freudian and feminist reading of the text would certainly want to speculate on the meaning of Maudlin for Jonson; in its full spelling of Magdalene her name has New Testament connections with sexuality as well as the sentimentality of the word 'maudlin' – and a possible implication of papism. It is striking that this is the only Robin Hood text until recent times that actually shows Robin and Marian as being in sexual rapport, in an impressive scene when they meet and display credible affection:

> *Rob.* My Marian and my Mistris.
> *Mar.* My lov'd Robin!
> *Mellifleur.* The Moone's at full, the happy paire are met
> *Mar.* How hath this morning paid me, for my rising!
> First, with my sports; but most with meeting you!
> I did not halfe so well reward my hounds,
> As she hath me today: although I gave them
> All the sweet morsels, Calle, Tongue, Eares and Dowcets!
> *Rob.* What? And the inch-pin?
> *Mar.* Yes.
> *Rob.* Your sports then pleas'd you?
> *Mar.* You are a wanton.
> *Rob.* One I doe confesse,
> I wanted till you came. But now I have you,
> Ile grow to your embraces, till two soules
> Distilled into kisses, thorough your lips
> Do make one spirit of love.
> *Mar.* O Robin! Robin! (I. 6. 1–13)

The lively sensuality of the scene has attracted Anne Barton's praise; she finds the relationship 'ecstatic, blameless and both emotionally

and sensually fulfilled' (1984, p. 346); it is also conceivable that the
witch-centered strain that enters the relationship later is a negative
response to this realization of sexual contact. Jonson is too powerful a
writer for his text to remain empty; without the conflicts of politics,
like the earlier Robin Hood texts, or the elaborations of satire, like his
own other work, the text does not remain at the simple level of
mechanical entertainment and performance routines, as do most other
early gentrified plays dealing with the outlaw hero. It will be not until
modern feminism begins to reshape the legend that a Marian will be
as strong-minded, or as dangerous to the hero.

Another strand that Jonson draws out from Drayton provides the
first clear sign of Robin Hood being in some way a figure of national
identity. In his magisterial prologue, he makes it clear that part of his
purpose is to use English material in a text that can claim to match
the international levels of subtlety:

> He pray's you would vouchsafe, for your owne sake,
> To heare him this once more, but, sit awake.
> And though hee now present you with such wooll,
> As from meere English Flocks his Muse can pull,
> He hopes when it is made up into Cloath;
> Not the most curious head here will be loath
> To weare a Hood of it; (Prol., 7–13)

The strained metaphorics themselves proclaim rhetorical complication
of a Europe-wide character, and that is one of the ways in which this
text will become 'a Fleece,/To match, or those of Sicily, or Greece.'
(Prol., 13–14) But such nationalism is here only a cultural force; a
deeper and longer shadow will be cast by the race-based nationalism
that will enter the myth with Ritson's analysis and Scott's fiction.

It is presumably no accident that the two completions of the unfinished play to have been produced in the stage both appeared in a
context of high conventionality and constrain Jonson's conflicted text
towards a quietist end – Francis Waldron's version for Drury Lane in
1785 and Alan Porter's for Vassar College in 1935. Waldron, as Greg
comments 'takes too much trouble to marry every good personage of
the drama at the close, and to convert every bad one' (Jonson, 1905,
p. xxiv). Porter, an Adlerian psychologist as well as an English professor, was equally keen to resolve all problems in a version that was
closer to Jonson in style, but based on Waldron's plotting (1944).

By solving all the issues, these completers arrest the tradition. The unfinished text indicates more accurately the inherent complexity of the outlaw myth. Jonson's play testifies both to the attraction of Robin Hood as a theme and the difficulty in giving this elusive hero a substantial active part in any extended genre, especially one that is inherently conservative. As a figure of opposition, he must act against substantial forces: merely frustrating a witch, like impersonating a lady, is a reduction for a previously political figure and also demeans the hero in minor skirmishes. To solve this problem, to realize Robin Hood as a fully active political figure within the world of hierarchy, a way had to be found to make the process of noble and active resistance actually align with authority. The balladeer Parker had solved that problem by making him an enemy of the corrupt church, but a Trickster's success in confronting the clergy was itself hardly the stuff of theatrical glory.

The power of royalty was too great for the Elizabethan playwrights to go far in making Robin the libertarian enemy of princely oppression – although the idea was hovering about the figure of Prince John, it would not be fully realized until the weight of history and the growth of bourgeois democracy had made royalty an easier target than in the period of autocracy. In those circumstances the hierarchical idealisms of Elizabethan and Jacobean neo-pastoral produced the hero's own inactivity, and that was the pattern that continued throughout the light theatrical modes of the eighteenth century.

But before that sequence of reduced intensity, the tradition produced one unique political play, in which Robin Hood was decisively brought into line with the conservative structure, while at the same time being recognized as a potentially rebellious force. *Robin Hood and his Crew of Souldiers* was printed in 1661 and the title page proclaims that it was acted on the day of his majesty's coronation in Nottingham itself, see illustration 8. The text is unpaginated (see Knight, 1993 for a fuller description and a reprint of the text, also available in Dobson and Taylor, 1976, pp. 237–42).

This short play was described by Ritson as an 'Interlude of a few pages and no merit' (1795, p. lxxii) and while that view arises rationally from both his aesthetic taste and his radical politics, the play is nevertheless fascinating for the way in which the tradition is consciously, even aggressively rehandled. Nelson could only see it as a 'Restoration Curio' (the title of his chapter 7, 1973, p. 236) but it has

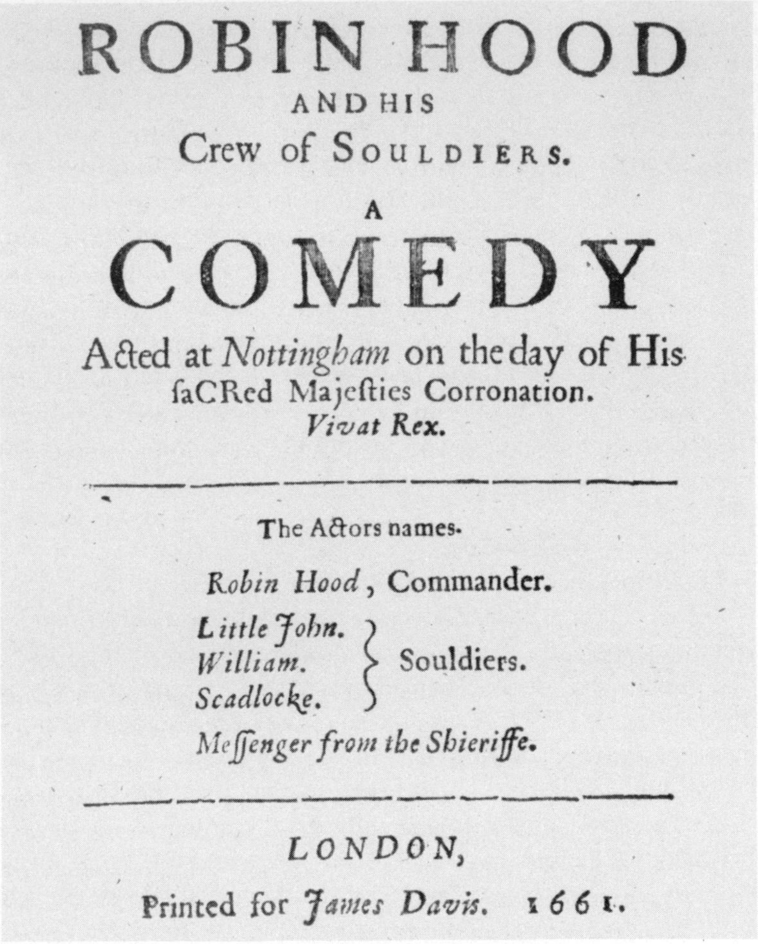

ROBIN HOOD
AND HIS
Crew of SOULDIERS.

A

COMEDY

Acted at *Nottingham* on the day of His
faCRed Majefties Corronation.
Vivat Rex.

The Actors names.

Robin Hood , Commander.

Little John.
William.   } Souldiers.
Scadlocke.

Meffenger from the Shieriffe.

LONDON,

Printed for *James Davis.* 1661.

Illustration 8   Robin Hood suppressed by Royalism, 1661
(Courtesy British Library; photo Lensmedia.)

greater significance than he implies, because here the idea of hierarchical fidelity is in overt conflict with the outlaw's insistent, though
often constrained, role as a figure of anti-authoritarianism.

Most striking of all this play's innovations is Robin's final confes-
sion of his past treasons to the crown:

I am quite another man; thaw'd into conscience of my
Crime and Duty; melted into loyalty and respect to vertue. (p. 311)

The action, such as it is, itself confirms Robin's weakness, and the recent and important nature of his enfeebled state. He is presented in military terms as Robin Hood Commander, while Little John and Will are 'Souldiers' – though the title page seems to present them as three, namely John, William and Scadlock (see illustration 8). To call them a 'Crew' has its own implications; this meant originally a detachment of armed men (reinforcements, or an 'accrual' of strength) but by the Civil War it had clearly attained the sense of a disorderly crew. These soldiers are potentially hostile to newly-established order.

Very little happens; at the opening, the outlaws are taken aback by loud offstage shouts of 'general joy'. In an epic simile – a form foreign to the outlaw tradition – Robin expresses 'wonder and astonishment' like that of villagers facing an ocean in flood, and immediately admits his own weakness:

> And thus it is with us; the guilty breast
> Still pants and throbs, when others are at rest. (p. 309)

Little John returns in a darker mood: 'Gives and Fetters, Hatchets and Halters, stinking prisons and the death of dogs is all we can expect' (p. 309). The outlaws have never, even faced with the sheriff's worst connivances, been so low-spirited. But this text has a different position: John explains the events offstage: 'Tis the Kings Coronation; and now the Sheiriffe with a band of armed men, are marching to reduce us to loyalty, and the miseries of an honest life; this Messenger here can tell you a rufull tale of obedience, that is expected' (p. 309). Nobody assumes the sheriff is to be resisted; authority is accepted as the only structure of force and value and the outlaws implicitly acknowledge their criminality: this text provides no space for a counter-authority of any value.

The messenger formally requires 'a cheerfull and ready submission to his Majesties Laws, with a promise of future obedience', to be followed by 'the rest of our lives running in a smooth stream of loyalty and honest allegiance'. With that in view, he brings 'pardon of all past misdemeanours' but otherwise they are to 'expect the miseries of a sudden destruction' (p. 309).

Robin is silent and the other ranks exchange lengthy and vulgar paragraphs of regret, but then they begin to speak in a language which in 1661 was very much worth dismissing. John suddenly sounds like a leveller: 'Every brave soule is born a King; rule and command o're the fearfull rabble, is natures stamp; courage and lofty thoughts are not ever confin'd to Thrones, nor still th'appendages of an illustrious birth, but the thatcht Hovell or the simple Wood oft times turns forth a mind as fully fraught with Gallantry and true worth as doth the marble Pallace' (p. 310).

Those words would have come well from a social bandit, but when Robin finally speaks it is in a different mode, one that strangely, and perhaps just as threateningly, condenses the worst features of acquisitive royalism with lower-order insurgency. His speech takes a position that is partly one of aristocratic self-will and partly one of Hobbesian rapacity, and so through the rejected leader the play realizes and disavows what might be taken as the worst case ideologies of both sides in the civil war.

First Robin asks in terms of egalitarian individualism:

Why then should the severities of obedience, and the strait niceties of Law shackle this noble soul, whom nature, meant not onely free but soveraigne . . .' (p. 310)

Then, sounding more like a Prince Rupert who has read *Leviathan* than a Cromwellian trooper, he rejects this passivity in fustian style: 'No we have Swords, and Arms, and Lives equally engaged in our past Account, and whilest these Armes can wield our Swords, or our uncurdl'd blood give vigor to those Arms, hopes of submission are as vain as is the strange request.' (p. 310).

This is the moment of encounter with the enemy. Now, the ballad Robin would blow his horn and so condemn the force of conservative authority to accept another defeat. But in this different and highly-contained situation, the messenger – not even a fighting man – responds with a long prose speech, which carefully refutes the points Robin has made and concludes that the outlaws are indeed in the wrong – 'your disobedience betrayes a boundlesse pride' – and then repeats his opening point about the aura of majesty: 'This Great, this Gracious Prince is this day Crown'd, and offers Life, and Peace and Honour, if you will quit your wilde rebellions, and become what your birth challenges of you, nay what ever your boasted gallantry expects of you, that is: loyal subjects' (p. 311).

Robin, for once, simply gives in. All he says is 'Ha! Whence is this sudden change?' and then admits his sense of 'Crime' and his new devotion to 'loyalty and respect to vertue' (p. 311). The play is over; the former rebel Commander leads forward his two outlaws and they sing thanks to Heaven which

> hath (not only to our land
> Restor'd but) crown'd our KING. (p. 311)

And so the formerly rebellious and violent 'crew' agree they shall:

> to joy and generall mirth
> This glad day set aside. (p. 311)

Holiday is the final note, as in so many Robin Hood ballads, but here it is not in the spirit of power-reversing carnival. This is the play-game of royal authority. Restorations are common enough in the myth, from the annual reappearance of the Summer Lord to the more political re-instalment of King Richard himself and the more fraught reassertion of kingly power after the tensions of the King and Subject encounter. This play, though, sees and dramatizes a different kind of restoring, the reinstitution of a genuinely embattled royal authority, and the play's stridency and urgent destruction of all the usual formations of the outlaw myth are to be traced to the special circumstances of 1661, and indeed of Nottingham itself.

King Charles raised his standard there at the beginning of hostilities; Nottingham, which Drayton called 'the North's eye' (song 26.6) was the most southerly point of Charles's power base in the north. And yet the city was never entirely royalist and returned solidly parliamentarian members. As the war ended Francis Harker refused to concede and was executed; Colonel John Hutchinson, Nottingham's governor and a man of considerable standing in the county, who had been at the Banqueting House on the day of execution, was reprieved through a mixture of influence and repentance, but was soon enough arrested, refused further capitulation and died in jail in 1664 (Knight, 1993, p. 305). He and those who felt like him may well be the particular target of this fierce piece of political theatre; it has some resonances of Robin's proffered surrender to the king in Parker's 'True Tale' (see p. 91) but is essentially original in its rehandling of the outlaw and the genre, and in particular for the overt way in which

the question of authority, so deeply and often obscurely entwined
throughout the whole myth, is treated as a matter of overt concern.

The Nottingham restoration play remained unique as the flow of
gentrified performance continued into the next century. *Robin Hood,
An Opera* proclaims the title page of the 1730 renovation of the tradition, and its subtitle locates it firmly in the heart of London popular
theatre: 'As it is perfom'd at Lee's and Harper's Great Theatrical Booth
in Bartholomew Fair'. The context does convey some force to the piece
and in a book on the ballad opera form, E.M. Gagey speculated that
'the fact of its having been calculated for the meridian of the fairs has
tended to preserve some of the robust popular quality of the old Robin
Hood ballads.' (1937, p. 202)

This period, according to Nicoll, was one of 'trivial minded' theatre, a fact noted by a contemporary like Curll, when he deprecated
'Our present Polite Taste, when nothing will go down but Ballad
Operas and Mr Lunn's Buffoonery' (see Nicoll, 1965, p. 10). That
view certainly seems to fit well this amiable but relatively insignificant pastiche, though it does provide some surprises. The opera has a
simple framework, with two acts, one at court and one in the forest;
it tells how the Earl of Pembroke loves Matilda (sister to King Edward
– unnumbered again) and so causes his rival, the Earl of Huntingdon,
to be outlawed; Robin kills Pembroke at the end, but first the villain
proclaims his enemy's innocence. There is no clear source here, certainly not Munday; it would seem that an elementary libretto has been
constructed from memories of the *Gest* and the broad idea of a distressed lover earl.

As is common in these theatrical versions, an extra love interest is
involved, presumably so that more than one woman can appear; here
Marina, friend to Princess Matilda (and an anagram of Marian), is in
love with Darnel, Huntingdon's friend, who turns into Little John.
The outlaw band is easily identifiable as descendants of Peter Quince's
Athenian rustics and with a neat mixture of ballad narratives and
gentrified sentimentality the opera ticks along as a fairly uninteresting
reworking of the myth. Some new modulations occur, as when the
outlaws rescue Will singing a fine piece of contemporary military
chant, 'March on Brave Hearts', with the Whiggish, though gram-
matically strange, chorus 'And Liberty, with all Their Charms, Shall
smile and crown our Arms' (p. 15).

Strange things happen as authors try to fill up the need that extended genres have for narrative, especially when the anti-authoritarian actions of the earlier Robin Hood are not felt to be politically correct in a conservative context; here, as Gagey noted, the context provides a rough edge. Matilda and Marina wander, brave and frightened, into the forest – the influence of *As You Like It* is visible. But another visitor has a different origin, a miserly Puritan called Prim drawn from religious satire. Will Stutely robs him, which seems a predictable enough treatment for this modern representative of an oppressive church, and Robin gives the money to a poor couple. Suddenly, though, Stutely shows the harsher side of outlawry. He seizes Matilda and Marina, and plans to rape them: 'you are my prisoners by the right of Arms, and I must make bold to try my Manhood upon you' (p. 26). Worse yet, the formerly amiable men of the forest all want to join in:

1 Outl.   Come, come, Stutely, I must put in my Claim; all Prizes are to be shar'd in Common among us.
2 Outl.   And I mine.
3 Outl.   And I mine. (p. 26)

Robin is at hand, after a nervous while, to dispose of this disgraceful communalism, a touch of London-style mob rule in eighteenth-century Sherwood. But there is still need for more material before the triumphant end, and a sequence follows of almost zany transgressiveness; Little John, who it seems has wavered from his role as noble Darnel and lover of Marina, suddenly stars in a piece of broad comedy where, having been caught *in flagrante* with the Pinder's wife, he hides under the table in the guise of Towzer the dog, and is fed scraps by the amiable Pinder. Then after the husband returns suddenly again, Darnel/John moves to the baby's cradle and the affectionate Pinder kisses him. A comic sequence as old as the Second Shepherd's play rollicks around the stage for a while, until it is time to draw to a stately close with Robin reinstated and the outlaws entertaining the audience with the final dance.

In part trivial, in part conservative, but clearly marked with the multiple possibilities of the Robin Hood materials, the 1730 opera retained and recreated the elements of play and game in new form. This is even more true of the 1751 Drury Lane production *Robin Hood: a New Musical* written by Moses Mendez and identified as a 'ballad farce' by Ritson (1795, p. lxxii). Nicoll again has appropriate keywords for the text, describing this period as 'less rowdy and more highly decorous' (1966, p. 5). Although it is called farce it has none of the grotesquerie of the 1730 play; its humour is more towards a sour but also lukewarm form of satire.

There is no earldom to be lost here; Robin is simply discovered in the forest escaping from the sheriff. That may be derived from the ballads, but the hero's inactivity belongs to the gentrified tradition. The heroine is Clarinda, presumably related to Clorinda the queen of the shepherds, whom Robin marries at the end of the literary compilation 'Robin Hood's Birth, Breeding, Valor and Marriage' (see p. 87), but here her lover is the youthful Leander and the plot, such as it is, tells how Robin helps her escape the intentions of her father Graspall who wants her to marry Glitter, an unappealing wealthy man about town. The general source is clearly 'Robin Hood and Allen a Dale', where the hero helped a true wedding to occur, and here too Robin appears in disguise, though not as a priest but as another claimant for Clarinda, Sir Humphrey Wealthy, as whom he masterminds the final marriage.

Not much else occurs except the singing of a series of airs which are presented in a highly formalized mode. The piece is well-organized, tonally consistent, mildly satirical – Glitter suffers nothing worse than a chambermaid suggesting he might hang himself, after calling him a 'travell'd coxcomb' (I.4). In general this is a very minor piece of Hoodiana, in which the decorum of the period has constrained the usually heterogeneous materials into a fairly uniform if unexciting piece.

The much more elaborate comic opera *Robin Hood or Sherwood Forest*, first produced in 1782, with music by William Shield and libretto by Lawrence McNally, was performed at the Theatre Royal Covent Garden. Records remain of its thirteen performances in the 1783–4 season; on three occasions it took more than £200 and was therefore among the most successful productions of the time – and this was by no means an unusually short run by the practices of the day (Hogan, 1968, II, p. 638).

The opera realizes rather fully a version of the neo-pastoral ideal, as it represents 'a chearful rural life' where lovers and exiles can 'frisk it near the chrystal stream'. Robin Hood exhibits a manly sense of independence, with a song devoted to ale and many rousing exhortations like 'we are free from care, my boys.' This large-stage version of the eighteenth-century bucolic romances, has a whole series of loving pairs, introducing contemporary women's names – Stella for Scarlet and Margaret for Allen as well as an entirely new proto-Gothic pair called Edwin and Angelina. Love and pleasure dominate the action; there is here no sheriff, and no king, just Robin as a rural authority figure. But politics is not forgotten as there is recurrent reference to the sheer Englishness of this forest Eden, and Robin and Clorinda finally proclaim:

> Strains of liberty we sing
> To our country, queen and king.

But not everything in this text is a recreation purely in terms of contemporary convention; the opera is touched by the new interest in the past and the nobly 'national'. In 1777 Thomas Evans published his collection of early ballads, including twenty-seven Robin Hood texts, and the growing interest in the medieval, the Gothic and the antiquarian is discernible in the 1782 opera: in addition to a song from Milton ('O Nightingale') there is also one taken 'from a new ballad collection'.

This re-orientation towards the past made fullest use of the older narratives and so re-energized the enfeebled, over-gentrified outlaw myth when Joseph Ritson in 1795 published with widespread impact his authority-bearing and fresh-seeming set of what were apparently quite ancient Robin Hood ballads. Many of them were of course already available through other anthologists like Evans and in the still thriving eighteenth-century garlands; while theatrical Robins spoke of nobility and gentility, the ballad hero had continued to roister in the streets. But the two traditions, rebellious narrative and gentrified authority, were about to come together with a dynamic impact whose reverberations are still felt today in Robin Hood reconstructions.

The last two of the eighteenth-century Robin Hood performances mark the change. In 1788 Frances Brooke's *Marian*, a comic opera, was produced. A distinctly rustic Robin the Boatman loves a teasing flirt, Patty Clover the milkmaid, but he also performs the role of marital go-between to which Robin was reduced in the 1751 'ballad farce'. In *Marian*, the possibilities of nautical stagecraft have swamped the older tradition and the Robin Hood myth itself is almost capsized; indeed the opera seems closer to the general notion of Robin (rather than Robin Hood) as an all-purpose semi-comic lover, as found in Fielding's Walpole satire *The Grub Street Opera* of 1730. But then in 1795 comes *Merry Sherwood or Harlequin Forester* by John O'Keefe, the prolific comic playwright best known for *Wild Oats*. Even though this is called 'an operatical pantomime' it brings the outlaw myth suddenly in focus again. Material is drawn solidly from the ballad 'Robin Hood and the Tanner,' the Allen a Dale romance and the gentrified narrative concerning the Prince of Aragon. They are all ballads at least as old as the seventeenth century, and here they are fitted into the idea of a distressed gentleman whose world is both neo-pastoral and performance-oriented. It makes a hectic, overstuffed short piece, but also one rich with the outlaw tradition and modern reorientation of it, and in that sense *Merry Sherwood* is more substantial than the thin and mechanical pieces displayed on the eighteenth-century stage, where the dynamic tradition of Robin Hood performance had almost run into the sand of theatrical convention. As chapter 5 will show, from this new combination of the manifold narrative strands of the myth, now firmly inside the overarching concept of the displaced earl, stems the whole structure of the Robin Hood myth in the modern world.

5

'Undying Pastoral Liberty': Greenwood and Heritage in the Nineteenth and Early Twentieth Centuries

5.1 COLLECTING THE TEXTS

Robin Hood in his first few centuries had many affiliations: to the various forests of Inglewood, Sherwood, Barnsdale, Rockingham, and also to places great and small like Edinburgh, Leicester, Yeovil and Chagford. But although the hero has his sites of devotion right across the face of England, he was never identified with the nation itself. There are clear signs in the plays discussed in chapter 4 that nationalism is a growing feature of the context, but those stirrings of patriotic performance were little more than transitory in dramas basically devoted to love, clowning and property under threat, and the hero himself was not seen as a symbol of national values.

It is only at the beginning of the eighteenth century, as various social and economic forces conspire to make the 'national' a domain of value, an 'imagined community' in Benedict Anderson's terms, that the newly-powerful bourgeois professionals can find an ideal that conforms to their sense of self-conscious coherence. It is also a domain where writers begin to find the new construct, the nation, a useful means of supporting their own political values, of remarkably different kinds. Homi Bhabha has recently led the discussion of ways in which a 'nation' is created through its own forms of 'narration' (1989, pp. 1–7) and this is one of the major processes that dynamize the new patterns in the Robin Hood myth.

153

But history and nationalism alone are cool forces; they gain their emotive, indeed romantic, power through being a terrain on which the individual can stand alone, revelling in his – the gender is consistent – escape from the entanglements of the essentially collective and communal forces which Robin Hood, among other symbolic figures, has in the past represented, whether he is a social bandit or a briefly distressed aristocrat. Privacy and passion provide the inner dynamism that give emotive power to nationalism and historicism throughout a sequence of literary developments that in terms of the Robin Hood myth were, as the times suggested, revolutionary.

Robin Hood the national fiction is not a simple product; like all the other versions of the outlaw, from local play-game leader to renaissance pastoral figurehead, he is constructed in a set of interlinked and sometimes contradictory manoeuvres across a range of places and times. The process starts around 1800 in a context of raised socio-cultural awareness, when political and industrial revolutions are in the forefront of the minds of writers, even those – perhaps especially those – who merely rehandle aspects of the folkloric tradition. The innovator in this area, as in others, was Joseph Ritson.

He was not the first scholar to collect earlier literary materials – Thomas Percy had done that outstandingly a generation before and there were many less well-known collectors from the past, including Samuel Pepys with his broadsides, the Scottish collector and reworker of traditional materials David Dalrymple (Lord Hailes), and Ritson's immediate predecessor in offering Robin Hood materials in a organised series, Thomas Evans.

But Ritson did have two unique aspects to his position. He was the first collector to be a convinced radical, an enthusiast for the French revolution and for Tom Paine's insistence on the Rights of Man; and secondly he was the first major collector to work in a period when, for reasons of rapid social change, many of those who reflected on events and values were interested in looking back to contrast the turbulent present against what had gone before, whether it was imaginary, real, or a mixture of the two. At such a time, when overt political dissent was highly dangerous, a story from the past like that of Robin Hood was a suitable medium to convey feelings of a more or less critical character.

Those elements of a favourable positioning were fortified by Ritson's remarkable diligence as a collector, forever hunting out new sources and pieces of information and travelling energetically to consult people and their texts. That enabled him to gather what is still an impressive number of the major Robin Hood texts – he prints thirty-three of the thirty-eight in Child, the only early text missing being 'Robin Hood and the Monk' of which he only knew a fragment in 1795; it was inserted, apparently by the printer, as an appendix in the second edition of 1832 (II. 221–36). Ritson made the materials of the outlaw myth available to many readers and rewriters of the tradition; his first edition of 1795 in two volumes was reshaped in 1820 into a cheaper one-volume edition, and both were regularly reprinted throughout the nineteenth century.

But Ritson's impact was greater than that of a mere source for later re-modellers of the myth. He also shaped an image of the hero that was in one way or other to dominate almost all the treatments of the topic right up to the present. He opened his edition with a twelve-page statement entitled 'The Life of Robin Hood'. It drew together many of the elements of biography that had been gathering around the mythic outlaw for several centuries, but it was qualitatively different from the chronicle-style guesses of Grafton, the assertions of a balladeer like Martin Parker, or the random notes made by the antiquarian Dodsworth. This was a Life prefaced to a Works, so about a figure of importance, and it was written with what Marilyn Butler has called 'the full paraphernalia of scholarship' (1979, p. 143).

This hero was born at Locksley in 1160, by name Robert Fitz Ooth, Earl of Huntingdon, with Stukeley's genealogy reprinted to lend support to this tale rooted in antiquity and redolent with both identity and power. Ritson moves steadily through the quasi-factual moments of the early tradition – the associated places are named, the assistant outlaws mentioned. So are the hundred fine archers, and Marian. Improbability did not deter Ritson – he speaks confidently of a two-mile bow shot and just as firmly dismisses in a note Percy's rational argument that no early text mentioned the earldom (1795, p. xx).

In full-blown scholarly mode, Ritson provides a remarkably rich account of the hero's literary and folkloric career, and in his 'Notes and Illustrations' many long quotations from the major sources – most of the later rewriters of the theme worked from these, not the original texts. The pages seem like a concentration of the whole learned and aristocratized tradition, as the essence of Robin Hood the distressed gentleman is passed on with all the authority of a modern antiquarian.

But there is a difference from the previous stagy gentrification: Ritson the determined radical redirects this whole hierarchical edifice with a political purpose closer to the elusive figure of the social bandit. There is venom in his voice as he speaks of those whose power dominated the medieval world and, he feels, have suppressed a full representation of the people's hero. The passage of summary that comes after his account of the hero's death is justly famous as a piece of engaged history:

> Such was the end of Robin Hood; a man, who, in a barbarous age, and under a complicated tyranny, displayed a spirit of freedom and independence which has endeared him to the common people, whose cause he maintained (for all opposition to tyranny is the cause of the people), and, in spite of the malicious endeavours of pitiful monks, by whom history was consecrated to the crimes and follies of titled ruffians and sainted idiots, to suppress all record of his patriotic exertions and virtuous acts, will render his name immortal. (1795, I, pp. xi–xii)

This suggests a politics distinctly more programmatic and class-conscious than the naive anti-authority spirit of the early ballads, though it is generally in keeping with their dislike of abbots and sheriffs. But a note that is quite new is struck in the phrase 'patriotic exertions', and from this innovative national concept of Robin stems a great deal, both for Ritson and for subsequent treatments.

Through the eighteenth century there had been growing, in an uncertain and undefined way, the sense of Robin as an essentially English figure – his men are 'hearts of oak' in the 1730 comic opera, and as long ago as Jonson's preface the outlaw myth provided a local challenge to the power of classical culture. But there is something more specific behind Ritson's words than a general sense that Robin did his country proud. The concept of 'The Norman Yoke' was important to Paine and other early revolutionaries: as Christopher Hill has outlined (1965, pp. 50–112), radicals sought historical validation for their views in the idea, by no means entirely fictitious, that Anglo-Saxon England was a good deal more democratic in its institutions and attitudes than the political structure imposed at the conquest.

Ritson is cautious in this matter; he never puts Robin's resistance simply in terms of Saxon versus Norman, presumably because he argues forcefully for Robin's close descent from a conquest lord, as in Stukeley's genealogy, and he is well aware that Robert, let alone Fitz

Ooth, is a fully Norman name. Nevertheless, he lets the argument take a 'Norman Yoke' shape, especially when he argues about rights to rule. In a well-known passage he states: 'what better title king Richard could pretend to the territory and people of England than Robin Hood had to the dominion of Barnsdale or Sherwood is a question humbly submitted to the consideration of the political philosopher' (I, p. vi). And he goes on to link race to oppression: 'The deer with which the royal forests then abounded [every Norman tyrant being, like Nimrod, "a mighty hunter before the Lord"] would afford our hero and his companions an ample supply of food. . .' (I, p. vi).

Just as Ritson leaves the full nationalist and racist position unspecified, so even in the summary of Robin's behaviour the reasons for his outlawry and hostility to kings and priests is not made specific in this account. He communicates the aura of a need for reform, not any hard-edged analysis of Robin's politics and position. Such clarifications will be made by later writers, and many in ways that entirely elide the early socialist ideas of Ritson's Life; that is the easier to do because the structure is in itself inherently conservative, partly as Ritson accepts entirely the 'distressed gentleman' interpretation developed by Munday and also because this biography, being both individual-based and nationalist is itself basically anti-communal and so, in Paine's terms, anti-radical.

In spite of that contradiction between Ritson's attitude and the form of his representation, what comes across is a strong and solidly-based account of the outlaw hero. It is then all the more surprising to find that Ritson's influence is remarkably slight in direct terms; while almost everybody plundered his edition for narratives, ideas, facts and references, nobody simply took over his scheme and wrote an account of Robin Hood based on Ritson's Life.

Nor did his influence operate immediately. It was another generation before new versions of Robin Hood were created, and then they were, while recognizably related to the creation of the radical antiquary, both new in many ways and also to a considerable degree uncertain and riven with new kinds of strain. The reason for the generational gap may simply be that Ritson wrote as the late eighteenth-century wave of radicalism was broken, at least in England, by growing hostility to what radicalism had turned into in France. After 1793, when England declared war on republican France, few of the former British radicals held their ground overtly, and most moved to liberalism, especially the writers. Ritson's text came out just after its time, and it was not until after 1815, when postwar authors were reconsidering the structure of politics in England, that the Robin Hood myth, like a number of other ancient topics, provided a ready language in which to address with circumspection the issues of the turbulent years between 1815 and 1820, when England saw so much civil unrest and many districts came near revolt.

5.2   DEVELOPING A 'GREENWOOD' POETRY

Robin Hood poems only fill a slender space among the expanses of the myth in prose and play over the last two centuries. And yet they have a special importance, because it was non-narrative poetry that focused most sharply the issues at stake in the nineteenth century, as people who were more or less modern considered the meaning of a myth now distinctly ancient. The positions taken and the problems realized – not always consciously – by the few poets who then rehandled the outlaw myth give in fact a fine view of the core of modern responses to the tradition. From a surprisingly early date they shaped what we have slowly learned to call a 'heritage' position focused on the greenwood, a viewpoint validating an account of the modern world which is usually one of dissatisfaction, often sheer cultural escape, and sometimes one involved with aspects of national pride.

Robin Hood's existence was at least registered by Ritson's poetic contemporaries. Scott would not have needed his edition to know of the hero, and the discussion of Robin's skill in archery in chapter 13 of *Ivanhoe* actually draws on Scott's own account of Douglas in *The Lady of the Lake* (Scott, 1942 ed., V, strophe XXII, p. 257) where for the first time appears the strange, impossible image of splitting the opponent's arrow (presumably an imaginative extension or misreading of the old idiom 'to split the peg', namely land straight on the central peg which held the target on its straw base; there may also be some confusion with 'splitting the wand' the alleged practice – mentioned in the *Gest* – of using a peeled willow stick as the hardest target of all).

Another important contemporary, Wordsworth, refers specifically to the tradition in the opening lines of 'Rob Roy's Grave', composed in 1805–6:

A famous man is Robin Hood,
The English ballad singer's joy! (ed. De Selincourt, sec. ed., 1954, III,
   p. 79)

But his interest goes no further, and in *The Prelude* he merely mentions Robin in a list of improbable heroes:

Oh! give us once again the wishing cap
Of Fortunatus, and the invisible coat
Of Jack the giant-killer, Robin Hood,
And Sabra in the forest with St George! (1850 text, ed. De Selincourt,
   1926, pp. 155, 341–4)

Much more interesting material emerges later in a poetic debate between the two friends and collaborators J.R. Reynolds and John Keats. They seem to be chronologically the first to engage strongly with Ritson's materials, but only just: around 1818, as John Barnard puts it, (1989, p. 183) the Robin Hood story was 'one which seems to have been in the air' and the materials were drawn into what has been called 'The War of the Intellectuals' between 1815 and 1819 (Butler, 1981, chap. 6, pp. 138–54), when Leigh Hunt, Thomas Love Peacock, Walter Scott and Robert Southey were all at work in some way on the myth. The convergence of interest suggests some specific cause: a reprint of Ritson's collection in 1817 may have been a significant stimulus, but it may also be (as Marilyn Butler has suggested in discussion) that recent trials for sedition and blasphemy, especially that of William Hone in late 1817, may well have reminded liberals of the existence of a tradition of popular resistance.

Reynolds, the least-known name of them all, has the honour of starting the outlaw's new phase of romantic representation. On 3 February 1818 Keats received a letter from his friend containing two sonnets entitled 'To a Friend, On Robin Hood' – the second was merely titled 'The Same'. Like so much in the tradition, they are centrally concerned with place: it is one that now is empty of a presence, but Reynolds argues in the first sonnet that the imagination can recover 'the sweet days of merry Robin Hood' (the text is most readily found in a recent essay by John Barnard):

The trees in Sherwood forest are old and good, –
The grass beneath them now is dimly green;

Are they deserted all? Is no young mien,
With loose slung bugle, met within the wood?
No arrow found, – foil'd of its antler'd food, –
Struck in the oak's rude side? – Is there nought seen,
To mark the revelries which there have been,
In the sweet days of merry Robin Hood?
Go there with summer, and with evening, – go
In the soft shadows, like some wandering man, –
And thou shalt far amid the Forest know
The archer-men in green, with belt and bow,
Feasting on pheasant, river fowl and swan,
With Robin at their head, and Marian. (Barnard, 1989, pp. 183–4)

The opening image is of a deserted forest that can be peopled by imagination: it is at first a communal realization but the final couplet withdraws, as romanticism usually does, to a personalized viewpoint, seeing no more than Robin and Marian.

Examining both people and sharing their presence, vividly detailed, sensuously alive, is the thrust of the second sonnet:

With coat of Lincoln green, and mantle too,
And horn of ivory mouth and buckle bright, –
And arrows wing'd with peacock-feathers light,
And trusty bow, well gathered of the yew, –
Stands Robin Hood: – and near, with eyes of blue
Shining through dusk hair, like the stars of the night,
And habited in pretty forest plight, –
His greenwood beauty sits, young as the dew.
Oh, gentle tressed girl! Maid Marian!
Are thine eyes bent upon the gallant game
That stray in the merry Sherwood? Thy sweet fame
Can never, never die. And thou, high man,
Would we might pledge thee with thy silver can
Of Rhenish, in the woods of Nottingham. (Barnard, 1989, pp. 184)

John Barnard comments that 'Reynold's sonnets are really a nostalgic lament for a lost past' (1989, p. 184), but there is more than simple retrospection in mind here; Reynolds seeks a representation so vivid that a personal imaginative contact is made with these figures whose value is, in present time, seductive – the blue eyes through the dark hair give that notion full physical force.

Reynolds appears to be the first to imagine a personalized link with hero and heroine; it is a new departure in Robin Hood writing, where writer and character for the first time commune personally, though the possibility of such a link seems implied by the picturesque outlaw musing on the title page of Ritson's edition (see illustration 9). Reynolds, however, strongly develops the situation. In both concept and style, these poems show a finely-tuned romantic imagination of the past – and they also suggest that when Reynolds devoted himself permanently to the law, an interesting minor poet was lost to the language. Part of the impact of his treatment is that he disregards the directly communicating style of the ballads, and sets the outlaw and all perception of his meaning in the high-art, inward-looking and inherently private form of the sonnet.

Keats does not fully agree with his friend, in either meaning or form. His language is both easier and more powerful; the verse-form is a letter, that modern mode of direct communication, and the crucial point in this case is that the issues are conceived in a clear-eyed and fully socialized context. It was also immediate. On the day Keats received Reynold's two sonnets he wrote the poem entitled in most editions 'Robin Hood: To a Friend' (ed. Allott, 1970, pp. 301–4), but in his letter more sharply titled 'To JHR in Answer to his Robin Hood Sonnets'. As an answer it is both specific and forceful, opening by rejecting Reynolds' suggestion that the world of the merry outlaws is accessible through fancy:

> No! those days are gone away,
> And their hours are old and gray,
> And their minutes buried all
> Under the down-trodden pall
> Of the leaves of many years. (1–5)

Time has made Robin Hood distant; but other forces operate against a medieval summer dream-time. One is climate: Keats is one of the first to bring winter into contact with the myth:

> Many times have winter's shears,
> Frozen north and chilling east
> Sounded tempests to the feast
> Of the forest's whispering fleeces. (6–9)

ROBIN HOOD:

A

COLLECTION

Of all the Ancient

POEMS, SONGS, AND BALLADS,

NOW EXTANT,

RELATIVE TO THAT CELEBRATED

𝕰𝖓𝖌𝖑𝖎𝖘𝖍 𝕺𝖚𝖙𝖑𝖆𝖜:

To which are prefixed

HISTORICAL ANECDOTES OF HIS LIFE.

Illustration 9 **A romantic outlaw**
(From Ritson, 1795 ed.; photo Lensmedia)

But the images of death and oppression in the 'down-trodden pall' that has gathered through time are not only related to sombre weather. As Morris Dickstein says, this poem has 'a certain social consciousness' (1971, p. 171). The lines about winter carry metaphorical reference to a pastoral economy in the shears and fleeces, and these instruments have become wintry in effect and through time, as Keats startlingly asserts in the next line, 'Since men paid no Rent and leases' (10). In revision for publication he weakened this line to 'knew no rent nor leases' but the point still stands: new economic structures are causing the real inaccessibility of the past culture.

The speaker does, it is true, relish the world which has been lost to the present space where there is no 'bugle' or 'twanging bow', no sign

> of all the clan
> Thrumming on an empty can
> Some old hunting ditty. (25–7)

Such vivid recreation does not blind Keats to the present world and he uses Reynolds' notion of revivifying Robin and Marian to comment on what *they* would see in our time, not on what we would feel for them: Keats, though writing only in verse letter form, nevertheless brings into sharp and conscious focus the theme of sociocultural change that in most writers is left implicit in the Robin Hood texts. His power of concentration and sensuous argument develops the issues involved in the change from feudal to mercantile practices referred to before:

> And if Robin should be cast
> Sudden from his turfed grave
> And if Marian should have
> Once again her forest days,
> She would weep and he would craze.
> He would swear, for all his oaks
> Fallen beneath the dockyard strokes,
> Have rotted on the briny seas.
> She would weep that her wild bees
> Sang not to her – strange that honey
> Can't be got without hard money. (47–57)

Barnard speaks of Keats' dislike for standing military forces and other signs of an inorganic social structure (1989, pp. 186–7) and this is one of the poet's most explicit criticisms of the effect of the cash-nexus on direct sensual relations between humans and their natural productivity – a theme more fully developed in *Isabella*, especially stanzas xvi-xviii about the 'ledger-men' of newly mercantile Europe (ed. Allott, 1970, pp. 324–5).

The way in which the medieval 'organic' figure can act as a critique of the modern world will be a regular presence in modern Robin Hood realizations, and like so much else in the myth it can serve interests ranging from quasi-revolutionary left to highly conservative right. Keats has the imaginative insight and the politically dissenting position to isolate the point sharply. What he does not have is the energy or the context to press it further, and so he ends the poem by vowing 'Honour' to all of the denizens of old Sherwood and agreeing that he and Reynolds, and others too by implication, can at least provide a celebratory chorus to the intriguing myth:

> Honour to bold Robin Hood,
> Sleeping in the underwood!
> Honour to Maid Marian,
> And to all the Sherwood-clan!
> Though their days have hurried by
> Let us two a burden try. (57–62)

Keats leaves a space for cultural cherishing of the past, though the nature and significance of that 'burden' is not here spelled out. But in the same letter another poem dealt with that issue. It is a striking index of Keats' fecundity in this period that Reynolds by the same post received 'Lines on the Mermaid Tavern', which appears to have been drafted some days previously: Keats said it was inspired by a meeting with friends at the Mermaid itself. But as Allott indicates in her edition (1970, pp. 305–6), it was copied out after 'Robin Hood' in the letter, and may have been adapted in accordance with thoughts developed there.

When praising the tavern's food he says, in the same spirit:

> . . . Oh, generous food,
> Dressed as though bold Robin Hood
> Would, with his Maid Marian,
> Sup and bowse from horn and can. (9–12)

Here, though, there is no sense of what Robin or Marian might think of the present; that seems a position previous to the thoughts aroused by Reynolds' sonnets, but also one consistent with the Robin Hood poem's final acceptance of the value of trying a 'burden'. 'To the Mermaid Tavern' imagines a word of cultural contact with the past, across time, in celebration, through the personalized imagination. When Reynolds suggested he should 'pledge' Robin Hood, Keats answered 'No', with his sense of historical and political reality aroused. But after relishing the myth in poetry, there seemed to him no compelling reason against following it up with the simpler cultural heritage position envisaged in 'Lines on the Mermaid Tavern'.

The withdrawal from political acuteness may seem disappointing, especially because of the incisive historical imagination of the poem: Dickstein called the end of 'Robin Hood' a feeble gesture' (1971, p. 161). That relative withdrawal from a political argument should, however, be placed in the context not only of Keats' youth and innate tendency towards idealism, against which at this period he clearly struggled more than many other poets with less gift than his for sensuous idealization; it should also be seen against the wider context of the limits of thoroughgoing radicalism among the leftish sympathisers of the day (Butler, 1981, p. 154).

However clear was Keats' ultimate withdrawal from the political implications of his insights, Reynolds evidently took his point, as there is a third sonnet, written in answer to Keats and published at the head of the other two when they appeared in *The Yellow Dwarf*, the radical journal run by John Hunt, brother to Leigh. The sonnets, and especially the third, may have largely disappeared from knowledge except as a footnote for Keats scholars, but they had more status in their day and entered the mainstream of nineteenth-century poetry – for example, they appeared printed as a single poem down one column of the Melbourne 'Woman's World' of 2 March 1887, between the gossip column and a fashion feature on beaded tulles.

This sonnet, written third but printed first in later versions, has picked up Keats' phrase 'forest days' as well as his sociohistorical positioning:

Robin, the outlaw! Is there not a mass
Of freedom in the name? It tells the story
Of clenched oaks, and branches bow'd and hoary,

Leaning in aged beauty o'er the grass –
Of daz'd smile on cheek of border lass.
Listening against some old gate at his strange story;
And of the dappled stag struck down and gory,
Lying with nostrils wide in green morass.
It tells a tale of forest days – of times
That would have been most precious unto thee;
Days of undying pastoral liberty;
Sweeter than music old of abbey chimes –
Sweet as the music of Shakespearean rhymes –
Days shadowy with the magic greenwood tree. (Barnard, 1989,
   pp. 193–4)

Reynolds now conceives of 'a mass of Freedom' and the value of 'undying pastoral liberty' – it almost sounds as if Keats has sent him back to re-read Ritson's Life. But though the sonnet opens with the public attack of a ballad, it returns to privacy. Reynolds cannot elude his own sensualizing eye: the cheek of the border lass and the tragic details of the dead stag are realized with almost pre-Raphaelite personalized realism. 'Pastoral liberty' here is not the directly emotive organicism touched on by Keats; it outlines rather the alienated pleasures that Williams called 'neo-pastoral,' and this poem, like Keats' own, winds its way towards a conclusion which is purely cultural, in no way social or political, in the final presentation of the 'magic greenwood tree'.

If Reynolds and Keats touch on and then elide the political implications of the Robin Hood past for the modernizing present, they do much more for both poetry and politics than other early verse versions of the hero. Peacock did write a fine song, 'Bold Robin' but it is no more than a lively fragment of the fuller consideration of the myth found in his novella *Maid Marian* (see pp. 181–6); the only other lyrical piece from this period is Bernard Barton's poem, which Gutch calls his 'dirge-like lines on the death of Robin Hood' (1847, II, p. 429). Barton was a Quaker, sympathetic to reform, and while he lacks both Keats' skill to energize the threatened plod of ballad metre and also his verbally lucid sensual perceptions, he does at least see the hero as inherently a social figure.

Published in Barton's collection *A New Year's Even and Other Poems* (1828), the poem is romantic in its immediacy and simplicity of language:

> His pulse was faint, his eye was dim
> And pale his brow of pride;
> He heeded not the monkish hymn
> They chaunted by his side.

Barton simply tells the story of Robin Hood's last arrow, and sees it, as most do, as a reconnection with the natural, when they lift the dying outlaw to shoot through the open 'casement':

> . . . where it fell they dug his grave,
> Beneath the greenwood tree;
> Meet resting-place for one so brave,
> So lawless, frank, and free.

This is not a complex poem; it simply states the naturalness of Robin's resistance, identifying no hostile force greater than the 'monkish'. This kind of enemy-free freedom has both an automatic beneficence and a distinctly blurred effect. It may be 'the truth of nature in modest guise' as Lamb said in a letter, feeling Barton to be a kindred calm, even downtrodden, spirit (ed. Talfourd, 1837, II, p. 75) but it is a reduction of Robin Hood the active outlaw to a passivity that is effectively as conservative as any social gentrification.

A different path to stasis was found by two poets who attempted to turn the newly available story materials into verse narrative. Leigh Hunt may well have seen Keats' 'Robin Hood' poem the day after it was written (Barnard, 1989, p. 198), but while he said his collection called *Foliage* (1818) was 'written in a greenwood mood', it did not mention the outlaw. However, he must have soon set to work on the topic, as early in 1820 he published in his magazine *The Indicator* a sequence of 'Ballads of Robin Hood' though they were not anthologized until *Stories in Verse* in 1855: the usual subtitle 'For Children' was not in the original version.

These poems are effectively the first part of an up-to-date Garland. The first and longest is 'Robin Hood a Child', then follows 'Robin Hood's Flight' which explains how he becomes an outlaw because of the malice of abbot and foresters whom he kills – Hunt has reworked 'Robin Hood's Progress to Nottingham' in an anti-clerical mood. 'Robin Hood an Outlaw' more briefly celebrates Robin's power without any narrative and then 'How Robin and his Outlaws Lived in the Woods' summarizes Robin's activities in pleasure and noble robbery, without following a particular story line.

It is a curiously unfocused sequence and should also be considered in the light of Butler's comments about the lack of radical follow-up by intellectuals in this period (see p. 165). Hunt was a man of impeccably reformist instincts, and he suffered for them like any Hollywood leftist, including a two-year jail sentence for publishing what was adjudged a seditious libel on the prince regent. Hunt's health was poor, his finances disastrous, but he stuck to his views. This itself is the theme that emerges from the third of the 'ballads', when after detailing those who flocked to Robin's side, Hunt cannot refrain from speaking of false friends:

> Lord! that in this life's dream
> Men should abandon one true thing,
> That would abide with them. (1855, p. 160)

Drifting quite away from his outlaw theme, he goes on to note the pressures laid on age and ill-health to conform with existing power-structures:

> We cannot bid our strength remain,
>   Our cheeks continue round;
> We cannot say to an aged back,
>   Stoop not towards the ground. (p. 160)

And the topic of 'Robin the Outlaw' leads Hunt finally to state his own tired but determined faith in a life if not outside the law, at least against bad law:

> But we can say *I* never will,
>   False world, be false for thee;
> And, oh Sound Truth and Old Regard,
>   Nothing shall part us three. (p. 160)

Moving as this is as a commentary on Hunt's personal courage, it is far from a dynamic realization of Robin Hood, either radical or conservative, and when he writes the last ballad, with the non-narrative title 'How Robin and his Outlaws Lived in the Woods', Hunt is in

fact constructing a position just as inherently conservative as that
Reynolds offered, and Keats at least half espoused:

> The horn was then their dinner-bell;
>> When, like princes of the wood,
> Under the state of summer trees,
>> Pure venison was their food. (p. 161)

But Hunt stiffens his sinews and does at least provide this sunshine
rebellion with a real enemy:

> Only upon the Normans proud,
>> And on their unjust store,
> He'd lay his fines of equity
>> For his merry men and the poor. (p. 162)

In that stronger vein Hunt's poetry gains edge, and he reverts in
metaphor at least to the ferocity of the opening ballad:

> A monk to him was a toad in the hole,
>> And a priest was a pig in grain,
> But a bishop was a baron of beef,
>> To cut and come again. (p. 163)

With a remarkable resemblance to Keats' challenging imagery of social
change Robin returns 'plump new coin' to the workers whose labour
was alienated to provide such luxuries:

> Well, ploughman, there's a sheaf of yours
>> Turn'd to yellow gold:
> And, miller, there's your last year's rent,
>> 'Twill wrap thee from the cold. (p. 164)

Finally, choosing a name suggestive of the Peasants' Revolt, Hunt
combines economic restitution with a more political version of merriness
than is usual:

> And you there, Wat of Herefordshire,
>> Who such a way have come,
> Get upon your land-tax, man,
>> And ride it merrily home. (p. 164)

Hunt's 'Ballads of Robin Hood' are both incomplete as a sequence and uneven in tone and poetic vitality; their influence has been entirely absent in later years, and what they show most, apart from the personal strains of Hunt's own life and moments of radical insight, is the difficulty faced by anyone trying to work the Robin Hood narratives now made available by Ritson into a sequence that was consistent and thematically focused – as was desirable in terms of the kinds of literary form that held prestige.

At least Hunt did publish his efforts, and they did have some political force. A writer from the other side of the political fence was even less successful in organizing the material and making his own political point. Robert Southey, poet laureate and Tory ideologue, was seen very much as an enemy by the romantic radicals and was frequently attacked – so much so that Butler (1981, p. 145) notes it as 'one of the injustices of literary history' that he seems a malicious buffoon, when the actually vicious Hazlitt and waspish Byron appear as heroes of liberalism.

Southey did not sparkle in the Robin Hood myth, quite failing to bring out the conservative potential that many other less assuming artists, like Munday and Parker, had contrived to produce. But it was not for lack of forethought and ambition. In 1823 Southey wrote to his sister Caroline about 'the memoranda which were made many years ago, for a poem upon Robin Hood'. He wanted to avoid a resemblance to *Ivanhoe*, first published in 1819, and was later to insist that their plan had been 'dreamt of ten years, at least, before Scott wrote any of his tale' (1847, p. xi). The scale was large: like a grandiose version of Hunt's garland-like structure, it was to be a full epic life, modelled it would seem on the French medieval romances Southey knew well – his introduction to the 1817 edition of Malory's *Le Morte Darthur* is a fine piece of scholarship, highly helpful to Tennyson in his own Arthurian work.

The result of the Southeys' 'memoranda', *Robin Hood: A Fragment*, was published in 1847. As an outlaw biography, what exists seems closer to *Parzifal* than Martin Parker. Part 1, by Southey himself, starts with the sombre wedding of Robin's parents, followed by his mother's death in childbirth. The father goes on crusade (Sir William FitzHood, Ritson with a difference) and in proper epic pre-tale mode, dies.

Of part 2, by Caroline, only a little survives. The child outlaw is found with his nurse:

> . . . the little Robert throve apace
> From baby-hood to boy-hood
> Making fast progress
> And of excellent parts
>   Gave promise (1847, p. 33)

The verse is as banal as its content, but elsewhere Caroline does manage an engaging jog-trot, a naively detailed engagement of the kind Reynolds kept at the distance of sensual perception:

> Whereas, strange to tell,
>   And true as strange,
> Let Hubert the old huntsman but fling down
> (Humouring the child)
>   His arrows all a-heap
> And lo! at a glance the tale was told,
>   True to a feather. (p. 34)

As this suggests, the problem of focus weighs heavily on Robin Hood poetry in the early nineteenth century, whether it is lyric manoeuvering for a viewpoint and appropriate theme as with Keats and Reynolds, or intended narrative failing to establish an appropriate structure and tone through the intractability of the material as connected narrative. The poetry wavers between emphatically moral and almost trivial, simply because the myth has been little more than an attitude and a context, filled out in various ways, from comic business to the polemics of gentrification.

Though post-Romantic poetry did not suit the outlaw myth, there were other new genres to engage with the material. Since the novel was the newly-powerful genre when Ritson published it would seem in retrospect likely that with all the narrative details now to hand, with a single hero as the obvious focal point, and the historical novel emerging through Edgeworth and Scott, Robin Hood must find a significant place in the new form. That this was far from the case indicates both the inherent difficulty of moulding the outlaw hero into a form highly committed to many kinds of constraint, thematic and aesthetic, and also the remarkable lack of individualistic potential in the figure, in spite of Ritson's organized biography. For all his accreted genteel respectability, Robin Hood proved a rough diamond among the novelistic jewellers.

5.3   Outlaws in the Novel

As far as prose was concerned, before the nineteenth century Robin
Hood was not a figure of fiction. Historians and antiquarians had used
prose to record references or speculate on the origins of Robin Hood
and there were in print and manuscript several prose accounts of the
hero, but verse was employed for fictional adventures of Robin Hood,
unless the genre was drama. The garland tradition of ballad collections
did continue into the nineteenth century but surviving examples are
either early – the last London publications are from 1810 and 1821
– or from more distant regions, like York (1809) and Derby (1850).
But even old-style garlands can derive from the new antiquarian tradition rather than from popular transmission at street level, like the
Life and Exploits from Halifax in 1858 which drew on Ritson as a
source. There were a few prose garlands, or chapbooks, in the old
colloquial style like that from Manchester in the 1840s, but most
fictional prose about the outlaw followed the new form of the novel,
and this generated a new range of problems. The rise of the novel, as
many a lecture and essay has pondered, in part depends on the notion
that a single life has sufficient interest to sustain a story, and this
raises the question how to construct a lengthy narrative in a way that
foregrounds and also develops in depth that individual figure.

These were problems that the Robin Hood myth had not encoun-
tered before. The Robin who plainly commands the *Gest* can do so offstage as well as on it, and his disseminated force in large part derives
from the generality, the non-individualism, of his personality. He
exemplifies a set of values, not a specific person of value. When a hero
– or a heroine as the novel was discovering – is foregrounded and
isolated, the central character's motives and meaning are put under
testing scrutiny. Moll's are enticingly obscure, Pamela's an object of
argument still, Tom Jones's masculinist enough to have been once
consoling and now, for many readers, discreditable. Robin Hood is,
like them, a single figure after whom a text can be credibly named,
but he lacks the inner tension and the personal trajectory which the
novel constructs as central.

There are, then, both political and formal reasons why Robin Hood
does not leap simply into the forefront of the novel, and indeed his
entry into the form is both sideways and uncertain. Even though the

recent Penguin Classics edition of *Ivanhoe* (1986) carries on the cover the central detail from Daniel Maclise's 'Robin Hood and his Merry Men', showing an ebullient Robin entertaining King Richard, who seems almost overpowered with delight (see illustration 10), the novel in fact marginalizes the outlaw hero. He is named 'Locksley' for most of the action, only identifying himself to the king as Robin Hood on p. 464; he does not indulge in any of his traditional adventures, though his ballad encounters with wealthy clerics and his exchanges with the king seem sources for the action of chapters 32–3 and 40–41. Locksley's major role is to act as military support and security officer to the forces of good throughout the story, especially at the siege of Torquilstone Castle where he plays the part of the gruff non-commissioned officer who really runs the show in a 1940s British war film. He takes control in a crisis and is rock steady, but he is also illiterate, and therefore not officer-material (pp. 260 and 264). As 'Robin' he disappears from the final sequence where Scott rather strangely consigns him back to the popular genres from which he has come:

> As for the rest of Robin Hood's career, as well as the tale of his treacherous death, they are to be found in those black-letter garlands, once sold at the low and easy rate of one halfpenny –
> Now cheaply purchased at their weight in gold. (p. 475)

Intriguingly, the passage both states the origin of Scott's knowledge of Robin Hood in literate scholarship and also can put a price on him in those cash terms which Keats and Hunt both deplored.

The image of gold itself will help to explain both the marginalization and the power of Locksley. But before considering that structure in detail, it is necessary to establish what the role of the outlaw is in *Ivanhoe*. Is he, as in *Edward I* or *Looke About You*, an instrumental character in a plot that is not basically that of the Robin Hood myth; or is the whole structure actually a displaced Robin Hood text, where the central elements of the outlaw myth have been retained but are located in a different leading character because Robin Hood carries a message inherently hostile to the interests of the producing and consuming context? That, as has been established previously, is the case with *Gamelyn, George a Greene*, and *As You Like It. Gamelyn, George a Green*, Orlando – or more precisely Rosalind – all bring into the

Illustration 10 Daniel Maclise's forest feast
(Courtesy Witt Library.)

anti-authority pattern a new value, symbolized and enacted by them; by supplanting the hero who bears the authority in this structure they enforce their own innovative validity as bearers of a new set of values which oust the unacceptably anti-authoritarian Robin Hood.

It is quite clear that *Ivanhoe* deals with a conflict against authority, that this is new in its terms and that it focuses on Ivanhoe himself. The major opposition is between Saxon and Norman; Scott acknowledged in the 'Author's Preface' (p. 537) his debt to Logan's *Runnamede* (1783) which opposed Saxon and Norman barons in the context of Magna Carta and also gave a powerful ideological account of British worldwide power. This island was presented as entirely benevolent, different from rival countries, those 'great destroyers of the globe' unlike which Britain:

> . . . fights and conquers in fair freedom's cause.
> Her song of victory the nations sing:
> Her triumphs are the triumphs of mankind. (p. 101)

On a local rather than global scale Scott clearly means, like Logan, 'to add the Patriot's to the Poet's fame' (1783, p. v) and intends his tale to be read through the conventions of patriotic history: in his 'dedicatory Epistle' he refers to Chaucer's time in militaristic fervour, as well as scholarly spelling, as 'the age of Cressy and Poictiers' (p. 528).

However internationally conservative, *Ivanhoe* is not bemused by noble blood. Athelstane is the grandest of the Saxons in lineage but has a definite strain of noble idiocy; Cedric may be the weightiest in terms of personality, but it is the youthful Wilfrid of Ivanhoe who carries the hopes of the true English, in large part, it seems, because he has mastered the art of chivalry in addition to his pure Saxon blood.

As a focus of nationalism, Ivanhoe has replaced the deeply localized Robin Hood – this is a grand version of the displacement perpetrated in *George a Greene*. But the model for the new hero is, not unironically, itself a French one. When Ivanhoe is wounded in the opening tournament, he fails to claim his prize, and suffers agonies, to be succoured by a young woman who loves him but whose feelings he cannot return. It is obvious that Scott is drawing on Malory's 'Knight of the Cart' sequence (*Works*, 1967, Bk. VII, pt 4). Much like Ritson's pro-English outlaw lord who carried a Norman name, Ivanhoe has the sophistication of chivalry but the virtue of simplicity.

Robin Hood was never a figure of mounted warfare and elevated chivalry was clearly central to Scott's idea of a medievalism grand enough to attract a substantial audience in this his first English historical novel. But other reasons may also have led to Scott's demotion of the hero. His comments elsewhere on Robin Hood suggest that he saw him as a distinctly anti-authoritarian figure and in that case may well have wanted to restrain the force of someone so inherently threatening from a Tory viewpoint. Scott knew Ritson's work well, and had little taste for the man or his politics. In his Dedicatory Epistle he likens Robin Hood to Rob Roy, but in the processes stresses the rebellious characteristics of both (p. 523), and most pertinently, when he wrote a note about Robin Hood and the May Games in *The Abbot* (1820, see 1898 ed.), he seemed uncomfortably aware of the character's propensity for what a Tory would see as public disorder: 'The representation of Robin Hood was the darling May game both in England and Scotland, and doubtless the favourite personification was often revived when the Abbot of Unreason, or other pretences of frolic, gave an unusual degree of licence' (p. 175).

This may imply that Robin was less licentious than the Abbot of Unreason, though in the text of *The Abbot* the May Games themselves are seen to be run by a group of serious troublemakers, and in some way through all of the presentation of Locksley in *Ivanhoe* there is an ominous aspect to his strength, with none of the playful or Trickster elements usually found in Robin Hood, even in his most gentrified form. This disturbing power comes across frequently in the novel, and may be the key to Robin's deliberate marginalization. Though Locksley is sidelined in the plot, when he appears he has great impact, at Torquilstone, in the encounters with the Black Knight – who is actually King Richard, his only equal in authority in the text. Scott seems almost to have an approach-avoidance relationship with Locksley's character, his power seeming too great for him to be handled too much.

Ivanhoe on the other hand, though ideologically the linchpin of the text, is in general passive, wordy and remarkably insignificant: for this reason it has proved impossible to make an interesting or dynamic version of this novel in film. Whereas the figure is actually based on Lancelot, it is his least active aspect that is employed; in Malory the great warrior can be very different and his most powerful appearance comes in the middle of the Tristram book when he is a wandering, bruising, mysterious black knight — just the role appropriated here for King Richard. The effect is that although Scott has structured the novel in correct aristocratic nationalist terms, the weight of feeling is with the yeoman class — just the group, of course, which figured so prominently in his series of Waverley novels outlining the forces of Scottish history. Locksley, it can be argued, is the undercover hero of the text, and so the Penguin Classics cover of *Ivanhoe* has its own outlaw-like air of covert rectitude.

But this effective doubling of the hero is not the only inherently anti-aristocratic movement in the novel. More striking to many readers, in the time of publication and ever since, is the doubling of the heroine. The lovely, fair, rich, passive Rowena, she of true lineage who must marry the hero, is found distinctly boring by many people when set against the dark, volatile, passionate, intelligent, active, vividly beautiful Rebecca, daughter of Isaac the moneylender of York.

He too has qualities. Abba Rubin has written about Isaac's treatment as 'the most realistically favourable portrait of a Jew that had yet appeared' (1984, p. 123). Although his physical features are grossly stereotypical and his greed is extreme, he is also depicted as enduring, determined, loyal to his friends, passionately devoted to his daughter and brave in her defence. She in particular is as dramatic and noble, not to mentioned as physically enchanting, a heroine as a text in this period is likely to have. Most people felt her a better match for Ivanhoe than Rowena, and, as Scott indicates in the last lines of the text, Ivanhoe apparently felt the same way: 'it would be inquiring too curiously to ask whether the recollection of Rebecca's beauty and magnanimity did not recur to his mind more frequently than the fair descendant of Alfred might altogether have approved' (p. 519).

The origin of this favourable treatment must to some degree be *Harrington*, by a writer Scott much admired, Maria Edgeworth (1817); an American reader, Rachel Mordecai, had written to complain of the stereotypical hostility shown to Jews in Edgeworth's previous work and in conscious atonement she wrote the story of a young man who is brought up to despise Jews, but grows to love a young Jewish woman — though, as in Scott's story, the plot contrives finally to sideline her and her attractions.

But there seems more power in Rebecca than mere deference to Edgeworth: the Jewish characters represent, as Rebecca wisely says at the end to Rowena, those people for whom wealth has been 'the source both of our strength and weakness' (p. 518). The description fits remarkably well the new urban bourgeoisie, among whom Scott has a major place and who, above all, found new value – and of course false consciousness – in his fables of antique honour. Just as Robin is a dangerously fascinating artisan, the Jews represent a social role equally close to, and ultimately rejected by, Scott himself. Underneath the simple nationalistic ideology surge the forces of actual social innovation, seen in the awesome competence of the artisan and yeoman classes symbolized by Locksley and also in the vulnerable, innovative and yet fascinating force of capital and those who lived by its systems, represented by figures like the Jews, characters who are outside the old world and are at once in part despicable, in part deeply impressive.

The political weight and historical detail of Scott's representation of the outlaw hero, however secondary his role might be, is substantially more serious than in a curious contemporary version called *Robin Hood: A Tale of the Olden Time* which not only has a Scott-like title but like many of the Waverley novels employs a pretended mediator, Goody Clifford, who is introduced to the author by an Oxford friend and offers to tell a tale handed down in the family about 'Robin Hood the freebooter' (Anon, 1819, I, p. 27). Though this was published in Edinburgh and is presumably a 'cover' for *Ivanhoe*, it uses history quite differently from Scott, emphasizing the emotive and sensational possibilities of medievalism by locating the sister of the heroine in a convent, beset with anxieties. Her name, Ruthinglenne, is one of the few memorable things about the book, in which Robin is both handsome and theatrical rather than formidable as Scott had made him: 'about twenty five years of age, tall, and elegantly formed; and of a countenance distinguished by an unusual degree of masculine beauty. His dress was green, like that of his companions; but it was enriched by a purple scarf thrown across his shoulders, and by a knot of plumes of a similar colour, which waved in his cap' (1819, I, p. 131). This cynosure plays a mostly passive role in the story and the book seems to have been completely forgotten by commentators on the tradition, which is perhaps unfair to its lively style and curiosity as a pastiche of period effects, too successfully Gothic to be historical.

Several other novels were soon to follow Scott, at some distance, in using Robin Hood as a functionary in a medieval romance. Lacking his powers of complex invention, the authors make the outlaw no more than a two-dimensional figure, without any underlying social meaning other than simple service to the overt ideology of the plot; as a result their efforts remain almost completely unknown.

Thomas Miller, the son of a carpenter and himself by trade a basket weaver, produced a range of largely fabricated historical novels, and early among them is *Royston Gower* (1838), where the central figure is a 'brave old soldier who had looked on death a thousand times without blenching' (p. 90). He is helped in his efforts to regain his rights and protect his family by a band of outlaws; their leader is a stern, tall man, not named until p. 85 as Robin Hood. The action is mostly a fanciful version of history with story-book characters like Hereward the Ready, Walter the One Handed and Druth the Dwarf. More familiar in the tradition is the presentation of a beautiful and peaceful greenwood in a style partly sensuous and partly stilted:

> The scene was worthy of the pencil of a Genius! The rays of the setting sun gilding the long forest glade, which was engirded with almost every variety of tree; some of them receiving a portion of the red golden light, while others were thrown into a greater depth of shadow, and contrasted beautifully with the deep yellow sunbeams which fell upon the greensward in unimaginable and picturesque forms. (p. 19)

The most unusual feature of the text, and one presumably related to Miller's humble social origins, is that he resists the notion of an aristocratic hero, whether a Robin or an Ivanhoe. Much of his work was popular in both audience and attitude – he went on to write volume V of Reynold's *Mysteries of London* – and he resolves his story in a spirit of lower-class resistance. In the final pages he tells us that the outlaws will all fight on against King John and he has Robin marrying the brave, brown-skinned Saxon peasant girl who drives her cattle into just that red-golden glade.

Miller is, by making Magna Carta the focus of his politics, typical of much nineteenth-century liberalism and reinterprets Robin Hood's connection with King John's period. But there was another time and place for the hero's reformist activity, and that was exemplified in a historically more sophisticated but rather less heart-warming novel by G.P.R. James, *Forest Days* (1843). His title suggests he had read Keats or Reynolds, or both; he had certainly studied an extensive article by 'G.F.' which appeared in the *London and Westminster Quarterly* in March 1840. It revived Bower's argument (though imputing it to Fordun) that Robin Hood had lived in the mid-thirteenth century, was active in support of Simon de Montfort's attempts to limit royal power, and after Evesham, where de Montfort died, Robin took to the forests as one of the 'disinherited' (see p. 36).

If there was anything in Victorian liberal hagiography which challenged Magna Carta as the symbol of reformist antiquity, it was the myth that de Montfort established a version of parliamentary democracy through the 'Provisions of Oxford' in 1258. As Earl of Leicester he had played an honest part anachronistically in *Looke About You*; he has more to do, and more accurately, in Victorian historical fiction.

Forest Days was written by the man identified by the *Dictionary of National Biography* as 'the most prolific and in some ways the most successful novelist of his time' (XXIX, 1892, pp. 308–10). James wrote a novel about every nine months for eighteen years; his hallmark was a welter of names and places that are identifiable with history as taught in Victorian schools, with some local empiricism to add conviction – he has, for example, one interesting paragraph about how the weather was warmer in the middle ages, and speculates if deforestation was a cause of the change (p. 146).

Within that structure of credibility James, like almost every writer on this topic from this time, offers the idea of greenwood as a refuge from modernity: 'Wide forests waved their green boughs over many of the richest manufacturing districts of Great Britain, and the lair of the fawn and the burrow of the coney were found, where now appear the fabric and the mill' (pp. 1–2). The story is a fabricated conflict within the family of the Earl of Ashby – Scott set his great joust at Ashby-de-la-Zouch, and this sort of name transference is very common in the chain of relationships to be found in recent Robin Hood publishing. In James, the heir of Ashby has the curious name Alured, though he is not identified as Saxon.

Robin Hood will help the wronged, whether they are village folk in need of a strong friend, or de Montfort requiring a leader for his archers at Evesham. The outlaw's full name is Robert of the Lees by Ely, something of a conflict of references. Presumably the knight of the *Gest* provides Lee, and Munday's hostile bishop gives Ely. Equally spurious is the grand feast in Sherwood where they enjoy bittern soup, peacock, 'many a roasted pig of tender age' (I, p. 183) and a baron of beef, but, being democrats, have no salt cellar to have to sit below.

G.P.R. James's Robin, though in touch with simple folk and a supporter of de Montfort the liberal peer, is no radical. Social disorder, he believes, is all a matter of poor leadership by those born to lead: 'Would that the nobles of England but consult the dictates of the heart, and keep that heart unhardened – would they remember the oath of their chivalry, and act as that oath requires, there would be less mourning in the land – there would be more happiness in the cottage, and some reverence for men in higher station' (I, pp. 275–6).

Yet this Robin is not entirely servile, and James, for all his conventionalist rhetoric, does finally recognize some political sting in the outlaw, though after a long period of inactivity. Eventually the villainous Richard of Ashby is caught, but pardoned by the king because of his nobility. As he moves off, a tall figure appears, and smoothly shoots dead the villain. Robin gnomically states: 'Whom kings spare, commons send to judgement' (III, p. 302).

That is presumably a defence of the House of Commons, its rights and history, and in that sense consistent with the role of Simon de Montfort in the story. Although Thackeray pilloried G.P.R. James for his servile rhetoric, renaming him as the mock-genteel 'G.P.R. Jeames' (*Dictionary of National Biography* 1888, p. 210), there is at least some sense of politics, however orderly and tame, in his version of the Scott tradition of patriotic rewriting and effective marginalizing of the outlaw myth.

Other novelists, however, made the hero and his narratives, as handed down by Ritson, central to their fiction, though this process too was beset with difficulties, unevenness of tone, and led to no acknowledged masterpieces of the literary canon. The first and in many ways the most interesting of these Robin Hood novelists is that intriguing figure Thomas Love Peacock. The Robin Hood material offered Peacock both the opportunity to speak in ways consistent with his reformist sentiments but also, because of its antiquity, to withdraw to a more generalist position in his satire. The text expresses so much that both fascinates and irritates about Peacock: the stylist's edge to the writing, the probing scepticism of the true radical, the almost angry rejection of simplicities right and left, clear signs of genuine sympathies for the oppressed: and yet at the same time an elusiveness on the practicalities of a liberal politics, a tendency to leave the scene with a perfectly judged exit line. Like Wilde, Peacock has all the talents of the major political writer and very little of the Shavian endurance needed for genuine impact, in either literature or politics. The elusive and anti-authoritarian hero of the outlaw myth meets in Peacock an author equally hard to pin down.

He was working on his version in 1818, but appears to have stopped to concentrate on writing materials which would gain him a lucrative place in the East India Company. He returned to the outlaw myth after *Ivanhoe* appeared, and *Maid Marian* was published in 1822. The relations between the two books are complicated. Peacock added a prefatory note to say 'This little work, with the exception of the three last chapters, was all written in the autumn of 1818.' The point would seem to be to distance himself from Scott, but Sir Henry Newbolt wrote a lengthy essay on this issue, suggesting three areas in which Peacock seemed to draw on *Ivanhoe* well before the last three chapters – the major siege (Torquilstone and Arlingford), and two treatments of the theme of a returning pilgrim, one relating to Ivanhoe and one to Peacock's Robin and Marian (1925, pp. 420–4). In fact as Dawson points out (1970, p. 229), a major siege is a basic incident of medievalizing stories, and the disguise of a pilgrim is an even more familiar motif. Dawson suggests a closer link with Gay's *The Beggar's Opera* and sees Robin's role as a version of Macheath (1970, p. 231), but this appears improbable. There seems no reason to think Peacock deliberately drew material from Scott, but it may well be that he revised his manuscript under the implicit influence of the sonorous simplicities of the wizard of the north – a point Newbolt picks up well (1925, p. 424).

The satirical thrust of *Maid Marian* is to criticize and undermine the growing use of medieval material as a conservative manoeuvre with, as Butler remarks 'its nostalgia for the feudal, Catholic, Middle Ages, and its mystique of monarchy' (1979, p. 140). Those like Scott who both used and loathed the appurtenances of the modern world were reconstructing a middle ages rich in organic simplicity and innate nobility, drawing their ideological support from Burke's *Reflections on the Revolution in France* and employing nationalism as a rationale for injustice. Peacock was less easy to bemuse with such legitimist versions of history than many of his contemporaries and wrote to Shelley in the spirit of Ritson about his work on *Maid Marian* (quoted in Butler, 1979, pp. 140–1): 'I am writing a comic Romance of the Twelfth Century, which I shall make the vehicle of much oblique satire of all the oppressions that are done under the sun.'

Peacock's innovation is not only political. He is the first, and in some ways the most successful, writer to rationalize the Robin Hood narrative materials into one structure. Essentially he fitted much of the ballad stories into the framework devised by Munday. His story opens, like The *Downfall*, with the wedding of Robin and Marian disrupted by the king's officials; Robin goes into outlaw exile; various adventures occur, many of them taken from Ritson's ballads, involving Robin, Marian, the Gamwell family and a decidedly upmarket version of Tuck, Brother Michael. Eventually King Richard does return and restores order but at the end Munday's sombre story is picked up as John is king at last and the forces of good take again to the forests.

The whole is shaped well, with a major central scene in the siege of Arlingford, Marian's home, and a mixture of brisk action, entertaining songs and Peacock's usual intermittent irony. It seems strange that the text has been so little known. Part of this must relate to Peacock's overall genre; it is hard to describe *Maid Marian* as a novel, because it is too short, and yet it is not really that elusive form, the novella. George Saintsbury understood the genre fully in his introduction to the Macmillan edition of 1895, which is still (an irony which Peacock would have enjoyed) in print when Saintsbury's name is the opposite of canonical among the newest modes of criticism. Partly through his extensive knowledge of French, partly through his pre-modern positioning, Saintsbury comprehends the essence of Peacock's mode. Like the work of the early Edgeworth, it is essentially that of the *contes moraux*, shortish stories told for their suggestive and exemplary powers, not for the value of their narratives as imitations of what readers might like to think of as life. Seen in this way *Maid Marian*, like Edgeworth's *Castle Rackrent*, is no longer a lightweight, with a comic scene or two, but a testing exploration of worlds and modes – again Butler has cleared the path for modern readers in her fine introduction to *Castle Rackrent* (Edgeworth, 1992).

The other reason why *Maid Marian* lacks recognition for its innovative reshaping of the Robin Hood tradition is, of course, that in the period of copyright and the rising evaluation in both critical and market terms of originality, no authors now follow the patterns of a previous text as closely as they once did. Authors, though aware of the convention in which they are working, seek to innovate for personal advantage; the natural process of reshaping in contemporary terms is accelerated by the need to be original in every conceivable way.

This seems especially unfortunate, because of Peacock's formal and thematic subtlety. Unlike Scott, Peacock makes Robin and Marian central to his story; but like him he is in no doubt that royal and aristocratic malice is the essential enemy. Scott and Peacock both pick up from Munday (the details seem drawn from Ritson's full account in his 'Notes and Illustrations') the idea that Prince John is Robin's true enemy and rival for Matilda/Marian. Scott sees this in terms of national politics while Peacock, like other romantics, inherently more concerned with the personal realization of forces, sees the loss of love as the major threat. In spite of this limitation Peacock is capable of a fully political statement, as when he reflects on the rights of possession in terms of equity rather than inheritance: 'What title had William of Normandy to England, that Robert of Locksley has not to merry Sherwood? William fought for his claim. So does Robin. With whom, both? With any that would or will dispute it' (p. 82).

The political and egalitarian edge of that analysis by Friar Michael is highly Ritsonesque (see p. 156), but Peacock's natural tendency is to work by mockery, as when he pictures Richard I as a conservative figure, but one not nearly as oppressive as his modern would-be imitators. The Lionheart is presented as:

> that most legitimate and most Christian king, Richard the First of England, the arch-crusader and anti-jacobin by excellence – the very type, flower, cream, pink, symbol and mirror of all the Holy Alliances that have ever existed on earth, excepting that he seasoned his superstition and love of conquest with a certain condiment of romantic generosity and chivalrous self-devotion, with which his imitators in all other points have found it convenient to dispense (p. 71).

Against that sense of a modified oppressiveness, the figures of real evil are, rather as in the early ballads, the officers of state, an abbot of Doncaster condensed from Munday's villains, and a sheriff called Sir Ralph de Montfaucon, whose name looks forward to the gothic menacers of Victorian melodrama as much as back to simple Norman bullying. Yet as Peacock's tone is always, with that of the *contes moraux*, one of bantering analysis rather than emotive re-creation, and both the politics and the oppressions seem less than serious. The contemporary world is only mentioned in jesting passing, as when the servile royal bard is called 'Harpiton', and this is given a footnote to indicate it comes from the Greek for 'a creeping thing' (p. 73): the reference to

Southey, poet laureate and himself a Robin Hood aspirant, is both clear and clearly trivializing.

Butler has discussed the ways in which this *conte* is distinctly less *moral* in modern terms than Peacock's other work. Although they resist bad government, Robin, Marian and Brother Michael are all no more than 'freedom loving individualists' (1979, p. 141), and like many highly conservative texts of the modern period, the only true positive is found in the greenwood as a natural refuge. Peacock takes the position of both Keats and G.P.R. James, but his typical verbal felicity seems to emphasize the unserious nature of the irony:

> So Robin and Marian dwelt and reigned in the forest, ranging the glades and greenwoods from the matins of the lark to the vespers of the nightingale, and administering natural justice according to Robin's ideas of rectifying the inequalities of human condition: raising genial dews from the bags of the rich and idle, and returning them in fertilising showers on the poor and industrious: an operation which more enlightened statesmen have happily reversed. (p. 126)

The image of 'fertilising showers' invokes a burlesquing interpretation, and makes Robin's idea of 'policing' with his lady as partner seem strange.

The title of the text itself is, of course, a significant moment, for all Peacock's ironies. Davenport had titled his play *King John and Matilda*, retaining one male figure first in the title after the death of the other and Drayton's poem of 1594 had in its title identified Matilda as Fitzwalter's daughter in a similarly enclosing manoeuvre. Peacock appears to be the first to use the woman's name as a title in anything approaching a serious account, though Frances Brooke's opera of 1788 had apparently been the absolute first. Yet here too, there are limits to Peacock's radicalism; Butler argues that this representation of Matilda/Marian is limited, being essentially that of a 'natural woman' and not in any significant way in tune with the feminist position already established, as Peacock quite well knew, by Mary Wollstonecraft. In the first half of the story, Butler says, the heroine's connotation 'is not much more than that of a nature-loving, emancipated girl' (1979, p. 152) and as she goes on she becomes more of a forest sprite than a figure of resistance. Peacock shows here another tendency to avoid reality through mysticism, a serious-minded parallel to his sliding into burlesque. Butler finds in much of his later work a tendency to move towards a form of mythical idealism quite outside politics. It makes the connection with the later 'Georgians' the more comprehensible, and even gives some context – if not credibility – to the end of Newbolt's essay on Peacock and Scott in which he appears to be suggesting in all seriousness that the two writers shared ideas by some kind of thought-transference (1925, pp. 427–32).

Whatever its sources, either inherent flippancy, political exhaustion, concern for a career, a mystical tendency, or perhaps just the difficulty of using the *conte moral* form for material that is basically politico-historical as it comes through Ritson's hands, Peacock's *Maid Marian* is, with all the enigmatic elusiveness characteristic of the Robin Hood tradition, both a remarkable achievement and also a dead end in literary terms. His ironic touch is too light for lesser writers to imitate, his structure too economically interlinked for the three-volume men to expand with success. There is no enduring model of a Robin Hood novel descending from Peacock, and those who continue to attempt the form produce new versions of narrative, each with its own innovations and eccentricities.

The most popular of all the fictional reworkings of the outlaw myth in the nineteenth century was by Pierce Egan the Younger, who shortly after the success of his first effort in medieval melodrama, *Wat Tyler*, produced *Robin Hood and Little John: or, The Merry Men of Sherwood Forest*, published in book form in 1840, and serialized from 1838. In *The Penny Dreadful* Peter Haining remarks on its enormous success, saying it sold 'hundreds of thousands' (1975, p. 24). It came out in forty-one parts, with a text reproduced in newsprint column form, with some of Egan's own naively effective pictures (see illustration 11).

This is the sort of book that people seem to have described rather than read. *The Dictionary of National Biography* found it an 'extravagant narrative of feudal society' (XVII, 1889, pp. 144–6) while J.C. Holt calls it the 'first comprehensive story deliberately written for children' (1982, p. 185). Neither of these opinions seems fully valid. Though normally bound in one volume and less than five hundred pages, the novel is very closely printed, and is actually of three-decker length, running to nearly four hundred thousand words, beyond most children then and now. The style itself might not be as off-putting to a literate child as length might be, but the size, the sombrely informative tone and the grisly nature of a good deal of the material, including some of the illustrations, indicates that a mass adult audience is the essential target, as Haining implies.

Illustration 11   Egan: Victorian melodrama
(From Egan, 1840 ed.; photo Lensmedia.)

To call it an 'extravagant narrative of feudal society' is closer to the theme, though extravagance really consists more in the book's free hand with fact and rapid lurching from topic to topic rather than any large-screen tendencies, and the account of feudalism is similarly without historical depth or analytic point. This is essentially what is nowadays called a 'page-turner', where the narrative races along from drama to drama, with many sudden turns of personality, character, fortune and passion. As in contemporary soap opera, an enormous quantity of material is consumed, and Egan's real extravagance is in the amount of incident he invents.

It is clear he is familiar with Ritson, and equally that he has disagreements with the radical anthologist; Ritson is in fact the first named character in the book, and one of the pleasures of reading Egan

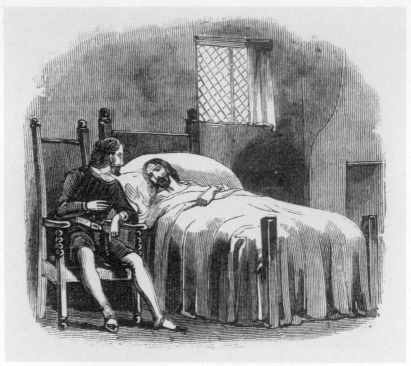

Illustration 12   Egan: Death of Ritson, the character
(From Egan, 1840 ed.; photo Lensmedia.)

is to find this is one Roger Ritson of Mansfield, a sneaking traitor to
his own kin who dies in confessional agony on page 40 (see illustration
12). The novel is rarely so amusing; it is replete with melodramatic
incident: the Earl of Huntingdon, connoisseurs of nineteenth-century
fiction will not be surprised to hear, has been misplaced as a baby; the
Gamwells of Gamwell Hall are pressed into narrative service to thicken
the plot over many pages, but Egan does not hesitate to cast his
novelistic net more widely. Lady Christabel, evidently from Coleridge,
is the vulnerable heroine of book I, but other characters have less clear
sources. This is certainly the first time the Robin Hood myth has
included a minor villain called Caspar Steinkopft who dies, in another
free-floating historical reference, with a King Harold-type arrow in his
eye (see illustration 13).

Scott's kind of nationalist narrative is taken as a model, with troop
movements and sieges, particularly one of Gamwell Hall, while the

Illustration 13   Egan: Caspar Steinkopft dies like King Harold
(From Egan, 1840 ed.; photo Lensmedia.)

narrative incident of many of the ballads is woven into what is effectively a skilful compilation of traditional materials and innovative
elements into a rapid, thrilling and frequently sensational sequence.
The whole is spiced by a martial version of the Gothic, which might
remind readers that Pierce Egan the Older had made his name as a
producer of boxing novels: 'Smarting with pain, foaming with rage, in
an agony of half-blindness from the effects of the blazing torch dashed
in his eyes, Lambie followed his men as they, not very conversant with
the path, pursued Robin' (p. 130).

The same kind of wordiness for affective purpose is at its most
breathless yet also its more decorous when Marian Clare is described
at the opening of book II:

her conduct to all, both her equals and inferiors, was of one uniform sweetness – a kindliness of bearing which created in the males a veneration even to the death, while the females felt not the jealousy which her superior attractions excited, because she never made them feel that such was the case; each year had more fully developed those beauties which, when she was first introduced to the acquaintance of our reader, were comparatively budding . . . (p. 167)

These 'budding' and 'superior attractions' are however not made as physically real as pain, death and exultation are among the men or indeed as is the male physical presence, especially that of Robin:

the beauty of the boy had settled into the handsome countenance of the man; his dark hazel eyes shone with brilliancy; his brown hair fell in curls upon his shoulders; his moustaches and beard of the same colour gave a manliness and nobility to his countenance, begetting great admiration, especially from the fair sex. (p. 256)

It is not that Egan does not know about the evaluative underpinning of the legend. There are Norman dogs in plenty to be fought, and as Robin dies he does reflect in briefly lyrical terms on the greenwood, but it is to tell John that this sylvan resource continues after he will be gone:

And you, Little John, thou noble heart, thou more than brother, grieve not that I have quitted the old green wood for ever; the birds will sing as sweetly, the sun shine as brightly; the flowers, the leaves, and the grass be as green, as fresh and fair, when I am gone, as ever, my old friend. (p. 473)

In mediating the heroism, the vigour, the tradition of Robin Hood in all its muddled modernity, to a huge audience, Egan has done it a major service, bringing forward the material so it can be plundered and renovated over and over again. None of the radical politics is present to any degree; but nor is any of the overt conservatism either. In the simplicity of this two-fisted egalitarianism we see a nineteenth-century version of the hectic transgressions and positive populism of the ancient play-game, and Egan consciously relates it to Keats' location of something of value in Robin Hood for the present: Egan ends by quoting the poem from 'Honour to the old bow-string' right through to 'Honour to Maid Marian And to all the Sherwood clan' (p. 474). Thereby he states his claim to be a broad-based part of the transmission of the outlaw tradition to the present, and not without some humble part of that honour himself.

A much less well-known, distinctly less coherent, but markedly more amusing version of the Robin Hood novel was produced as a conscious parallel to Egan's book by Joachim Stocqueler in 1849, entitled *Maid Marian or, the Forest Queen*. Stocqueler was an all-round writer; he spent the years from 1821 to 1841 in India and most of his work was in the military and historical mode, long forgotten now, but sympathetically represented in the somewhat historico-military *Dictionary of National Biography*. That ignores his contribution to the Robin Hood tradition, probably because it seemed less than serious (LIV, 1898, pp. 395–6). His novel combines elements from all the major sources: Marian Fitzwalter of Arlingford castle comes from Peacock, while Prince John's chief instrument of human evil is a Norman in the spirit of *Ivanhoe* but called, with a Stocquelerian sense of fun, Hugo Malair.

The air of the novel, like the plot, grows thicker. William of Goldsborough is a character here, that mysterious figure who is said to have shared a grave with Robin Hood; no doubt Stocqueler was up to glancing through Ritson for occasional stimulus. He may though, have simply invented Leila, a beautiful but seriously at risk foreign girl, and Minnie Eftskin, the witch who troubles the wood in a sub-Jonsonian sequence. Where Egan plodded on through combats and intricacies with determination rather than pleasure, Stocqueler cavorts among the source material. He creates a jester called Gurtha by condensing Scott's humorist Wamba with his heavyweight Saxon friend Gurth, and the ultimate in Norman villainy comes straight from the music hall stage, Baron de Berkem: in the author's mind and panto-mime tradition, it must be 'Burke'em', referring to the slang term for 'smother'.

The sheer lack of seriousness may have invalidated the text for some of the three-decker audience, though it is highly enlivening for modern readers. Scholar and joker, Stocqueler as a novelist is no more than a sport in the tradition, though one who reminds us aptly of the Victorian capacity for fun as well as sober self-consideration. But if his *Maid Marian* is no more than an entertaining interlude in the sequence of the myth, he has a good deal more significance when he turns his irreverence and capacity for ironic contemporaneity to a genre in which such impromptu commentary and transgressive wit is authentic, namely the Victorian equivalent of communal performance, the musical hall tradition and its most formal realization in pantomime.

5.4   ROBIN HOOD ON THE VICTORIAN STAGE

Stocqueler was one of the authors – and judging by his novel, his hand was a major one – of one of the earliest recorded Robin Hood pantomimes, *Robin Hood and Richard Coeur de Lion*, apparently from 1846. This marks the beginning of a new stage in the myth, or rather our knowledge of it, when fully popular material has been recorded, and so it is possible to trace how exotic and also contemporaneous this modern play-game actually was. It built upon a long-standing tradition. Robin Hood had appeared regularly on the musical stage throughout the eighteenth century and Peacock's *Maid Marian* was produced as a very successful opera in the year of publication in a version organised by J.R. Planché, skilfully cut down from Peacock's text and with his songs preserved. This is well organized and high style theatre compared with the random tendencies of the eighteenth century operas and especially with the riotous characteristics of the nineteenth-century pantomimes.

In a lighter vein, Stocqueler's pantomime offers literary reference, burlesque and a comic version of resistance:

> Scene II – Sherwood Forest – Distant Village. Outlaws lying about, stringing bows, and chatting.
> Nuthook, Scut, Kestrel.
> (As the curtain rises to the music of 'Those Evening Bells', the village clock strikes and curfew tolls.)
> *Nut.*   The curfew tolls the knell of parting day!
> *Scut.*   The curfew may be toll'd, we shan't obey!
> *Kest.*   The Norman, like his bell, is crack'd who thinks
> His chains shall ever come across *our* links. (pp. 4–5)

Jokes of this kind give way soon to a barrage of contemporary satire as Scarlet arrives with bad news:

Our greenwood home, old Sherwood Forest's sold.
Sold by Prince John, the imp of all impiety,
To the New Nottingham Building Society. (p. 6)

The beginnings of the present-day brickish suburb of Sherwood are
referred to; but in fiction there is release and Nymphaline, 'Fair sylvan
guardian of the outlaw race', promises to solve the problem.

Another threat appears: it is the sheriff, grandly named Front de
Boeuf a La Mode – Scott was rash enough to name his most thuggish
Norman Front de Boeuf and wit of the Stocqueler kind does not look
such gift jokes in the mouth. The villain, this sheriff-cum-property
developer, sings, to the popular tune 'Rumpti Bumpti':

Parlour, and kitchen, and drain,
With houses the forest we'll cram,
Opposition to me is quite vain,
I'll let the world know who I am! (p. 7)

The pantomime sweeps on, filled with comic action rather than
even a ludicrous form of satire; King Richard has a row in an inn
about the bill; Abd el-Kader, the Algerian nationalist hero known as
'The Old Man of the Mountain', plays a large role in a frenetic plot
of misunderstandings, songs and love affairs, including the extensive dalliance of Blondel, Richard's legendary minstrel with Almea,
another helpful nymph.

Little John and Robin appear and argue. But these are not the
touchily dangerous outlaws of 'Robin Hood and the Monk'; Little
John starts to cry. This strange turnabout is due more to Victorian
stage conventions than a farcical gender reversal: both Robin and John
are in this production played by women, as are Blondel and all the
outlaws. It is not uncommon for Robin to be the classic principal boy,
filling out the green tights to the customers' delight, but this turns
into something more like a girls' own adventure. Act 3 starts in
Fairyland, and then after rescuing King Richard from prison, a coali-
tion of king, heroic beauties and a few miscellaneous characters attack
in Birnam Wood style the sheriff turned developer and an army of
railway navvies. All ends in a flurry of stage mechanics, explosions,
spectacle and fairy splendour.

For the modern reader perhaps the best part, and the best reason to honour Stocqueler as a forgotten talent, is the first scene which, presumably anticipating the shape of the conclusion, owes much to *Macbeth*. Three authors enter a blasted theatrical heath. The third possesses a cheque cashable only if he has a script ready by Monday night. His fellow scribes of the stage agree to help, and they all invoke their art in richly comic style:

> *1st Auth.* Arise, thou charmed pot, which mortals call
> An inkstand – rise, with all thy magic gall!
> (Inkstand rises, with goose quill)
> *All*: Now round about the inkstand go,
> And in it our materials throw.
> *1st Auth.* Tale of Fairy – joke of Hood –
> Squibs from Punch, not understood –
> An evil Djinn, a host of sprites,
> By Coryphees in silken tights. (p. 2)

Finally, Mr Keeley, actor manager, whose wife will play Robin, appears, the author-wizards conclude their spell, and a stage direction to equal the hero's appearance in Lady Fitzwater's nightgown follows: 'A small Robin Hood rises from the inkstand.'

The figure keens 'Keeley! Keeley! Keeley!', hands him a manuscript, the inkstand sinks, and the pantomime begins. Its comedy, reference, and sheer vigour are in full contact with the tradition of reversal and misrule that was inherent to the earlier Robin Hood performance. We cannot know what has gone unrecorded or lost in the popular Robin Hood theatrical tradition; but when it first appears in print, in this version, it is obviously a lusty, strongly hybridized and deeply theatrical growth, without the conservative nationalism of Scott or the enfeebled gentrification of the earlier recorded theatrical tradition.

Other pantomimes lack the conscious flair of Stocqueler and the crazy speed of *Robin Hood and Richard Coeur de Lion* but they maintain the practice of localized carnival. In 1858 the Theatre Royal Manchester saw a 'New and Original Grand Christmas Pantomime' where both Marian and Robin were played by men but Alan by a woman – Jack a Lanthorn and the fairies provided other female attractions. This is more plot-oriented, though still highly innovative and especially notable for its costly and spectacular effects. They are not separate from the localized theme, however: Robin is captured by Auriferrissimus, the Gnome Demon, who is master of the mines, and whose name means 'most gold-bearing', a clear, if jocular, pointer to industrial profit.

There is much play with fire and forge, and obvious displacements of industrial imagery cluster around the Gnome Demon – this is inherently a Manchester kind of villainy. Robin's triumph, intriguingly, is associated with the good side of the industrial dialectic. Although Richard I appears as the Black Knight – Scott is one of the sources the anonymous author has rapidly traversed – the actual release from the dungeons is brought about by the Queen of Bowerland, leader of the fairies. That seems a fully pastoral and anti-mechanical form of magic, but as the play bill proclaims, her triumph is both realized by and celebrated in the height of contemporary theatrical machinery, technical marvels which fill up much of the time spent in the performance – the script is short and there are no more songs than usual to occupy the time. The change of scene to fairyland is a classic transformation, with gauzes flying in, lighting changing from front to back, and heavy multiple flats being swiftly flicked across from castle to forest under the cover of flashes, explosions and cymbal clashes. The triumphant release is celebrated with 'The Peal of Cast Steel Bells' from Sheffield, which, for added technological impact, are 'Rung by the Patent Machinery of Jones Pendleton, Manchester'. In the same spirit the grand finale is a miracle of culturally transplanting the natural, a set-piece that remains popular in mass-audience theatre to this day, namely the water spectacle. 'A Fountain of Real Water' fills the stage; music, lights, nymphs in flimsy dampened clothing, all celebrate climactically in modern form the quite ancient significance of Robin Hood.

Some of these pantomimes seem, from this distance, simply silly; in 1871 E.L. Blanchard went to see *Robin Hood, or The Maid that was Arch and the Youth that was Archer* (Scott and Howard, 1891, II, p. 185). But then terrible puns played an important and inherently subversive role in the discourse of Victorian popular art. The *dramatis personae* page of many of the Robin Hood pantomimes is a mass of highly-contrived verbal comedy, even outdoing Stocqueler's playfulness. A prime example is from Sir Francis Burnand's *Robin Hood or the Forester's Fate* (1862), a fairly conventional run-through of events derived from Peacock and Egan, with extraordinary efforts made to contrive some verbal humour (emphasis original):

QUEEN MAB (who I'*m ab*by to say will appear in her Draytonian chariot) . . .   Miss Newham

ROBERT, EARL OF HUNTINGDON (who, *Early* in the piece, appears as *a peer*, and subsequently as Robin Hood . . .)   Miss Latimer

SHERIFF OF NOTTINGHAM (not the same Sheriff as the one in the Robin Hood ballads, as this is the Sheriff of *Not-in-'em'* – this character, being a *She*-riff, is played by . . .)   Mrs W.S. Emden

Robin Hood clearly filled a role in comic theatre throughout the century, and not all the farce was scripted: all the long tradition of performance would have been alive in vigorous visual form in 1888, when Dan Leno played the Baroness in a show rejoicing in the name *The Babes in the Wood and Robin Hood and his Merry Men and Harlequin Who Killed Cock Robin*. (Disher, 1925, p. 176) The comic and eclectic tradition was widespread: for Christmas 1858, at the height of the roaring days of the gold rush, the Theatre Royal, Melbourne, offered *Harlequin Robin Hood, or The Bold Hunters of Sherwood and the Fairy Localotta*, which according to *Bell's Life* (1.1.59) included both attacks on the government and an Aboriginal corroboree.

But if the material on offer tended to range from pompous melo-drama to satirical hilarity, the motifs of nobility and nationalism that had been re-established in the myth by the likes of Scott and Keats, did also come through in nineteenth-century theatre. John Oxenford's *Robin Hood: An Opera* of 1860, with music by 'Professor' G.A. MacFarren took a patriotic position with two of the first three songs being 'Englishmen by birth are free' and 'Confusion to the Norman'. Such chauvinism indicates the full development of the nationalistic dragon's teeth sown by Scott; radical ideas of the Norman Yoke have been turned into something close to fascism in a song like:

> Our fathers were of Saxon race,
> With Hengist here they came;
> And when they found this resting-place,
> They lit a sacred flame.
> It did not blaze from altar or from pyre;
> But burning in the English heart is still that deathless fire.

Against the excesses of the mid-century fun merchants and the strains of jingoist frenzy, the more sober delicacies of the later nineteenth-century Robin Hood theatre seem at least acceptable, if on the tame side. Reginald De Koven's *Robin Hood* was highly successful in 1890 and was produced in London as *Maid Marian* (perhaps because Robin Hood was so common a title by then: more confusingly yet, De Koven wrote a follow-up which in America was called *Maid Marian*, but seems not to have been produced in England). The plot was simple, emphasising a love-triangle with Guy of Gisborne as Robin's eventually violent rival for Marian. From the traditions of popular romance, this neat condensation of the old conflicts focused everything on hero, heroine and feeling, and was to be a dominant structural idea in later versions, though sometimes it was the sheriff, rather than Sir Guy, who played the moustache-twirling villain.

De Koven's version, especially the song 'O Precious One', was a national success, and no doubt this prepared the way, in America at least, for the version that rounds off the tradition of nineteenth-century Robin Hood theatre, Tennyson's *The Foresters*. This play with music combines much of the early material, has conscious links with Keats and the romantic representation of Robin Hood, and is also a work which appears to have been unfairly denigrated.

Apart from Tennyson's own relative rejection in this century and the present disregard for poetic drama, there has been special feeling against the play, and even those who still admire Tennyson's drama feel this is his weakest work. Historically it has a negative context in England as Irving, who commissioned it, refused to mount a production in 1881 (Martin, 1980, p. 525). It was produced with great success in America just before Tennyson's death in 1892, with music by Sir Arthur Sullivan, and a lavish production by Augustin Daly (Eidson, 1964). But the English production shortly afterwards was a distinct failure, and a typical modern assessment is that by Jerome Buckley, who feels the play exhibits 'story-book naiveté' and 'the sentiment and derring-do are incredibly juvenile' (1960, p. 209). Yet to turn to the play expecting an inert sequence of nebulous nationalism – the image given by commentators – is to be positioned for surprise. It seems, rather, that in this play Tennyson sought honestly, and with some success, to represent the popular and even political elements of the tradition, in a way which was neither to Irving's grandiose taste nor in tune with the lyrical and elitist sympathies of many of the laureate's later critics.

The play certainly lacks the sensual edge and the tense introspection of Tennyson's powerful earlier poetry, from *In Memoriam* to *The Idylls of the King*, and it lacks the drive that authors as varied as Scott, Peacock and the pantomime writers brought to the myth, but there are also solid virtues. As usual with Tennyson, there are many signs of intelligent scholarly work behind its creation: he is only matched by Peacock as an intelligent combiner of earlier materials, bringing together the *Gest*, Munday, and a number of ballads. Tennyson follows and amplifies with some skill the Peacock-Planché separation of the two stages of the Sir Richard Lee story from the *Gest* to provide the opening and the climax of his drama.

The underlying politics of the play are basically the national liberalism developed in the popular novels, which absorbed and deflected Ritson's radical edge – though the *People's Journal* of 1846 reprinted the *Gest* in its first issues as an ancient validation for modern populism. Tennyson's position was less divisive: he summed it up as: 'I have sketched the state of the people in another great transition period of the making of England, when the barons sided with the people and eventually won for them the Magna Carta' (H. Tennyson, 1897, II, p. 173).

Baron Tennyson has no difficulty in siding with both lords and people. Vice, though, was, as elsewhere in his work and his period, identified more with sexual liberty than political oppression; Robin's loathing of Prince John is 'for his want of chivalry' as one

> . . . that can pluck the flower of maidenhood
> From off the stalk and trample it
> And boast that he hath trampled it (1965, I. 2, p. 573)

Equally characteristic of Tennyson's attitudes is that the hero expects to rule in the forest; after he is attainted by Prince John, Tuck tells him of the 'good fellows' in 'merry Sherwood' and Robin replies immediately 'Have they no leader?' (p. 756, I. 3). With hierarchy goes national pride. The opening view of these 'stout hearts' who 'hold by Richard' is simplistically patriotic, though not as crassly so as in Oxenford's opera. The Foresters sing, 'as they disperse to their work':

> There is no land like England
> Where'er the light of day be;
> There are no hearts like English hearts
> Such hearts of oak they be.

There is no land like England
Where'er the light of day be;
There are no men like Englishmen
So tall and bold they be. (II. i, p. 757)

Tennyson, perhaps as a way of rationalizing such naivety, makes Robin's new location closer not to political liberty but the freedom of heaven, in one of the speeches that might remind readers this is indeed the author who negotiated with real flair and fine poetry the ideological complexities of the Grail story and the passing of Arthur. Robin says he is

> ... all the better
For this free forest-life, for while I sat
Among my thralls in my baronial hall
The groining hid the heavens; but since I breathed,
A houseless head beneath the sun and stars,
The soul of the woods hath stricken thro' my blood,
The love of freedom, the desire of God,
The hope of larger life hereafter, more
Tenfold than under roof. (II. i, p. 757)

However enticing as idealism, this is hardly the stuff of potent theatre, and for most of the rest of the play Tennyson searches for action that will detain the audience's attention. In the following sequence he chooses sheer comedy, taking from 'Robin Hood and the Bishop' the idea of Robin posing as an old woman, and inventing a ludicrous exchange between Robin and Prince John, which lacks both the business and the grotesquerie that the likes of Stocqueler and Dan Leno would have worked up for the occasion.

Ill-judged as some of his material might be, Tennyson sticks to his task and invents moments of high conservatism, as when Robin actually robs some sturdy beggars who do not deserve his charity (borrowed from the ballad of 'Little John a Begging'), and then, in a thoroughly bourgeois-pleasing sequence, treats generously a pair of 'Citizens' visiting Nottingham on entrepreneurial business. Such innovation aside, the neatness of this Robin Hood re-creation comes in part from its full reliance on sources. The lack of any directly contemporary material in the last scenes does remove the conservative gaucheries to which Tennyson was prone, as in 'Locksley Hall: Sixty Years After', but

equally makes the text somewhat lifeless. *The Foresters* only moves again
with influential vigour when at the end both Marian and Robin speak of
a surviving value in the land, one not realized now in terms of thumping
patriotic songs, but a patriotism displaced into the environment.

Reynolds uncertainly and Keats with cool-eyed passion were the
first to construct the beginning of a heritage realm of value, a site of
'undying pastoral liberty'. It was a new form of what Raymond Williams
terms 'neo-pastoralism' (see p. 134), a world without any of the messi-
ness of real people and actual history, a structure at the core of the
Robin Hood myth for their times. Developing the position fully,
Tennyson first puts into potent language the essence of the greenwood
myth where something that can pass for English immortality and
permanence may be found. True to the *Gest* the scholarly Tennyson
makes Robin move, reluctantly, to the king's court. But his heart, and
his hope, remains in the forest in a sequence whose optimism is made
persuasively uncertain by Tennyson's easy skill with the run-on line:

> And we must hence to the King's court. I trust
> We shall return to the wood. Meanwhile, farewell
> Old friends, old patriarch oaks. A thousand winters
> Will strip you bare as death, a thousand summers
> Robe you life-green again. *You* seem, as it were,
> Immortal, and we mortal. How few Junes
> Will heat our pulses quicker! How few frosts
> Will chill the hearts that beat for Robin Hood. (IV, p. 782)

Finally Marian speaks the same theme in less nervous mode and
with a lyrical clarity that had a special impact on poets to come:

> And yet I think these oaks at dawn and even,
> Or in the balmy breathings of the night,
> Will whisper evermore of Robin Hood. (IV, p. 782)

She does claim that there are social benefits in their story:

> We leave but happy memories to the forest.
> We deal in the wild justice of the woods.
> All those poor serfs whom we have served will bless us,
> All those pale mouths which we have fed will praise. (IV, p. 782)

But this has an automatic feeling compared to the mystic timelessness in which she feels they participate:

> And here perhaps a hundred years away
> Some hunter in day-dreams or half asleep
> Will hear our arrows whizzing overhead,
> And catch the winding of a phantom horn. (IV, p. 782)

The concept of a timeless value connected with moral rectitude,
English triumphal history and the beauty of the countryside is a
potent notion towards the troubled end of the nineteenth century.
What Tennyson has finally shaped in *The Foresters* is the scheme for
the 'Georgian' representation of the outlaw, more or less fully formed.

Intriguing, uneven, both triumphant and disastrous, *The Foresters*
has all the enigmatic attributes of Robin Hood literature; and unlike
many other of the fascinating dead ends of the tradition, it did have
a considerable afterlife in what poets and dramatists made of the outlaw
myth before and after the Great War. But that was not only because
of Tennyson's transmission; it was also to do with something that in
part informed his text but found its strongest realization elsewhere,
the development of Robin Hood stories as part of the new flood of
instructional and moralizing material in the booming industry of
secondary education, a phenomenon which needs to be explored before
the Robin Hood renaissance of the 'Georgian' period can be outlined.

5.5   HERITAGE, EDUCATION AND 'GEORGIAN' POETRY

As with many other aspects of culture in early periods (like clothing
and decorum for example) the Robin Hood myth before recent times
did not have separate categories for children and adults. While there
can be no doubt that children long enjoyed the outlaw story, it was
not part of a separated infantile library. The Duchess of Newcastle,
now better known as Margaret Cavendish, the Restoration poet, is said
to have read as a child 'horn books, then Aesop's fables, Robin Hood,
Cervantes and the Bible' (Jones, 1988, p. 10). Much of this lack of
generic definition remains into at least the early nineteenth century.
As has been argued above, Pierce Egan was not primarily a children's
writer, in spite of the naivety of his procedures, and the simplistic

The·Merry·Friar·carrieth·
Robin·acrofs·the·Water:·

Illustration 14   Howard Pyle's merry outlaw
(Courtesy British Library.)

nature of much in the Robin Hood pantomimes seems to have been
directed to the puerile of all ages. But clear signs of a category separation
are becoming visible by the mid-century: in 1851 'H. Weir' produced
a Robin Hood text in a series named 'Treasury of Pleasure books for
Young and Old' – the title is cautious, hedging its bets on the development of a small readers' market. The publisher was Cundall and

Addley, and John Cundall, writing as 'Stephen Percy' had been quickly in print for Bohn with *Robin Hood and his Merry Foresters*, a cover version of Egan's novel in 1840.

According to the records in J.H. Gable's very full bibliography of Robin Hood materials up to 1935 (1939), Robin Hood collections for children only begin to gather in numbers in the last quarter of the century. George Emmett's *Robin Hood and the Outlaws of Sherwood Forest* appeared in 1869 in 'The Young Englishman's Edition'. In about 1870 (these ephemeral texts often carried no dates and left no traces elsewhere) 'Forest Ranger' wrote a series called *Outlaws of Sherwood Forest* in forty numbers at eightpence each. 1865 had seen a *Life and Adventures of Robin Hood* by Richard Lewis, writing under the nursery-tale name of 'Peter Porrence', with seventy pages at sixpence, and more of these were serialized in *Boys' Own Tales* in 1878 as the youth literary market began to organize its production and delineate itself from the wide-ranging 'simple reading' materials which, in a period where many were barely literate, might include many adults.

It is intriguing to note that America is nearly as productive of such material as Britain: the anonymous *Robin the Bold* of 1876 was co-published by Pott in New York and Young in London, and fifty cents was the US price. Tennyson's New York success was obviously based on widespread familiarity with the materials (as well as De Koven as precursor), especially from what is still the classic anthology of Robin Hood stories for children, which was the work of a young American illustrator, Howard Pyle, whose compilation *The Merry Adventures of Robin Hood of Great Renown in Nottinghamshire* was in 1883 published by Scribners in America and Sampson Low of London, and at $4.50 was a full-scale production, a volume to be cherished rather than an easily damaged throwaway pamphlet.

Pyle was a Quaker, not the first or last of his persuasion to have an interest in the stubborn reformist strength of the outlaw, and while he took the most trouble over his bold wood-cut style of illustration (see illustration 14), which shows the clear influence of William Morris, who admired their 'decorative craftsmanship' (Nesbitt, 1966, p. 35), he also assembled a well-written and lucidly structured text; his mother owned a copy of Percy's *Reliques* and his biographer, Elizabeth Nesbitt, says 'he steeped himself in the original sources of the Robin Hood stories, the old ballads' (1966, p. 41). She judged that he combined a 'slightly archaic flavour' in the language with much more modern-seeming kinds of 'sharply delineated physical descriptions and character portrayals of Robin Hood and his men, each of them strongly individualized' (1966, p. 41).

Pyle's text is still in print; his strong, dramatic yet old-world illustrations have been a major attraction, but his confident, jovial style has a Chestertonian ring that has seemed both manly and good-humoured to those who value such qualities: 'Here is a stout lusty fellow with a quick temper, yet none so ill for all that, who goes by the name of Henry II. Here is a fair, gentle lady before whom all the others bow and call her Queen Eleanor' (1883, p. 3). The structure is as appealingly simple as the analysis; Pyle describes his outlaws as: 'all living the merriest of merry lives, and all bound together by nothing but a few odd strands of certain old ballads . . . which draw these jocund fellows here and there, singing as they go' (p. 4).

Pictures, text and structure have a bracing simplicity and naive strength. But a subtler reason for success lies in the technique of narration: he is the first to realize in emphatically spare style a recounting of the stories based on character in action, that is, a novel-like relating of the material. And he did this without encumbering himself with the intractable problem of reshaping this compartmentalized and action-based narrative into the deeply-focused moralized contours of the novel. No doubt that was a matter of good fortune for Pyle: at the age of thirty and as an occasional producer of text for his illustrations, he was unlikely to be a masterful narrative theorist. But then most of the major successes in the Robin Hood tradition have come from just such technically-skilled and unassuming artists, from the composer of 'Robin Hood and the Monk' right through to the most memorable of the film-makers.

Apart from good luck and authentic skills with his form, Pyle had something else to add, a theme that he touched on with the right amount of delicacy, where Tennyson and G.P.R. James had laid too heavy a stress. He threaded through text and illustrations aspects of that heritage and greenwood value that Reynolds and Keats had been the first to detect in the stories, and he did that not only with deft persuasion, but also at a time when those very values were taking on a meaning of much greater significance than they had borne in the time of the personal and youthful sensitivities of the romantic 'co-scribblers', Reynolds and Keats. Pyle was the first to make Robin Hood a part of the 'English heritage' mainstream, when that set of values was new, potent, and about to claim a place in the massively-expanding domain of the educational industry.

As Brian Doyle has outlined in *English and Englishness* (1989), a number of social and cultural factors came together in the late nineteenth century. One was the observed decline in religious attendance and so in the power of religious feeling as a means of social control – Matthew Arnold is the classical source on this in *Culture and Anarchy* (1869) and he also was a major theorist in planning to deploy cultural systems to operate with the constraining power of religious sanctions in the past. At the same time as the vote was extended through the male population and higher levels of basic skills were being required in the workforce, the provision of education beyond elementary literacy and numeracy became a widespread and increasing need. In the first stages this was mass primary education, state-provided; but even before secondary education was launched on a widespread scale it was necessary to increase massively the provision for teacher education simply to staff the new primary schools throughout the growing cities of industrialized Britain.

This education could no longer follow the model of elite male instruction in Latin and Greek – the subject was too hard, teachers were too slow to train and it was felt that such a mandarin discipline was not appropriate for the basically female personnel who were, rather like nurses, to make the massed youth of Britain suitable for a society resonant with docile health. The new or 'modern' subjects were above all history, geography and English, but only the last needed curricular clarification; the material of history was already largely available in the description of the deeds and processes of the powerful through the ages, and imperial considerations provided most of the facts thought necessary for geography.

English literature however had not been an instructional subject before, and whereas the universities went through various contortions to try and make it seem like Latin and Greek – mostly through philology, source studies and an emphasis on early literature – in the schools not much was attempted beyond a reading of classic literary texts in heavily diluted form. None of those forces themselves brought Robin Hood onto the school stage, but they were the context in which such 'old world' material could be adapted for widespread use.

The trigger to a remarkable expansion of Robin Hood anthologies, appreciations and recreations lay in the development in the same period of a sense that an essential source of value, at once nationalistic, democratic and vaguely humanist, lay in the English heritage. Here was a setting to generate a sense that the country had once been great and powerful in simpler and more admirable ways than the modern world permitted, and that this force could be communed with through the landscape, ancient monuments, noble buildings and literary realizations of that past world. The 'heritage' movement was anti-urban, anti-modern and in some sense anti-democratic; however much it also made available for widespread consumption works of high cultural value, there was an underlying intention of social control, civilizing the mob through art.

The Tate Gallery was founded in 1897 to exhibit the finest of English art and so create a domain of patriotic value that could quite obscure the conflicts of history, including investments in slave-worked estates like some of those which had generated the Tate fortune. The National Trust was started in 1895, providing support, maintenance and restricted public entry to the great houses and castles and churches which had in the past been built to exclude and dominate many sectors of the public, whose successors were now invited to share in this new cultural domain of national value. Everyman's Library, less directly tied to the oppressions of power, began in 1906 to print the best of English writing, with occasional non-English parallels thrown in, and so helped to shape at the level of thought a whole image of national achievement, and made it available in the education industry.

Heritage replaced religion for many as a value, and also it both focused and emphasized the newly strident nationalism that could assuage some of the fears that arose from international threats to Britain's place in the international market. Englishness was constructed as an instrument of eliding conflicts at home and abroad, just as chivalry or bourgeois morality had in other times and genres – romance and novel especially – been ways of resolving social and ideological conflicts.

In this context Robin Hood material began to emerge more strongly than before. It included a major French contribution from an earlier period. The two outlaw novels attributed to Alexandre Dumas the Elder had remained untranslated since 1872–3, but *Robin Hood: Prince of Thieves* appeared in 1903 and the shorter *Robin Hood: The Outlaw* in the same year. The first began with a brief and quasi-scholarly preface borrowed from Scott's fiction and using Ritson through the mediation of Augustin Thierry (1825) and Edmond Barry (1832), two French cultural historians who employed Robin Hood as a suitably anti-aristocratic model of liberal reform during the period of anti-royal bourgeois ascendancy. But a glance at the text indicates the over-whelming influence of Egan, Dumas's avatar in the English pulp fiction market. Here again are Margaret and Gilbert Head, foster parents to the dispossessed infant; Ritson the character has now become gallicized as Roland but remains villainous. The skilled narrative technician who wrote this, whether Dumas or not, has great use for the complicated relations of the Gamwell clan, and it is a pleasure to rendezvous again with Egan's finest villain in the modest alias of Gaspard Steinkorf.

The French texts provide general assurance of the value to be found in the English past; a much more specific, not to say crass, version is provided in the Aldine produced series 'The Robin Hood Library' in which between 1901 and 1906 forty-six pamphlets appeared in thirty-two page form at twopence each. Alfred C. Burrage wrote the first and many others. In the medieval forest, with much use of words like 'immense' and 'vast', among 'bubbling streams' and 'the fragrance of flowers', acts brave Robin, son of a Franklin, yet evidently having had a classical education – he owns two hounds called Hector and Vulcan. He also has learnt how to put a woman in her place: Marian is worried that something has happened to Will but Robin responds firmly: 'Tush! Tush! You think like a woman and talk like a woman' (1901, I, p. 3).

So masculine a hero faces without flinching what he calls 'the biting steel of these Norman ghouls' (I, p. 5) and incites his 'henchmen' to use the war-cry which provides the title for this issue: 'Sweet Liberty or Death' (I, p. 7). In spite of this tub-thumping tone, cultural heritage is not forgotten; apart from the flowers and stream there is mystic history, as when Robin escapes to Robin Hood's Cavern 'from which, perchance, the bearded Druids had culled the mystic mistletoe with silver sickles beneath the light of the moon' (I, p. 5). The cynical scholar may, perchance, smile at this melodramatic posturing; yet it is a short journey from here to the cultural chauvinism of Sir Henry Newbolt's 1917 volume *The Book of the Happy Warrior* which extols pleasure in war and an acculturated form of bloodlust through a series of hero stories, among whom Robin Hood has a place. The dedication, in that sombre year, is, chillingly, 'To All Boys'.

Brian Doyle speaks of the constrictions of mentality brought about by the curriculum of English, in which what seem like an innocent aestheticism and a nostalgic love of country are in fact shaped into a repressive structure of political certainties (1989, pp. 21–3). Robin Hood has been in the past at the service of bodies as conservative as the Catholic church, reforming zealots, the aristocracy, even Munday's London aldermen and Scott's proto-nationalists. Now the outlaw myth is retold in child-sized chunks as part of the creation of a controlling curriculum for a modern secular state seeking orderly and tractable citizens.

Should that interpretation seem strained, it would be instructive to read the essay on Robin Hood published in 1892 by W.C. Hazlitt in *Tales and Legends of National Origin*, a set of essays on English mythology (and published by the remarkably mythological-sounding firm Swann and Sonnenschein of London). The author was the grandson of the essayist who had brought his considerable intellect and sharp tongue to bear on conservative targets of the early nineteenth century, especially the unfortunate laureate and failed Robin Hood writer Robert Southey.

Hazlitt the younger moved immediately to identify heritage as the issue, and one firmly and metaphorically linked to property: Robin's is 'an imperishable name, one which is part of our history and our birthright' (1892, p. 250). After sketching in a historical biography rich with individualist empiricism, Hazlitt dealt firmly with the possible embarrassment of what seemed like ancient leftism: 'If in his political sentiments and principles Robin leaned in the direction of socialism, it must be remembered that it was a very different state of parties, of which he was a witness and contemporary, from that which at present has to reckon with the socialist as a problem and a danger' (1892, pp. 251–2).

Robin would, given his chance of living in the present, clearly be a national liberal:

The Barnsdale outlaw saw before his eyes only two main orders or ranks of life, the patricians and plebeians. The great Middle Class, which has made England what it is, and which can alone maintain us in our position as a State, could be hardly yet said to exist as a mature potential future; and Robin laid down for himself the rule and maxim, not that all were equally entitled to share the national lands and wealth, but that the circumstance justified him in holding the balance between those who were too rich and those who were too poor. (1892, p. 252)

Liberal conservatism had, in cultural terms, appropriated to itself the art of the past as well as the profit of the present, and used the former to validate the latter. Robin Hood the right wing liberal patriot was born fully armed.

The flood of educational texts representing Robin in this way is remarkable. Gable's bibliography records between 1900 and 1935 many items that appear to be oriented towards schools and younger people's instructional usage, and not only in Britain. Against the fifty-three British titles in this category, Gable gives the strikingly high figure of forty-two in the USA. At this time, East Coast mandarin culture, as Mark Twain had good reason to regret, remained very European in its orientation; Henry James and T.S. Eliot, like Howard Pyle himself, sprang from soil nurtured by the English myths mediated by north-eastern publishers, and the Ivy League universities were leaders in developing the academic subject of English culture.

In Britain a major innovation, directly related to the 'Newbolt Report' on the teaching of English in schools, was Nelson's 'Teaching of English' series, edited by Newbolt himself. It included a number of Robin Hood items in its list: no. 20 (1925) was E.C. Oakden's *Pattern Plays* including a 'Robin Hood and Allan a Dale' drama; no. 40 (1925) was Newbolt's own *The Greenwood*, a set of patriotic paraphrases and critical essays; John Hampden's no. 164 (1931) reprinted John Drinkwater's playlet of 1912, 'Robin Hood and the Pedlar'.

Robin Hood was not only to be found in children's reading editions and specially prepared school materials. Major items of the cultural canon spoke up for the hero in a modern way. *The Dictionary of National Biography* gave him an honoured, if strangely fictional, place (see p. 13); Sir Arthur Quiller-Couch published an influential collection of *Robin Hood Ballads* with Oxford University Press in 1908, and then his *Oxford Book of Ballads* of 1910 had a whole section on 'The Greenwood' dominated by Robin Hood; the famous eleventh edition of the *Encyclopedia Britannica* in 1910–11 carried a long article by J.W. Hales and F.J. Snell giving a full account of the hero and his inherently mythic meaning (vol. XXIII, pp. 420–1).

The educational positioning was crucial for the new status of the myth as part of heritage culture; but it was the creative writers, as usual, who indicated most fully the significance of the outlaw tradition in this new context. Several of the lesser poets associated with the 'Georgian' movement wrote something on Robin Hood. The least remodelled version was Drinkwater's occasional piece *Robin Hood and the Pedlar*, with music by James Brier, which was performed at Bournville on 25 June 1914; the early summer date is a revealing connection with the play-game, and a Quaker connection appears again, in the location at least. This was a fairly simple creation of a 'new' ballad based on the 'Robin Hood meets his match' model merged with 'the King and the Subject' – the pedlar turns out to be King Richard. At first Robin sings in favour of the simple life:

> Let life go unforbidden
> Straight-limbed among the green,
> And laughter be unchidden,
> And gravity unseen; (p. 5)

Soon enough the tone turns to a form of forest mysticism, albeit one whose poetic style seems almost playful:

> I'm brother to the beech tree
> I'm brother to the oak,
> And glad the little beasts be
> And glad the feathered folk. (p. 5)

The king punishes the sheriff after Marian beats him in a fight – the influence of Tennyson seems clear, and the king gives a ring to the ballad singer who sums up a position more purely aesthetic than the chauvinism, national and masculine, relished by some of the other 'Georgians':

> I have no falcon on my wrist
> Nor any beakers made of gold
> But lips as kind as any kissed
> Are mine to kiss, and mine to mould
> In shapes imperishably fair,
> The brain's tumultuous beating throng
> The wonder of the world I snare
> In shining nets of love and song. (p. 20)

In the same period, Noyes, author of a poem sequence on Drake and the patriotic recital piece 'Forty Singing Seamen', wrote the verse play *Sherwood* in 1908 (apparently not professionally performed until in 1926 it was shortened and made a little more colloquial and mystical, as *Robin Hood*). The famous anthology piece 'Sherwood' sums up this quite complex condensation of romantic nostalgia and political conservatism, a new version of 'neo-pastoral.'

The poem opens in a spirit like, if less crisply attentive than, Reynolds' sonnets:

> Sherwood in the twilight, is Robin Hood awake?
> Grey and ghostly shadows are gliding through the brake,
> Shadows of the dappled deer, dreaming of the morn,
> Dreaming of a shadowy man that winds a shadowy horn.

This is a hero-centred dream, not a sensual reverie of past and possible relationships, as Reynolds proposed. The worm of nationalism is firmly in the bud of greenwood beauty:

> Merry, merry England has kissed the lips of June:

And this imaginary nation is rising in youthful revenance:

> Merry, merry England is waking as of old,
> With eyes of blither hazel and hair of brighter gold:
> For Robin Hood is here again beneath the bursting spray
> In Sherwood, in Sherwood, about the break of day.

Keats' historical common sense and his communal culturalism have been elided out of the picture, as has Tennyson's scholarly pastiche of socially attuned – if determinedly conservative – narratives. For Noyes, a domain is created of culture alone, where there are glimpses of some obscurely comprehended ideal state, as in: 'Marian is waiting with a glory in her eyes', or: 'Round the fairy grass-rings frolic elf and fay.' Yet in these misty surroundings there are strains of masculine comfort: 'Friar Tuck and Little John are riding down together', and their context is one of yeomanly militarism: 'With quarter-staff and drinking-can and grey goose feather.' 'Grey goose feather' is of course a reference to Agincourt and the like, and, as Noyes now acknowledges, patriotism is coded into all this material:

Softly over Sherwood the south wind blows.
All the heart of England hid in every rose

Such a visionary re-enactment of the Sherwood outlaws is, like
'Georgian' poetry itself, a fiction of the past used to obscure the fact
of the present, and only at the end does the poem partly admit its
ideological function. The noise and celebration of the outlaw troupe is
high:

... from aisles of oak and ash
Rings the *Follow! Follow!* and the boughs begin to crash,
The ferns begin to flutter and the flowers begin to fly,
And through the crimson dawning the robber band goes by.

Noyes does not clarify why these notionally secretive outlaw-
robbers make so much noise; in image they are a fox-hunting pack
or a group of privileged louts, educated bourgeoisie at play like some
of the 'Georgian' poets themselves on a country visit. But against
that vigorous presence the last stanza has a dying fall and admits this
is a dream from which even the author must wake:

Robin! Robin! Robin! All his merry thieves
Answer as the bugle-note shivers through the leaves,
Calling as he used to call, faint and far away
In Sherwood, in Sherwood, about the break of day.

In *The Greenwood*, published in 1925, Newbolt asserted that 'Where
Tennyson utterly failed, Alfred Noyes has succeeded'; his success lay
'in dreaming to life' what Newbolt called 'the natural legend'
(p. 215). It is certainly true that Noyes is more like the early Tennyson
than the mature poet chose to be in *The Foresters*, but Newbolt's
purpose here is to stitch together a seamless web of greenwoodery, to
suggest there is a wide flowing movement of natural patriotism: it is
a one-book analogue to his editorship of the Nelson Teaching of English
series and his crucial guidance of the 1919 'Report on the Teaching
of English', a bureaucratic intervention of the highest importance in
constructing a heritage culture (Doyle, 1989, chap. 2). The most creative moment Newbolt achieved was to produce dramatic poems of
chauvinist educational sentiment like the tub-thumping 'Drake's Drum'
and *Vitae Lampada*, better known as the poem offering the notion that

in various crises, in battle, cricket and life, the best exhortation is 'Play up, play up and play the game'.

Not all 'Georgian' material was quite so simple in tone, but complexity did not come easily. When a 'Georgian' attempted irony, it tended to express hostility, not the satirical bonhomie found in most pantomimes. J. C. Squire, the influential editor of *The London Mercury* and invader of villages to play cricket – with much of the disruptive impact of Robin's band as described by Noyes – produced in 1928 a play called *Robin Hood* which reveals the patronizing, sexist conservatism of the 'Georgian' position, especially interesting in a man who had toyed with Fabianism, stood for Cambridge in 1918 as Labour and then for Brentford and Chiswick in 1920 as a Liberal. By 1928 he had settled into stereotypical certainties, as indicated by the *dramatis personae* of *Robin Hood*. Particularly telling descriptions are:

Little John (Tall and very big; Newfoundland dog type)
Much the Miller's Son (A lump, elderly; good-tempered, stupid, North-country accent)
Alanadale (Very elegant, tall, unperturbed, precise, high voice, foppishly dressed at first appearance)
The Knight (Armoured, bronzed)
His Squire (Bright, manly, luxuriant hair)
Marian de Burgh (Rosalindish, vivacious, but more daring and male)
Clorinda (Chief Shepherdess; Dresden and pert)

The text is compounded with elements from the *Gest*, *The Sad Shepherd* and something of *The Foresters*, but mostly it is a self-consciously witty modernization of the tradition which develops the class confidence and gender instability revealed in the characters' descriptions. Even the greenwood escapism so beloved of the 'Georgians' is here undermined with a weak form of pantomime wit:

Robin:
In Sherwood a man may live without lying, and breathe without taking in foul air. He may trust his companions, and consort with nothing that he hates, and if he must rob, it is at least openly and with an eye to justice.
Knight:
Fie, fie, I must not listen to this, or I shall have protests from all the Chambers of Commerce. (1928, p. 112)

Between the simplicity of Noyes and Newbolt and the lightweight hostility of Squire is traced the political anxiety of the 'Georgian' reworking of Robin Hood. It is a version that has largely been lost, but it did have its own quite influential constituency. There are from the period many relatively feeble and clumsy 'poetic' reworkings of the myth, with some sense of woolly patriotism, some idea of greenwood value – an English greenwood of course – and varying amounts of liberal democracy enshrined in the hero, usually amounting to little more than distaste for town life and the morality of merchants.

Some of this might seem rurally appropriate, like Ronald Gow's *Five Robin Hood Plays* of 1932, commissioned by the 'Village Drama Section' of the British Drama League. More obviously inauthentic were the para-Georgian greenwood dramas that flourished overseas, like Owen Davis's American edition of *Robin Hood or The Merry Outlaws of Sherwood Forest* (1923); the French's acting edition is in the same series as US classics like *The Charm School* and *Daddy Longlegs*. Not only America celebrated the displaced delights of a well-groomed greenwood; the University of Sydney's highly respectable Women's College (basically for the daughters of wealthy landholders from many miles away) mounted *Robin Hood and His Merry Men* by Elizabeth F. Matheson in August 1913 (the beginning of Spring in that hemisphere), based on the *Gest*, but with a maypole and Jack o'the Green added.

Local or international, Georgianism caused a definite Robin Hood renaissance, however little contact it had with the early rebelliousness of the outlaw hero. But the period was not entirely in the hands of conservatives. A striking example is the ballad opera *Robin Hood* composed in 1933 by Michael Tippett, with book and lyrics by David Ayerst and Ruth Pennyman, described as the work of 'David Pennyless' (Chase and Whyman, 1991, pp. 21–5). Tippett became associated with the scheme to establish work-camps and cultural activities for unemployed ironstone miners in Boosbeck, North Yorkshire. David Matthews describes it, in *Michael Tippett: An Introductory Study*, as a work 'in which aristocratic power and oppression are trounced by the romantic hero of the people' (1980, p. 24) and both the overall idea and the detailed text are close, if somewhat playfully so, to Soviet ideas of the period, as in the chorus:

So God he made the outlaws
To beat the devil's man;

To rob the rich, to defend the poor
By Robin's ten year plan. (Chase and Whyman, 1991, p. 23)

An equally vigorous reversal of the modern orthodoxy was Geoffrey Trease's novel *Bows against the Barons* (1934), which in its title firmly separated Robin from the Magna Carta popular front invented by the Victorians, and developed a rebellious outlaw story which leads up to the Peasants' Revolt. A similar Maoxist stance was taken by Jack Lindsay, the poet, novelist and left-wing scholar, in *Robin of England* which, according to Bernard Miles, was produced with great success by the Unity Theatre in 1938 (Miles, 1984, p. 226).

The genre of poetry was itself not entirely given over to the right-wing Robin Hood. America had its pasteboard Georgianism and its mass enthusiasm for diluted Robin Hood educational tracts, but other views were possible. In the context of the *Gest*, Thoreau had spoken in his usual tone of enigmatic dissent of England's wilderness 'as a green wood — her wild man a Robin Hood' (*Excursions*, 1880, p. 164). In *The Saturday Review of Literature* for 15 November 1930, pride of place on the first page is given to 'The Death of Robin Hood', a new poem by William Rose Benet, best known as a literary journalist.

Intriguingly this poem seems to go right back to the ideas of Barton, Keats and even Ritson; it draws the phrase 'wild justice' out of Tennyson and defines it much more firmly:

There hangs the long bow, the strong bow, once was bent,
To cleave the clout, to split the willow wand;
Till the quiver's shafts were spent
The bow that wrought wild justice in this land.

The politics of this 'wild justice' are not only liberation in 'the wild wood', but expressly anti-authoritarian action:

. . . king and clergy knew
How sure its clothyards flew
To right the poor and lay oppression low.

The trees of the greenwood are seen here not as media of mystical union, but a defensible base for hunted men:

> There grows our great oak, our girthed oak . . .
> The hunted and the hounded knew its ground
> For refuge, knew who stood
> A stiff yew hedge in the wood
> Around its bole, when that the horn was wound.

The dying Robin, who envisions all this from his past, asks to be lifted to see again the 'forest walls', and to find with an arrow the site of his grave. He leaves a message of armed watchfulness, with the readiness for violent resistance:

> Go soft then, saying naught; but hark ye! kneel
> When the evil hour would awe, –
> Kneel and bend bow and draw
> And loose your shafts in a whistling sleet of steel!

This fierce poem looks back to 'Robin Hood's Progress to Nottingham' for a parallel, and has had nothing modern to match it. But if Benet renders outlawry in direct action terms, another writer not known as a radical was shaping a subtly different meaning for the greenwood in a book that is not in any direct way a Robin Hood text, yet uses the patterns of the 'Georgians' in a consciously new sense. In his 'Terminal Note' to *Maurice*, E.M. Forster speaks with quiet clarity of this long unpublished novel:

> it belongs to an England where it was still possible to get lost. It belongs to the last moment of the greenwood. *The Longest Journey* belongs there too, and has similarities of atmosphere. Our greenwood ended catastrophically and inevitably. Two great wars demanded and bequeathed regimentation which the public services adopted and extended, science lent her aid, and the wildness of our island, never extensive, was stamped upon and built over and patrolled in no time. There is no forest or fell to escape to today, no cave in which to curl up, no deserted valley for those who wish neither to reform nor corrupt society but to be left alone. (1971, p. 240).

The story is of an educated bourgeois who finds a fully realized life in his love for a rural man, not in the mechanical processes of office work and polite society. For Forster the image of greenwood offers a radical release into the true self – an idea which, as he wrily notes, in

Lady Chatterley's Lover, Lawrence took more operatically and (as Forster surely means in a reference to his 'prickly gamekeepers') more crudely.

Forster, and finally Maurice himself, understand 'greenwood' in the personal sense that Reynolds perceived, and Keats was willing to admit, though the subtler poet reserved a place for historical understanding as well. Forster, not unlike Tennyson but with much more depth in analysis, does have a social meaning for the greenwood, but it is fully personalized in the authentic modern, and indeed modernist, mode, whereas the 'Georgians', with whom he should not be associated just because he used the forest image, shaped the greenwood myth into a conservative fantasy.

Forster's quietly manoeuvering style, the deeply introspective mode of his novel, above all his theme of homosexual liberty, all make it clear that there were many innovations in early twentieth-century culture and society which the 'Georgians' and the educational movement had not touched on in their Robin Hood realizations. Nothing would be so innovative, however, nor as far-reaching in its impact on the outlaw myth, than the revolutionary medium of cinema, which would give new life to some of the oldest features of the myth, and dominate the representation of Robin Hood in the modern period.

6

'We Saxons Just Aren't Going To Put Up With These Oppressions Much Longer': Robin Hood in the Modern World

6.1 THE EARLY FILM TRADITION

The special significance of Robin Hood in film is not merely the number of productions – the same kind of popularity is found in ballad or popular theatre in some periods. But in the cinema medium, the myth has considerably higher status and wider dissemination than in prose, verse or drama. It is still a 'popular' topic in the evaluative sense, as art houses have rarely shown the films, though critical analysis has been known to deal with them and the myth is structurally important within the genre of film as several 'classic' productions have come from the tradition. But that quality is added to remarkable quantity, and it would seem that this century has achieved a well-recorded parallel to the lively and variable patterns of performance that previously were in play-game, harlequinade and, becoming better recorded last century, comedy and pantomime.

The potency of the Robin Hood story in the cinema is revealed by a simple but dramatic statistic: five Robin Hood films were made before 1914. In that almost primitive period the subject had already emerged as part of the repertoire, with repetitive patterns that were, in varied forms, to survive through to the present. Those early films showed a strong relationship with theatre itself, which was booming

218

in the same period – the Lord Chancellor's records reveal seven new British stage productions between 1900 and 1910. The earliest of the films was 'Robin Hood and His Merry Men', a one-reeler released in England by Clarendon in 1909 (some records indicate 1908, but that was presumably the production date). The plot is about the outlawed earl 'going to Sherwood Forest with Maid Marian and gathering his band to fight injustice' (Behlmer, 1965, p. 91), and it, like many later films and some plays, uses the gallows rescue as the climax (Richards, 1977, p. 194). There is no single ballad source: this is a brief 'round-up' narrative of the kind often used in the contemporary school plays, which suggests that the tradition of Robin Hood playlets used by barnstorming companies fed directly – like the players themselves – into the early films.

A similar catch-all narrative was the basis for the single reel 'Robin Hood – Outlawed' from British and Colonial films in 1912. The title suggests the second novel attributed to Dumas, *Robin Hood le proscrit*, which was translated in 1903 as *Robin Hood the Outlaw*, but that was a sequel; here the emphasis was on how Robin formed his band and rescued Maid Marian from a knight with evil intentions – a situation harking back to Victorian stage melodrama and much used in the early cinema (Richards, 1977, p. 194).

The outlaw film moved to a higher level of sophistication with the Hollywood three-reeler made by Eclair in 1912 (1913 is the release date) called simply 'Robin Hood'. This was a studio-based production with Californian exteriors, and there was more plotting to fill out the greater length. Here the triangle story was derived from De Koven's musical and set out the basically new idea, much imitated in later cinema, of a conflict for Marian between Robin and a Guy of Gisborne who was both wicked and lustful.

The personalization of the myth, which had begun with Reynolds' empathetic representation of Marian and Robin, here develops its reflex, the emotionally-realized villain. The earlier stories had never contained a fully focused individual enemy for Robin Hood, just a generalized institutional hostility embodied in a character, whether it was an abbey sketchily personified by abbot or prior, or the growing statist powers represented by sheriff or forester. The nineteenth century period of emotionally individualized fiction had changed the context for conflict from the political to the personal, though the essentially depersonalized forms of pantomime and historical novel did not realize that to any degree; it is the emotionality and closely focused form of film that recasts the ancient conflict between Robin and authority into fully private terms.

A less innovative structure was used for another Californian picture produced by Thanhouser in four reels, also just called 'Robin Hood', also from 1913. This developed the 'filmic' possibilities of the older narrative, bringing to the screen the archery contest that Scott developed and ending with the well-known sequence of the king in disguise.

These two well-mounted productions set in place the twin elements which Robin Hood films since then have generally combined, some more successfully than others. There will be a certain amount of epic setting, with splendid scenes, exciting battles, amazed crowds and thrilling chases – a combination of the history spectacular and the western, sometimes right down to the ponies used. But also the plot focuses on a boy-meets-girl story with a proper villain, a lustrous-eyed heroine, and a final reconciliation made all the more satisfying in that, as the couple are reunited, so the king is restored to place. The cinema's capacity, indeed hunger, for rapid montage between long shot and close-up, external and internal, suits very well a story which has previously been difficult to handle in any of the major genres, and has thrived in those forms which can emphasize the intensity of a conflict and also suggest further generalized dimensions, such as play-game and ballad. The number of early films indicates the potential that was seen in the story by cinematographers from the very beginning – and there is another English version from 1912, a Kinemacolour 'In the Days of Robin Hood' which was actually shot in Sherwood and seems based on a Pyle story about Robin being disguised as a monk to rescue one of his men from the sheriff (Richards, 1977, p. 194).

While early film scholars might have perceived that the Robin Hood myth fitted precisely the cinema's need for public spectacle and personal tension, they could not have predicted how fully and powerfully those two elements were to be projected and combined in the 1922 Robin Hood film which Douglas Fairbanks Senior helped to write and finance and, most of all, illuminate with his star quality. This, of all the Robin Hood texts that had been produced and performed over the centuries, is the first major success in any genre; here the myth moves into the big time in terms of both professional and market acclaim. With due respect to the skill of the author of the *Gest*, admiration for the terse power of the best ballads, overdue praise for Tennyson's solid effort in *The Foresters*, none of these ever claimed major status or survival value as an artistic text. But Fairbanks' *Robin Hood* still holds enthralled an audience of hardened film students, and is remarkably rich for discussion whether it is at the level of costume and setting, performance and direction, or, the matter of most interest here, the psycho-social messages being encoded in the text.

Fairbanks was already a highly successful artist fresh from playing in *The Three Musketeers* and *The Mark of Zorro* and with his own team of advisers and specialists – he was in effect an actor manager at a new level of success. He and United Artists were looking for a major project and Robin Hood was mentioned. Fairbanks at first was cool, and is reported to have said 'I don't want to look like a heavy-footed Englishman trampling around in the woods' (Hancock and Fairbanks, 1953, p. 191) though another version has him saying 'The spectacle of a lot of flat-footed outlaws in Lincoln green . . . did not strike me as anything to make a picture about' (Behlmer, 1965, p. 95). He evidently disliked the idea of humble immobility, two features which the film resolutely exorcized in its highly active flamboyance. It also managed without any of the ancient elements of rebelliousness, including the nationalist simplifications so popular in the preceding century.

While it is not clear what brought Fairbanks to agree to do the film in addition to the pressure for Robin Hood from United Artists' marketing department (Schickel, 1976, pp. 73–4), two features have been mentioned in discussions which seem to have had importance, and both project a combination of grandeur and personal identification. One of Fairbanks retinue was, apparently, named Lotta Woods (though especially in the Robin Hood context one must suspect such a name as being produced for the occasion by this group of famous pranksters). In preparing material for him to consider, a crucial element was apparently her prose paraphrase of Alfred Noyes' play *Sherwood*. This presumably communicated the spirit of Zorro and D'Artagnan and made the outlaw theme seem less 'flat-footed'.

But there was another, more important and more revealing moment of acceptance. Fairbanks went on holiday to Europe while preparation began. His brother, a trained engineer and Wilfred Buckland, a leading stage designer, prepared a huge set at the Fairbanks-Pickford studios on Santa Monica Boulevard. It dwarfed pre-skyscraper Los Angeles, ninety feet high, with a main hall four hundred and fifty feet long. The star was 'somewhat daunted' (Schickel, 1976, p. 75) by the size, and is reputed to have said 'My pictures always had the intimate touch, We'd look like a bunch of Lilliputians in the halls of a giant if we used that set' (Hancock and Fairbanks, 1953, p. 193). The response is, as usual with actors, concerned with perceptions of the self, but is also acute about the essentially personal impact of cinema. However, Alan Dwan, the director, evidently understood, and had pre-empted the anxiety. Immediately, he showed Fairbanks how a series of hand-holds were built into the set so it could be easily climbed and in particular how a huge hanging tapestry had a track built behind so Fairbanks could dashingly, almost magically, slide down it. The actor was fascinated, seeing instinctively how this permitted him to show a personal mastery of the huge set.

The grandiose scale and the personalized focus are technically built into the film, perfectly expressed when Robin scales the building in what seems like a few bounds and at the top turns in a purely Fairbanksesque moment and gives the gymnast's salute to his audience, one arm stretched high, chest out, a broad grin on the face. The remarkable technical skills of the designer and director had found a way to express the newly humanized essence of the Robin Hood story: gigantic funding and massive modernity on the set, were themselves used as a springboard for the supple individual to triumph. It is an achievement to parallel Chaplin's in *Modern Times*, and an anecdote makes it clear that these artists understood in some way just what they were doing.

One morning, apparently, Fairbanks and entourage were driven down to the set and told to wait outside. As they watched, the great drawbridge to the castle creaked down and then, after a pause, a small figure in a nightgown and cap wandered out, stretched, yawned, put down a milk bottle and a kitten, went back in and the drawbridge ground its way up. It was of course Chaplin, playing a 'gag' (Schickel, 1976, p. 75). But Chaplin was a comedian of genius and the gag had meaning; the 'little man' could naturalize gigantic modernity just as well as a swashbuckling hero.

The first half of the film is devoted to the grand scale of the filmic spectacular – a joust, the great hall, preparations for the crusade, the army on the march and in camp. Some thought this slow-moving, but all found it splendid, as cinema flexed the muscles that D.W. Griffith had been the first to exercise fully. The influence for the early involvement of the king is more likely to be *Ivanhoe* than the somewhat similar royal engagement of *Looke About You*, but the close friendship between Richard and Robin and the king's essential boyishness makes it conceivable that someone had followed up the earlier sources, available in Ritson's edition.

Many reviewers commented on the fact that it was only in the second half, when Robin was an outlaw, that the true Fairbanks appeared, the prankster gymnast fighting for a thoroughly respectable sort of freedom (see illustration 15). Some were relieved when that part of the film arrived and the massive gave way to the private. But there are other structural meanings in the plot than merely waiting for our hero to emerge in single splendour; the film dynamizes a whole set of new issues in the myth which come in part from the American setting and also from the new capacity to deal with sexuality and its discontents that arise from the post-Romantic personalization of the myth.

As is clear from the success of *The Foresters* and the prevalence of Robin Hood teaching texts, America had a strong relation with the outlaw myth: Robin Hood offers a special version of Jessie James or Bonnie and Clyde. In part this formation works because outlawry is always justified in the Robin Hood story and that appealed to a frontier idea of freedom, but also because of the American approach-avoidance relationship with royalty. The ancient motif that Robin goes to court but prefers the greenwood becomes, through America's complex relationship with ancient Europe, a new kind of myth. Like Fairbanks himself, this is the hero who can mix with kings and gilded aristocracy, but also be an active American prankster. Whereas Englishness was, and is, coded with class, so that in the original country for Robin to be a true rebel is a disturbing fact and must be coped with in various ways, in the USA the forest to which Robin escapes is very readily interpreted as the expansive liberty of America itself – and the fact that Californian woods provided both Sherwood and the Wild West for the cowboy pictures made the identification an easy one. But that idea of liberty goes with a contradictory relish for grandeur. Fairbanks extends the domesticated outlaw myth into a new kind of American imperialism through the royal pomp of the first part of his film, imaging himself and Mary Pickford as a new insouciant kind of royalty – it was widely remarked at the time how much like Pickford was Enid Bennett, who played Marian.

Illustration 15   Douglas Fairbanks 1922
(Courtesy Universal Artists; photo
Lensmedia.)

Illustration 16   Errol Flynn 1938
(Courtesy Warner Brothers, photo
Lensmedia.)

Illustration 17   Richard Greene 1955
(Courtesy ATV; photo Lensmedia.)

Illustration 18   Michael Praed 1984
(Courtesy Harlech; photo
Lensmedia.)

If the splendour of the opening half and the liberty of the second part bespeak American power to share in but not be tainted by European history and pomp, then another form of modern fantasy is encoded into the action of the first part and released through the second half, a pattern so obvious when the film is watched that it is remarkable it has not been discussed. It is common ground among analysts of westerns and American crime fiction from the between wars period that gender is a particularly strained territory. Robin Hood, like Shane, like Philip Marlowe, cannot cope with women. But, characteristic of this film, that problem is developed in a grand, visual and symbolically powerful way.

Richard I is played by Wallace Beery, specially cast by Fairbanks; Beery was a film heavyweight, usually a villain, and his choice presumably ensures that no male is more dynamic than the hero. Paternal in mode – or at least an elder brother – Richard urges all his knights to select a lady. Robin replies, in bold silent print: 'Exempt me sire, I am afeard of women.' The boyish Robin of the early ballads had, like other social bandits, no commerce with women. But as the story itself has become personalized and the bearer of individualist feeling, so the gender connection has become weightier and, at least in this context, needs to be stripped of its threat. This film goes on to show that Robin is quite justified in his fears. Just as Marlowe always discovers the crime was actually by a treacherous woman, for all Chandler's image of urban corruption, just as the western hero, to be a man, must elude the domesticating woman and let the tart take in her heart of gold the bullet meant for him, so Robin Hood in this new version is constructed as a self-defensive male.

In a striking sequence, after Robin's demurral to choose a lady, the young women of the court begin to close around him, moths to his chivalric lamp. Using the numbers, the size of set and the spectacular costumes that this highly-funded international theatre made possible, Dwan makes the women swirl and group around Fairbanks, looking in part like a civil riot, yet also like some strange amoebic life force. The hero breaks through their ranks and runs, to be pursued by what is now a troop of giggling schoolgirls, or indeed, fans. Finally he pauses on the edge of the river, and in an act of lone masculine display, dives into the water. Jungians would smile, arguing that his escape only leads him to immersion in the symbolized feminine, and that such resistance is eternally futile – as is itself implied by the recurrent obsession in popular forms of this period, especially the thriller and the western, with their need to represent and contain over and over again the danger perceived in the female.

There were structural reasons for that repetition-compulsion, related both to the power of woman in the family home where the male usually leaves to go to work, but also to the increasing number of women actively engaged in public life. It is noticeable, for example, that in the 1922 'Robin Hood' it is Marian herself who creates the links between the two halves of the film. Robin, in spite of his anxiety, has become linked with her because she is being brutalized by another man, Sir Guy, in the new triangular structure. But it is hardly a passionate contact, and in a quest for protection rather than love, Marian sends Robin a message about the parlous state of the country as Prince John exploits his position with Richard on crusade. The king refuses Robin permission to go home just for a woman, so Robin leaves anyway, coming under the slur of cowardice – a realization of the patriarchal fear that contact with women will reduce masculine esteem and power. However, Marian, herself under great threat, has faked her own death, so permitting both Robin's continued isolation and also his unthreatening idealistic fidelity to her, the absent sweetheart motif so common in war films.

Robin is therefore positioned for the merry men activities of the second half, where Fairbanks' boyish vitality comes to the fore, in what Shickel has called a 'comic opera style' (1976, p. 76) and creating the 'grown-up schoolboy' impact of the film (Richards, 1977, p. 196). Those comments imply criticism, but it should be noted that comic opera is the mode in which the myth has been most vigorous for several centuries and a schoolboyish positioning is often the focus of this American between-wars culture, from Hemingway to 'Mr Deeds Goes to Town'.

The film was a huge success with the public – a record 101,000 people saw it in the first week in the New York Capitol. It is said to have made Fairbanks five million dollars, and is generally regarded as the high point of his career. What it also did was translate the Robin Hood myth onto the screen as a real force; the tradition Fairbanks created that Robin Hood can be a major financial and artistic success has no doubt been the context for many of the films made since, whether or not they achieve anything in either category.

In terms of an overview of the whole myth, the intriguing factor is that the next major film maintained much of the Fairbanks mixture of the public and the private, the European and the American, but brought back into the newly confident film mode the political and nationalistic materials which had been discarded for the initial filmic reformulations.

6.2 FROM HOLLYWOOD TO THE LIVING ROOM

Only sixteen years after the silent, stagey, black and white Fairbanks film comes 'The Adventures of Robin Hood' starring Errol Flynn. While, as has been argued above, the traditions of the outlaw in prose verse and drama have no classical or vulgate version, this is not true of film: the Warner Brothers 1938 version is, for most people, *the* Robin Hood. It is still shown on television as a mainstream feature, not a curio from the past; its colour and dramatic action seem fully in accord with modern standards of large screen cinema; its score by Wolfgang Korngold is a powerful instrument of emotional excitement today. The performances in most cases have also been accepted as classic renditions: Flynn combining athletic bravado with the capacity for inspiration; Olivia de Haviland when very young, the image of flawless beauty and a heroine's spirit; Claude Rains a highly intelligent, even playful royal villain; Basil Rathbone as the enemy swordsman, Robin's ideal opponent.

This impact derives in part from effective casting – James Cagney was at one time considered for Robin, but Flynn's dash in 'Captain Blood' and 'The Sea Hawk' made him appropriate for the flamboyance that Fairbanks had stamped on the part, (see illustration 16). There was also a deliberate decision about the appropriate pace and tone of the film. William Keighley began directing but was removed after Warners felt his action sequences were too slow and too playful, and Michael Curtiz, already successful with 'Captain Blood', was brought in to reshoot some material and complete the film; Keighley retained a directing credit but contributed 'only a small amount of the footage included in the release print' (Kinnard and Vitone, 1986, p. 46).

But as has often been found, stars, a powerful distribution system and fine techniques do not necessarily make memorable art, in films as in other media. 'The Adventures of Robin Hood' has real inner strength, a good deal of which relates to its resurrection of some of the central features of the tradition, especially as it had been developed in the previous century. Although there had early been plans to start with a joust scene as in the 1922 version, this was abandoned (Behlmer, 1965, p. 98); the film makes a brief reference to the crusades, then opens with the scene where Robin, riding at the edge of the forest with Will Scarlet, confronts Gisborne over the forest laws on behalf of the peasant Much. The scene changes to the castle where Prince John asks with sharp irony 'Any more objections to the new tax from our Saxon friends?'

Through this remark, and the immediately following sequence, where Robin bursts into the hall and challenges the Normans, a sense of possible resistance is constructed from the start, and while there is a peasant-lord tension between Much and Guy, this social challenge is made less sharply class-based by being mediated through the hero, Sir Robin of Locksley, Guy's equal and not an earl until the very end: American democratism brings a populist touch.

But Robin's resistance is also highly individualistic. The overt breach between hero and authority here is not an assumed fact as in some of the early texts, nor is it the inevitable result of arbitrary power as at the wedding feast in Munday, nor yet the violent response to betrayals and brutality seen in texts as early as 'Robin Hood and the Monk'. Here resistance is the product of deliberate heroic choice: a highly self-conscious Robin swaggers into the heart of Norman power, dumps a dead stag on Prince John's table and in the ensuing discussion promises rebellion on personal terms, then escapes in a triumph of isolated agility, archery and cunning. The private hero is shaped for the first time in the myth: Robin is an identity in fully modern terms, an epitome of the personalizing of resistance in recent times, from Garibaldi to Gorbachev.

Ina Rae Hark has written about the visual symbolism of the banquet scene: the Normans are represented sitting and standing in lines, with vertical spears and horizontal table edges defining and organizing their power, and throughout the film they ride and march in straight lines. Robin on the other hand is relaxed, curved in his sitting posture, always both casual and mobile – and so are the outlaws throughout the film. Hark sums up: 'the Normans are controlled by an inflexible protocol, visually expressed through geometrical symmetry, which is all the more deadly because it masks sadism and greed' (1976, p. 9). Robin and his men, on the other hand are characterized 'by spontaneity of action and unrestrained motion; they generally create a dynamic mass within the frame' (1976, p. 8).

This perceptive analysis indicates the way in which Curtiz as director and no doubt Ralph Dawson the editor, who received an Oscar (as did the composer Korngold and the artistic director C.J. Weyl), had a clear sense of thematic form. Other examples of such visual modelling of meaning are evident: the outlaws inhabit and are filmed against the trees – in one very famous scene, developed from Fairbanks' gymnastics, the outlaws are hiding in a tree which seems itself to come to life and entrap the Normans by the forces of nature. In the opening sequence Robin and Will jump their horses over a low branch up into the forest like some form of animal spirit; the Normans on the other hand are usually filmed against the ground or oppressively dominating the skyline, and often from a dehumanizing distance.

In the same way fortress and forest represent the cultural and the natural set in opposition, but the natural also represents social culture at its most dynamic – the woodland feast is all movement and life against the stark lines of force evident in Prince John's banquet. What in the 'Georgian' poets was a thin version of anti-urban complaint has here become a fully realized dichotomy between social sites. The richness of this contrast in the film is certainly one of its considerable powers, but that in itself would not give it much political subtlety – it would be no more than a well-developed version of the naive anti-urbanism of the 'Georgian' poets. But inside the film there appear to be several more levels of conflict, dealing with contemporary anxieties across a wide field, from the international through the national to the distinctly personal. A number of contemporary references seem to exist and intensify the meaning of the film and its potent oppositions, and while their immediacy is largely lost now, their traces still sophisticate the film and deepen its range of reference.

Hark makes much of the friendship between Warner himself – previously a Republican – and Roosevelt, and has identified a New Deal kind of redistribution at the heart of Robin's activities: 'Clearly, FDR and New Deal democracy also lie behind the restoration of social equilibrium promised by King Richard's return' (1976, p. 6). But this may not be as clear as Hark asserts. In her argument, she refers to Jeffrey Richards' work on populism in the cinema, *Visions of Yesterday*, as support for the idea that Roosevelt could be seen as a statist liberal, rather than a grass roots radical, and so was acceptable to people like Warner. But in his other book *Swordsmen of the Screen*, Richards offers no such interpretation in a lengthy discussion of Curtiz's 'Robin Hood'. He sees the essential oppositions of the film lying in the way in which the scriptwriters 'utilized the Saxon-Norman rivalry to provide a strong dramatic axis for the narrative' (1977, p. 197).

Although Hark argues that the forest fortress is like a New Deal 'government camp', her reference is forward to 'The Grapes of Wrath' in 1940. A much stronger and more acutely political reference, as Richards implies, and more likely to be widely acceptable in contemporary Hollywood than pro-Roosevelt material, lies in associations related to the linear imagery and the civil violence that Hark has rightly seen as central to the ideological set-up of the film.

In 1938 the obvious response to both linear form and street violence would be Nazi Germany. Leni Riefenstahl's film of the 1936 Olympics, 'The Triumph of the Will', was a paean to linearity in idealized form; Krystallnacht and similar events were well known – especially at Warner's whose Berlin agent, Joseph Kauffman, had been beaten to death by a Nazi mob in 1935. When Robin, handsome and casual, natural and potent, declares his personal vendetta against the evident fascism of the Norman soldiers, then an image of European resistance is being created, though not one to be confused with communist or anarchist resistance in Spain; this is, rather, the height of liberalism set in a framework which is nationalist and so, with some irony, itself fully racist in basis.

The film also operates in a more personal sense of politics, bringing forward a whole range of images that may in part represent Robin Hood as a version of the 'green man'. The emphasis on the dynamic nature of the forest, Robin's consistent brown and green clothing, his playful nature, the strange imagery of splitting another man's arrow with your own – these are the most striking of the details which suggest that somebody in the making of this film knew, or re-imagined, the emotive impact of the forest and its images. But here, that masculine dynamism has a more complex direction.

The boyishness of Fairbanks' presentation is strongly continued in Flynn, though here it appears, in part through Flynn's personal reputation, to be linked with a fully adult masculinity – this Robin shows no fear of Marian, but rather handles her through a sexualized form of class conflict, and her own sympathy for him comes in part through his social commitment, as Hark points out (1976, p. 13). But if Marian's reaction has the effect of socializing the sexuality that Flynn conveyed so strongly, there is another area of emotive force where the film is not restrained. Callenbach notes a strong Freudian element inherent in modern versions of the story: 'Reduced to its story-conference level, *Robin Hood* is about the son who fights the evil father [the false king] and is rewarded by the good father' (1969, p. 43).

The lack of overt familial emotion, characteristic of earlier culture, has in the past restricted the myth's capacity to be read as a fable about bad and good fathers, but the theme comes through strongly for the first time in the 1938 film. This dynamic undercurrent deepens the range of concerns with authority into this familial mode of power, especially through the waspishness of this Prince John and the attenuated malice of Rathbone as Sir Guy, an elder brother out of the *Gamelyn* tradition. With Will Scarlet as very much a boyish companion and with the return of Richard to supervise settlement and the passage of the 'son' into marriage, the potential of the myth for this kind of paternalizing structure is markedly strengthened.

Made by a very highly skilled team who combine swift work with considerable subtlety, advised by a very knowledgeable scholar in F.M. Padelford, a sixteenth-century literary specialist, Curtiz's version of the Robin Hood story is, as Richards states, the 'definitive' form (1977, p. 196) and has been enormously influential in both popular and critical terms. It was itself re-released in 1948 with great success, and had a black and white version for television. Its dominance in the field is clear in that when studios in the following decades decided to profit from the popularity of the myth, they regularly deferred to this dominant version. Cornel Wilde starred for Columbia in 1946, but 'The Bandit of Sherwood Forest' was actually the son of the famous outlaw; incidentally the film called the villain Pembroke, suggesting a link back to 1730 – or more probably to some borrowing mediator. Richards calls this 'political, fast-moving and exciting' (1977, p. 214) and it is still to be seen on television. In the more ambitious 1950 Columbia production of 'Rogues of Sherwood Forest' John Derek also played Robin's son and this version also linked the story to an earlier formation by bringing Magna Carta into Robin's triumphs; it was especially close to the 1938 version because some stock footage was used from it and Alan Hale completed a remarkable record of playing Little John three times, as the youthful squire who did not over-shadow Fairbanks in height or personality, then as an apparently much taller man beside Flynn and finally as a senior warrior protecting his old friend's son.

Another prompt follow-up to the Curtiz picture was the widely criticized 'The Prince of Thieves' produced by Sam Katzman and Columbia, and directed by Howard Bretherton in 1948, which was indeed based on Dumas and was notable for a very complex plot, but it had little special weight or socio-political significance, other than to testify to the continuing interest in and marketability of the myth even when it appeared in, as Halliwell cuttingly remarks, a 'tatty second-feature version' (1990, p. 814).

Other routine representations followed with remarkable regularity in the high days of cinema, though as television began to have a major effect on audiences in the USA the low-budget films tend to appear only in England. In 1952 Disney, using funds frozen in Britain, pro-duced 'The Story of Robin Hood and His Merrie Men', starring Richard Todd, who seemed better suited to the stiffer acting style of British war movies. It did however link with modernity in the form of Elton Hayes as a wandering minstrel who told the story – both a contact with the emerging folk music tradition in which Hayes become well-known on television and also a link forward to the full-length cartoon version of Robin Hood by Disney in 1973. This is often condemned by film specialists for the simplicity of its animation technique and backgrounds, but has an amiable humour, a song track that appeals to children, and also employed some fine acting voices, with Peter Ustinov as Prince John and Phil Harris playing Little John as a large and stupid bear.

As with the high jinks of Fairbanks' film, sober-minded commen-tators sometimes find such populist transgressions distasteful, both as film itself and as a degradation of the Robin Hood tradition, but at least the cartoon version had some zest. This, and the high order technical skills of the earlier major versions, were mostly lacking from the routine Hammer picture 'Men of Sherwood Forest' directed by Val Guest, starring Don Taylor, and described by Halliwell as a 'fairly adventurous romp on a low level' (1990, p. 669). A similarly lacklustre effect rose from the Hammer version of 1961 (by another well-known commercial director Terence Fisher) called 'Sword of Sherwood Forest'. Peter Cushing played the sheriff to good effect, but Richard Greene was a somewhat overweight hero; Marian (Sarah Branch) is in better shape, though, as is revealed in the manner of 'continental' films of those Bardot days — she meets the outlaws after taking a swim in a forest pool, decorously face down in long-shot.

The most inherently unusual of these run-of-the-mill follow-ups to Flynn was another 'Son of Robin Hood' made by 20th Century Fox in Britain in 1958 and directed by George Sherman who had handled Cornel Wilde in 1946 with much better effect than this new 'son': perhaps in part because of the improbable script. Here the hero is actually a daughter, played in an unconvincing manner by June Laverick. Set in the days of Henry III and inventing a villain called 'The Black Duke des Roches', this was more pastiche than transgression; it is also called by Halliwell a 'romp', but he further defines this example of the genre as 'empty-headed' (1990, p. 941).

These films tend to be produced or at least made in England partly because of the 'Eady Money' structure of rewarding US companies for shooting in England, but also because television was eating heavily into the profitability of mainstream middle-of-the-road pictures in the USA. Naturally enough, that medium became part of the Robin Hood story, but not in the same way as the movies. A pilot was made by Hal Roach Jr but failed to convert into the expected series and so was released into the cinema as 'Tales of Robin Hood' in 1951. Because of its form it ran less than an hour, but did at least recognize 'the political overtones' of the myth (Richards, 1977, p. 202).

In spite of the growing Cold War anxieties, that was probably not the reason for its failure on TV and the lack of any later American television initiative in the myth. American television has little room, it seems, for the historical European costume drama outside the 'high culture' preserve of public broadcasting channels. What was carried in the cinema by colour, music, and a very high standard of finish in both the Fairbanks and Flynn version, could not survive in the small-scale, grittily-realistic mode of black and white television, from which more naturally emerged the modern detective and police series as a fiction of heroism and oppression.

But in Britain, things were different. As the country has weakened in power, the value of heritage has only grown, and if all round the world Robin Hood means Errol Flynn, in Britain and its dominions, the hero's name may equally mean the serious-minded and officer-like Richard Greene (see illustration 17) in the long-running series of half hour programmes made by Sapphire films for ATV which began in 1955 and ran till 1958. Some episodes have recently been released on video, but unlike the Flynn film, their appeal is distinctly antiquarian and sentimental.

The sets seem tiny, the cameras immobile in focus and position. What carries the series is the capable if restrained theatricality of an experienced English cast (though it included the youthful Paul Eddington as Alan a Dale) and the closely-worked, often serious-minded scripts which see authority and oppression from the viewpoint of a post-war reformist democracy.

Apart from a new form of ruling class oppression each week, there was a good deal of history; it was a serf versus lord structure, and few points were taken by the landowners. The audience, it might seem contradictory to note, were the emergent consumerists of what would soon be Macmillan's England, not least in possessing televisions, and there is little sign that the series was favoured only by the culturally inclined – it was after all on the 'commercial' channel, as it was then rather sneeringly called by many, the song in particular was massively popular among all strata of society, and the series was originally directed towards children.

What seems to have been the mainspring of success was the elegance with which the saga fitted the thirty-minute format (including advertisements) and the evident way in which it connected with a real depth of interest in, sympathy for and identification with the myth of Robin Hood among the populace – including that of Australia, where the programme was still running on some stations right up to the advent of colour in 1974.

It may well be, as Richards asserts, that 'production was skimpy and the action all too often clumsy' (1977, p. 202), but audiences were hardly demanding and the programme had a strong appeal. The song itself was well remembered: its verses were used to sum up each episode at the end, but the chorus was memorably simple:

> Robin Hood, Robin Hood
> Riding through the Glen
> Robin Hood, Robin Hood
> With His Band of Men.

Feared by the Bad
Loved by the Good
Robin Hood, Robin Hood, Robin Hood.

The resemblance between this and a line in Parker's 'True Tale of Robin Hood' which calls him 'Feared of the rich, loved of the poore' (Child, 1965, III, p. 232, st. 107) is presumably an accident, though some of the people involved in the scripts were more than capable of reading Child; Ring Lardner Jr has stated that he and Ian McLellan Hunter, being blacklisted in MacCarthy's America, contributed twenty scripts in the first year, under pseudonyms, including 'Oliver Skene' (1991). Bill Blake, the American Marxist writer and husband to Christina Stead, acted as researcher on some of the early episodes. The context in which this simple series was politically strengthened is outlined in the film 'Fellow Traveller' (1989), written by Michael Eaton, a script-writer and Robin Hood scholar, who interweaves the themes of modern betrayal and medieval resistance to create effectively an intriguing update of the myth.

Not only was the television 'Adventures of Robin Hood' inherently populist in mode; it came in a time and place where the restrained radicalism that had pervaded the myth from time to time was widely acceptable. Though the Labour government had been beaten in 1951, Britain was very much still a welfare state, with the moderate Conservative government and fairly right-wing Labour occupying a common ground sometimes called Butskellism, after Hugh Gaitskell the Labour leader and R.A. Butler, the very influential senior Conservative who never became leader. In that world oppressive practices were automatically rejected, both by socialists and by paternalist gentry, it was assumed that combination of the people was inherently a good thing, and also – where left-wing labour parted company – that it was natural for a leader of a higher class to supervise social improvement.

Apart from its relatively leftist politics, the other very striking element of the series is how well it fits television; the script writers tended to give one character a focal role in a particular episode, so that Bernadette O'Farell, a particularly managerial Marian and herself the image of a highly capable ATS officer, would have the story of her origins related along with her own response to problems of the sheriff's making. There was little intercutting between different strands as is now the mode in soap opera; each episode was a playlet, rather like an extended ballad or indeed like the two-scene drama that actually survives from the fifteenth century. If the television medium took the form back to quite antique fashions, so did the relative poverty of the production. The series was pruned down, like the spare narrative of the early ballads, and there was almost no plot decoration or elaboration; the feel of the early black and white drama had just the spare, impersonal character of the earlier ballads.

But if wartime social attitudes and habits of cultural utility lived on in that series, and formed a cyclical link back to the ancient days of Robin Hood drama, the audience was indeed in the teething stage of high consumerism and, especially after 1956, would encounter many new forces, in both international politics and the consumerist marketplace. As British self-confidence waned in the face of fading empire and weakening trade, so the old simple verities of narrative were under pressure from new techniques as well as radically shifting values in society and the fictions through which it contemplated itself. Always contemporary and always traditional, the Robin Hood myth represented these changes, and its next major reworking realized a very different world in both form and content.

A lack of simplicity in technique and belief is the keynote of three very different films that were produced in Britain in the following years. Whether it was Flynn in full colour or Richard Greene in tiny black and white, the tone had been quite reverential, the respect for the material clear and the presentation in its varying ways revealed a faith in traditional realism. But after the fifties the forms of popular art became much more experimental as modernist ideas and technical possibilities became more widespread, and at the same time a lack of faith in romantic and patriotic certainties was increasingly common. In various ways these developments were visible in the renovations of the outlaw myth on the screen.

The first was a striking return to carnival in its most free-floating, even naive form. Hammer kept on mining the successful vein of Robin Hood materials and in 1962 produced their third film in six years, 'A Challenge for Robin Hood'. Barrie Ingham was the hero, and his careworn earnestness of manner seems distinctly new for the elementally heroic figure, a touch of fifties pragmatism. This film is, like the ATV series, basically a fairly earnest and serious recreation of Robin as a friend of the people, but in addition to that familiar politics is some new hilarity as genuine artistic populism cuts across the politically-correct version. For most viewers a comic sequence must remain the high spot of the film, and one that thoroughly undermines it as a coherent piece, though hardly having the impact of a planned satirical transgression: this is closer to the anarchic chaos of true farce.

Robin has been trapped and caught; he is to be executed; rescue must be arranged, agree the outlaws. This is in part the time of plodding realism, and they wonder how they will travel to Nottingham as it is too far to walk. But this is also the time of Ealing comedies: what should heave into sight but a cart loaded with pies, and, if that is not enough of a threat to the heroic mode, one driven by Alfie Bass, malign imp of so many British comedies. Naturally, and with much comic interplay, the outlaws hijack the cart and rattle off to a rescue achieved in a hail of pastry.

If this disrupts the outlaw myth in the direction of street-level farce, another English film comes out of innovative comedy to apply new standards of hyper-reality. Richard Lester made his name in 1964 with a high-tension and hi-tech quasi-documentary comedy on the Beatles, 'A Hard Day's Night', but when in 1976 he turned to make *Robin and Marian* which Richards calls the 'first major Robin Hood film for over twenty years' (1977, p. 209) he took the position of anti-romantic realism. Especially he cut across the timelessness of the myth. The *Gest* recorded that Robin spent twenty-two years before his betrayal and death, but no version had ever considered time as real in the greenwood; equally, the Robin who quite often returned from the Crusades to take up his outlaw career was remarkably youthful and free from battle scars or military exhaustion,

Lester, though, made his film rich with autumnal credibility; Robin has been at war for a lifetime; the Marian he once loved and left for the Holy Land has long been a nun; he returns and they meet for a final conjunction in love and rebellion, and both are fated to failure. The fact that Lester was able to cast such entrancing ancients as Sean Connery and Audrey Hepburn gave the picture a special wistful appeal, but it was also quite disturbingly realistic in its final battle scene and aftermath. At the end it is indeed a nun who causes Robin's death: fatally wounded as he is, she gives him poison and takes it herself. The mysterious ending of the medieval hero becomes a moment of humanist passion enshrined by the fullest version of realism in the whole myth.

Moving and even searching as the film is, powerful attractions as its stars still are, it does not seem to have remained in the repertoire like lesser works of cinematic art in the myth, nor has its premise been adopted by anyone else. When it is replayed on television it is described as a radical reworking of the tradition, and it retains a 'one-off' quality. This must be because it breaks the mould by admitting time and reality, and indicates that these figures are in fact locked within the passing of human time. Lester has brought the myth out of the greenwood, out of its nationalist simplicities, given maturity and so obsolescence to the hero and his various loves, for country, freedom and a woman. While the film is politically quite radical, making Robin a man of the people standing against a corrupt aristocracy, and while it elides any special elitism that is in the heroic positioning (and that Connery might bring from his James Bond films), it also makes a deep-seated breach in the mythic conventions of timeless and symbolic activity; the myth is imprisoned by Lester within a cage of credibility.

Similar limitations, but less power of personality and lower production values, lie behind the limited success of the last of Hammer's many ventures into this topic, a television series which they planned in 1969 called 'The Legend of Robin Hood'. David Warbeck played Robin in realistic mode and considerable emphasis was placed on grainy reality in form and accurate political detail in the material. Richards summed it up:

> what we get is a film clearly concerned to be grimly realistic: no fancy hairdos or dinky Lincoln green suits, no scriptwriters' repartee and gaudy, multi-coloured costumes, no eternally sunny skies and purpose built Hollywood castles. Instead there is Welsh location shooting (damp woods, overcast skies, dark brown soil, mist), genuine weathered medieval castles, dull-coloured authentic-looking costumes, and a narrative which includes rape and torture. (1977, p. 209)

This was the style of the times: there was a 'realistic' King Arthur series from this period, 'Arthur of the Britons', with Oliver Tobias in the lead, but it had little lasting impact. The Robin Hood project fared worse; like Hal Roach Jr's previous attempt, the Hammer pilot never found a television outlet but surfaced in 1973 in a cinema version entitled 'Wolfshead.' The cause of the relative failure of these reworkings is not necessarily conservatism in the controlling bodies of television, as some radicals might tend to assume; there is, at least in this myth, and in this kind of audience, a limit to how much detailed realism the story can accommodate. Richards puts it simply with respect to 'Wolfshead': 'Perhaps the insistence on authenticity interfered too much with the free-ranging spirit of the legend' (1977, p. 209).

This notion can be developed: the myth relies on a positive realization of freedoms: if it is not summertime, the outlaw myth will not be liberatory. The audience knows about cold weather and defeat; the function of the myth is to offer an immediate sense of escape and also a more distant promise of Utopia. If the representation is too dark, no light can be seen at the end of the tunnel. But that does not mean all Robin Hood myth is desocialized fantasy. The glamour of romance does not preclude both realism and radical politics, as became clear in the most innovative and influential version of the myth in recent times, the series made by Goldcrest for HTV, starting in 1984 and starring the youthful Michael Praed, who had West End success in Gilbert and Sullivan and the looks of an unkempt matinee idol to recommend him for the part (see illustration 18).

This series had its origin in screenplays by Richard Carpenter, a television writer both fanciful and experienced, noted for 'Catweazle', a successful mix of magic and children's comedy. His Robin Hood is generically not unrelated, in that it has strict realism in costume and everyday medieval events but also offers great fluidity in its camerawork, natural beauty in setting and soundtrack; in thematic terms there is a similar mix, with a peasant-oriented politics as foreground but full value given to the supernatural as a domain of value. Glamour and realism are skilfully intermingled.

Robin is the son of serfs who have been murdered by Normans when he was a child. Now, when he is mistreated in early adulthood, he makes common cause with a group of other young outcasts, but he is also chosen for his role to lead resistance as 'The Hooded Man' by Herne the Hunter, a giant figure wearing stag's antlers and living in the fashion of pagan myth in a grove on an island in a lake. Herne apparently goes back to Cernunnos, the Celtic 'horned one' who is (in so far as the Celts had anything so inflexible) the lord of animals in their informal pantheon.

Carpenter keeps the two themes of legitimate rebellion and magical validation running in parallel and combining to make a mix which seems remarkably appropriate for a post-seventies context where political discontent and paranormal fascinations appear to have been almost coterminous in their concerns. But there are more specific signs of contemporary connection in the series. At the very beginning, a flashback shows the Normans on the rampage in a flimsy peasant village and the armoured men in their excessive brutality are very like a news film from Vietnam: the burning house, the fleeing child, all in an ironically green and fertile context, seem to speak as directly on contemporary ideas of international oppression as the brutality in the Curtiz film refers to thirties Germany.

In other ways the series combined late seventies reality and magical intoxications. Marian, as played by Judy Trott, is both a young, brave, sensitive woman, capable of firing an arrow and scheming in monkish disguise, and also a titian-haired, curl-tressed pre-Raphaelite beauty, with inspiration like an aureole around her back-lit head. Everything is young, as the culture had it in that time; the sheriff is himself a petulant mid-thirties, and Sir Guy of Gisborne, pink-cheeked, floppy-haired, is the model of any well-bred, ill-mannered public school bully.

Planning and technique worked well for this series, rather as everything came together for Curtiz; the sound track for 'Robin of Sherwood' was by Clannad, the epitome of new age music, somewhat Celtic, distinctly electronic, vaguely hallucinatory. That, with the quality and mobility of the colour filming, especially in outdoor sequences, made up for the limited thematic range that the absence of splendid aristocratic display imposed. The series, as it went on, did tend to become like a high-colour version of the old ATV offering, but just as it had combined political radicalism with the heights of magical culture, so it developed an effective multiplicity in the figure of the hero. Praed grew tired of the series, so he was killed off, with transcendent grief, memorial fire-arrows and Herne-related mysticism. But 'the hooded man' was not, unlike the Fairbanks or Flynn versions, irresistibly personalized. Another face could fill the hood, and Herne this time chose not a lad from Locksley but the youthful Earl of Huntingdon. With apparent signs of gentrification, as the eighties turned less hospitable to radical ideas from the past, Robin was transformed from the rawly romantic figure of Praed to the cooler, sterling-silver-haired Jason Connery, who, as a scion of film aristocracy, seemed like a natural inheritor to the role his father had previously held.

In music and magic, if not in politics, the series now seems rather dated, but although it is securely tied to a recent period and place, and the rather complex early eighties attitudes seem to be more old-fashioned than the thirties vigour of the Flynn film, the Goldcrest Television series remains one of the major innovative and compelling reworkings of the myth, especially interesting for its power to reveal that there need not be, as it had seemed in the hands of Tennyson and Noyes, a contradiction between magic and resistance politics.

Since 'Robin of Sherwood' there has been a considerable amount of cinematic action in the myth, but little of it has been in any decisive way innovative. The strongest contender for genuine revisionism has been the BBC television series entitled 'Maid Marian and Her Merry Men', which definitely re-evaluates some of the traditional positions, especially on gender, but because this is done in an essentially playful and self-negating way, it does not have the effect of a major repositioning in the legend.

The series starts by displacing Robin entirely as a figure of any authority. He is described in the comic book versions as a 'trendy go for it boutique owner' and his major function is to be a decorative and mildly enthusiastic aide to the determined, buxom Marian played with caricaturizing energy by Kate Lonergan. Feminism is obviously one of the positions from which this series works, but whereas the Arthurian legend is presented with a serious ideological challenge by Marion Zimmer Bradley's *The Mists of Avalon* (1982), 'Maid Marian and Her Merry Men' is in the tradition of English pantomime, where reversals and farce are part of the structure of jesting support to ideas of heroism (see illustration 19). Just as Marian plays the lead, Little John has become Little Ron, a dwarf who is fierce and brave, if fool-hardy and ultimately ineffective. The ingenu-cum-interlocutor roles of Will Scarlet and Alan a Dale are combined with good effect in a character named Barrington, a Rastafarian rapper with a finely wry style. Robin and masculinity are made farcical rather than satirized when he goes to the archery contest disguised as a chicken, a scene especially vivid in the cartoon version (see illustration 20).

This kind of reversal does not simply come out of pantomime, but rather from its updating into television's own mode of ironic farce. Tony Robinson, who played Baldrick in the television series of historical burlesque 'Blackadder', wrote the scripts, and took on the choice role of the diminutive, ferocious and incompetent sheriff. There are

Illustration 19 Maid Marian in charge
(Courtesy BBC Productions; photo Lensmedia.)

certainly traces of social comment to be found in this series, in the feminist reversal, in Barrington's consistent trouble with the law as represented by a pair of Norman louts called Gary and Graeme, but while the peasantry is certainly oppressed, the whole operates within the realm of the grotesque, parodying not only the idea of heroics but the notion of social reform as well.

As a contemporary television reviewer commented, this is 'children's television with street cred' though he also notes 'its humour gives its audience credit for some degree of intelligence' (Mangan, 1991). The printed form of the series, a BBC comic book, focuses neatly the multi-mode and inherently ephemeral nature of this series, being little more trenchant in social terms than another strip-cartoon of the myth, a long-running series entitled 'Robin Hood's Schooldays' from the *Beano* in the 1970s, which was basically a bow and arrow version of 'The Bash Street Kids' (see illustration 21). 'Maid Marian and Her Merry Men' indicates real possibilities in rewriting the myth that has not yet been developed at a more substantially feminist level.

There was little sign of such a development in the pair of major Robin Hood films that were released in 1991. Several studios were planning a big budget picture in the myth at about the same time, as if to confirm the 'one a generation' pattern of major re-presentations in the tradition. A number of actors were discussed as being suitable for the hero, with leading contenders Mel Gibson (continuing Flynn's Australian tradition) and Tom Cruise (the youthful, sub-Michael Praed option). Morgan Creek were the first to reach production, with Kevin Costner as Robin, but 20th Century Fox continued their project through the production company 'Working Title', with Patrick Bergin in the lead.

The Costner vehicle was entitled 'Robin Hood: Prince of Thieves', but it has no sign of relying on the Dumas story. It begins with a strong version of the 'crusade return' motif in which Robin is actually in an Arab prison, but he is helped to escape by Azeem, a noble black played by Morgan Freeman, direct from his success in 'Driving Miss Daisy'. He remains with Robin through the story. Though 'Robin of Sherwood' had an Arab ally for Robin, this one is much more attuned to a US audience: Freeman is an American black in person and his character is firmly Islamic, so a black Moslem hero is validated along with the white liberal one.

On the hero's return to Locksley, he finds the castle is destroyed, his

244

Illustration 20 Robin Hood disguised in feminist farce
(Courtesy BBC Productions; photo Lensmedia.)

Illustration 21 The schoolboy outlaw in *Beano*
(Courtesy D.C. Thomson; photo Lensmedia.)

father murdered and the evil sheriff and his cousin Guy are Robin's
dedicated enemies. He withdraws to the greenwood and takes up the
leadership of the outlaws, but not without some opposition from a
troubled young man, Will Scarlet, the focus for a motif from another
American liberal genre, the youth rescued from himself, as in 'The
Blackboard Jungle' tradition. Will, having resisted Robin's leadership
and been tempted to betray him, is eventually revealed as Robin's
half-brother, whom their father abandoned when Robin objected to
his foster mother. The old inheritance drama that focused on Will
Gamwell and the long-standing tradition of some tension between
Robin and other outlaws, which goes right back to 'Robin Hood and
the Monk', are both resolved through a positive model of the modern
blended family, realized in fully sentimental mode as Robin finally
says 'I have a brother'.

But such contemporary elements of fraternalization between sib-
lings and races are not permitted to have a major part in the story;
both Will and the black ally are minor elements, no more than a

market-oriented gesture. In any specific way, as Tom Shippey sharply remarked (1991, p. 6), the film has 'a total lack of political awareness' and plods mechanically through a series of familiar adventures. Such lack of structural imagination is matched by the technique: the film has a general air of being more like a set of fine adverts punctuating a long dull programme rather than a feature film: there are moments of visual power, like the arrow-mounted camera used in much of the publicity, or the burning of the forest fortress; similarly the sound track had one very successful song 'I do it for you', an international hit for Bryan Adams, but lacked the consistent level of pace and quality that Korngold and Clannad provided in other versions.

Such lack of drive is focused most strongly in the characters. Costner consciously sought to avoid the comic opera tradition by eschewing green tights and feathered caps and wearing the more realistic quilted jacket, leather trousers and heavy muddy boots, but the lack of heroic fire left the film flat. Costner's manner was summed up by Bob Ellis as 'a born Hamlet in a role demanding a born Hotspur' (1991, p. 12), and this undue placidity seemed basic to the actor's style: the much distributed publicity picture showed him as the only filmic Robin Hood to pose without a weapon.

Apart from that scarcely appropriate pacifism, Costner could not be said to have created a new Robin Hood in any substantive way, and the surviving memory of the film in public discourse is the heights of overacting achieved by Alan Rickman as the sheriff, who underlines the fact that apart from those rare talents who can fully energize Robin, this is the plum part. His ripe style, while splendid in its own way, quite unbalances the film, something both Curtiz and Rathbone were too professional to let happen. When the most quoted line from a Robin Hood film is the sheriff shrieking, in his fury at the peasants, 'And call off Christmas', it is evident that something is seriously wrong with the tone and overall balance of this version of the heroic myth.

In many ways better structured, with a more balanced impact, was the rival film, simply titled 'Robin Hood', directed by John Irvin and starring Patrick Bergin, with Uma Thurman making a considerable impact as a well-controlled, sexually-aware Marian. The script is a 'medievalized' version of the 1938 film: it opens with the saving of Much, but the enemy created in this way is Sir Miles de Falconet, who is out riding with his fiancee, Marian. After Robert Hode is tried for being an accessory to poaching, he and his friend Will head for the forest, but so does Marian, disguised as a boy to escape this unappealing marriage.

Robin takes over the outlaw band and makes an enemy in Harry, the former leader. The plot thickens with a 'false Marian' episode, laid on to trap Robin and the real Marian (coincidentally reminiscent of *The Sad Shepherd*), but their archery skills save them. In the final sequence Marian is captured by Falconet, but rescued by the outlaws who enter the castle in the disguise of an All Fool's Day procession, with Tuck as Lord of Misrule. The film ends with reconciliation between Norman and Saxon, and Robin and Marian marry, but it offers no simple resolution of the problems posed by Prince John.

This structure has woven a number of older features into the framework of the 1938 picture, but if the film has a well-shaped plot and considerable strength in its leads – Bergin has the looks and the arch wit to match his intense Marian – some found it tonally bizarre. This in part stemmed from its history: John McGrath, the radical British playwright was brought in to naturalize an American script by Mark Allen Smith, and he presumably emphasized the apparent links between Norman arrogance and Thatcherite restructuring of the 1980s. This film, as a result, does at least represent the tone of confused irritation that pervades British radical politics of the last decade, in a context that is faithful without too much filmic dilution to the notion of a hero with Trickster characteristics and a populist heart, and also presents, for once, a heroine capable of some authority and of taking a place in a political movement. Bob Ellis felt it was 'the only good film on this vexed subject yet made'; he characterized it as 'zestful, mud-caked, anthropologically exact' and he thought that Uma Thurman, as 'Olivia de Haviland on heat' gave 'androgynous gleam and beautiful arousing scorn' to a difficult role, while Bergin was fully convincing as being 'lustily belligerent, randy as a coot . . . and only incidentally a convert to Socialist redistribution' (1991, p. 12). Bob Ellis generates his own excitement, but it may be that he has accurately perceived genuine elements of carnival at the core of a film which could not claim to be a radical rewriting of the tradition, but is at least a competent, lively and in significant ways refocused version, a worthy challenge as few have been to the dominance of the Curtiz masterpiece of 1938.

There seems little likelihood that Robin Hood productivity will slow down in cinema, as visual narrative becomes increasingly the dominant form of story-telling on a worldwide basis and some of the versions have special audiences. That process goes back to the Warner animation team which picked up its own studio success in 1939 with 'Robin Hood Makes Good' (using squirrels playing outlaws) and then 'Rabbit Hood' (1949), starring Bugs Bunny. Consciously transgressive was 'Robin Hood Daffy' (1959) with Daffy as 'the Errol Flynn of Duckdom', but the show is stolen by Porky Pig as Friar Tuck; the Australian 'Robin Hood' (1971) was a more serious child-oriented animation.

A more mature spirit of fun came in the form of Hollywood burlesque, when the team who produced 'Love at First Bite', shaped the remarkable made for television film 'Zany Adventures of Robin Hood' from 1984, written by Richard Kaufman, with George Segal in the leading role. Notable for Morgan Fairchild's over-the-top performance as a Marian condemned to virginity – 'I'll soon be Old Maid Marian' – and Janet Suzman's presentation of an Eleanor of Aquitaine whose sexual aggression harks back directly, if accidentally, to the world of *Looke About You*, the film was most notable for its handling of the customary Marian rescue sequence. In order to release her from the castle, the less than heroic Robin goes to a character lifted straight from *Ivanhoe*, Isaac of York in the droll shape of Kenneth Griffith, acting his head off. Robin wants a loan for bribing guards. Business is bad, Isaac regrets, but he has friends. In one of the finest moments of Robin Hood transgressiveness, the hero enters the castle with a team of Israeli Commandoes, fully equipped as if straight from 'Flight to Entebbe'. This and other innovations of the film, including Segal's poorly-cut green tights, bring the high wit of Jewish-American comedy into the tradition, and provide one of its more diverting sports, a piece fully in the spirit of Joaquim Stocqueler.

A less ironic treatment is found in Mel Brooks's *Robin Hood: Men in Tights* (1993), which follows the familiar story in a determinedly farcical way. Robin is skilled and brave, though small and often unheroic; Marian is a beauty, but she, unlike the plot, is encumbered with a chastity belt. Brooks' speciality is Hollywood pastiche and many jokes are directed at other outlaw films: Costner's noble black fellow in arms Azeem here becomes Achoo, son of Asneeze, and other motifs are less obviously referential – a dungeon escape looks like that in 'Robin of Sherwood', a black rapper to introduce the film is very like Barrington of 'Maid Marian'. These links hardly amount to satire: robust comedy is the film's forte, with Tracey Ullmann playing an over-excitable witch called Latrine and Brooks himself presiding in rabbinical form as Friar Tuchman. Crass and comic as any pantomime, belittled by fastidious reviewers, *Men in Tights* is a thriving example of the most broadly comic side of the Robin Hood myth.

Other films could, with less confidence, be identified as part of the tradition, depending how far transgressiveness can go. Danny Kaye's 'The Court Jester' (1955) includes some lively parody of the Flynn-Rathbone sword-fight, and the Frank Sinatra vehicle 'Robin and the Seven Hoods' (1964) is a good deal closer to the structure of the myth, with Peter Falk as the rival gangster Guy Gisborne and Bing Crosby as the singing moralist Allan A. Dale who eventually marries Marian and leaves Sinatra, as Robbo, happy with his rat pack of modern outlaws. But these films, like the Muppet version of 1981 (Robin is a 'bold and chivalrous frog', and Miss Piggy makes an unusually forceful Maid Marian) are all parts of the ephemera of the Robin Hood myth, and in that way realize modern versions of the ancient play-games that are known to us only through dates, accountants' entries and the occasional outrage of over-serious citizens. The tradition of film has room for such sports in particular because it also has at least two major reworkings of the theme, by Fairbanks and Flynn and a respectable number of solid representations, with socially attuned variations.

The Robin Hood myth might well have survived to the present without the help of film, because of the continuing or ever growing need for a sense of resistance and its offer of an elusive symbolic hero who figures the natural against the oppressive aspects of the cultural. But there can be no doubt that the myth has gained dynamic energy in the modern period through the existence of a medium which is, like the ancient play-games and simple narratives, highly visual, excitingly active, able to encompass serial structures, and devoted to the construction of superficial images with deeply symbolic possibilities. Film seems made for the Robin Hood myth, but it is also true that the myth seems especially appropriate for film, and more in this most modern of generic traditions can be confidently expected in the future.

6.3 'THE HERO THAT LIVES IN YOU ALL'

If film has been the dominant medium for the myth this century, Robin Hood has still had many modern representations in other forms.

After the 'Georgians', poetry seems to have fallen largely silent, characteristic of the withdrawal of that genre into the domain of private communication, or the lack of it. However, in a period when fiction has continued to thrive, both in the high art form often publicly subsidized in various ways and also in highly popular international modes, it is notable that major Robin Hood novels have not been produced. This must testify to the difficulty with which the myth fits into the requirements of the novel for extended and interlinked plot and deep characterization. The relatively few examples of Robin Hood fiction tend to show up those difficulties and to indicate how authors have rarely been able to resolve the problems.

Most of the novels have been 'juveniles', as the trade would call them, devoted to action and without the detailed sexual activity that is apparently required for 'adult' fiction by publishers these days. There may indeed be an opening for a highly sexualized transgression of the myth's patterns; it would not be hard to graft the Lady Chatterley style of greenwood activity onto the outlaw myth, as E.M. Forster has implied (see pp. 216–17). Such prospects may be in the future; what has happened in the past is a series of fairly straightforward quasi-juvenile novels like Carola Oman's *Robin Hood: The Prince of Outlaws* of 1939, which is basically a reworking of the Child ballads with a rather thoughtful introduction. The same material, turned with some effort into a coherent narrative, forms the basis of Jay Williams' *The Good Yeoman* (1956) which explores with some stress on 'authenticity' the notion that in the days of Edward II a serf called John Nailer and a gentleman ultimately called Robin Hood join forces. The hero of the title is actually John, but the conflict between the two elides any social meaning and concentrates on a love triangle with Agnes, the daughter of a knight. A somewhat mechanical plot and over-antiquated style does little to save this from being a serious but rather plodding medieval tear-jerker.

Apart from these full-length novels, a wealth of reprints and reworkings have in a simpler mode kept the material before children. Any bookshop usually has one anthology, perhaps the three by four inch cut-down of Pyle for the very young in Deborah Kestel's adaptation from Playmore publishers, still using the Pyle illustrations and with a respectful one-page note about him, retailing at $1.25 in 1986. Or they could be pot-boiler rewrites like Enid Blyton's *Tales of Robin Hood* (1930), Puffin's *The Adventures of Robin Hood* by Roger Lancelyn

Green (1956) or remarkably late 'Georgian' versions like Edward Blishen's *Robin Hood* (1969) used in the BBC children's series 'Jackanory'. Then they might be straight re-tellings like Robin McKinley's *The Outlaws of Sherwood* (1988) or more upmarket, authorized by imposing names like Antonia Fraser (1957) or Bernard Miles (1979): both have illustrations by Victor Ambrus in a bold modern version of Pyle's clear linear style. T.H. White's treatment of the outlaw as Robin Wood in *The Sword in the Stone* (1938) is a more considered and original use of the figure as the spirit of forest lore, minor though his impact is in the whole novel.

Not all the youth audience is attuned to the simple re-delivery of antiquated material, however, and it is interesting to note that Robin Hood finds a place in the realms of what is now the recognized genre of 'Fantasy', which offers lengthy, complex, invented narratives, delivered with great attention to detail, but scant reference to probability, usually stressing parascientific speculation. Robert Holdstock's *Mythago Wood* (1984), which seems at the upper end of complexity and speculation, involves Robin in the process of time-travelling through the sympathetic magic of a particular place. The narrator explores his father's own explorations into the power of a place across the ages, and finds his notes very revealing; they are also a fair example of the special discourse of this genre: 'Hood is back . . . I cannot enrich the oak vortex sufficiently with the pre-mythago of the Urscumug' (1984, p. 37). Robin makes a similarly sudden appearance in a magical sequence in Peter Beagle's *The Last Unicorn* (1968, pp. 50–65) where on his journey to King Harfard's country to find the Red Bull, a character called Schmendrick falls in with outlaws, led by one Captain Cully, and the group's capacity for magic briefly conjures up the outlaw band – the moment seems almost out of Noyes's *Sherwood*.

Plainer fantasy appears in a volume in Robert Silverberg's Time Travel series entitled *The Robin Hood Ambush* by William F. Wu (1990); this is history with science, and the 'Databank' at the end includes among other items a note on 'The Walled Town of Nottingham' and an equally doubtful entry about 'Super Rebok Biotech Hightops', a form of electronic footwear. A wide-ranging anthology of *The Fantastic Adventures of Robin Hood* was edited by Martin H. Greenberg (1991), with items ranging from private eye pastiche in 'The Locksley Scenario' by Brian M. Thomsen to the realm of Dungeons and Dragons with Nancy A. Collins' 'The One-Eyed King'.

A less worldly-wise fantasy-oriented series was derived from the series 'Robin of Sherwood' and drew on another new genre, the 'tie-in-novel' which bears on its jacket a still from the film or television programme and invites viewers to relive their excitement in verbal form. The first was by Richard Carpenter himself, entitled simply *Robin of Sherwood* (1984); in an unostentatious way it justifies Carpenter's brief introduction in which he hopes to have provided a 'version that remains true to the spirit of Robin Hood while providing a few new ideas of my own' (1984, p. 5). Later examples were by Robin May (*Robin of Sherwood and the Hounds of Lucifer*, 1985) and Anthony Horowitz, who explains in print form the arrival of the new Robin in what is now called *Richard Carpenter's Robin of Sherwood: The Hooded Man* (1986). The screen versions have also generated titles in a different genre, the new choose-your-own adventure mode so popular with upper primary school children. The first from this stable was Graham Staplehurst, with the further extended title *Richard Carpenter's Robin of Sherwood Gamebook 1: The King's Demon* (1987), and Bantam Books quickly offered in their 'Choose Your Own Adventure' series *Outlaws of Sherwood Forest* by Ellen Kushner (1985).

Peter Vansittart hardly belongs in any genre, his fertility is so considerable, but his novel *The Death of Robin Hood* (1981) certainly has strong resemblance to modern fantasy, though its inheritance is further back, drawing on the Gravesian account of Robin as a natural force and combining it with many other motifs of natural resistance. After a fully mythic opening with 'Hodekin' and other numinous figures, 'Robene Hude' appears as a fertility dancer, and Marian appears in the same troupe; the novel moves on to deal with a General Ludd in Sherwood and the 'green dressed terrorists' of the Hardacre Riots of 1812.

The more conventional progress of the historical novel genre seems like firm ground under the feet after fantasy forms of the outlaw, and these have continued to appear, but hardly with rapidity or any great impact. Nicholas Chase in 1983 published *Locksley*, a full-length historical novel with an adult audience in mind and an 'I was there' orientation – the sort of novel that, descending from Scott's *Waverley*, places an imaginary central figure in historically real contexts. Locksley is on the crusades and through luck and skill in arms meets King Richard himself. The king's homosexuality is part of the narrative, and so is the attraction felt for Robin by the somewhat disgruntled

Queen Berengaria. After this unusually extended crusade opening, Robin returns to find Locksley itself burnt and joins the outlaws – the Costner screenplay may have been influenced. The narrative ranges widely, or even wildly, with Queen Eleanor showing a highly personal interest in the hero, and Robin becoming almost comically omnipresent at great moments in history: he kills Prince Arthur of Brittany on behalf of the queen, is there when the jewels are lost in the Wash, and finally settles down with the royal widow Berengaria to a productive life as a merchant.

The book was reprinted by Penguin in 1984, but has hardly made much impact. It was written in a competent enough style, but it shows up the sheer difficulty of fitting the myth to the special form of the novel, unlike the film genre. Chase has to flail about to find enough incident for a full-length novel. The traditional outlaw story does not permit the in-depth analysis that enables Jane Austen or Henry James to write copiously at length about very little action. But nor is there a great deal of condensed and unified action in the tradition: if many of the ballads are used, they usually will tend to have a serial, repetitive quality. To reach full length, Chase uses techniques basic to the modern historical novel – secret revelations, strained yoking together of separate incidents, inside stories on the lives of the great – but the effect is no more than pastiche of both the historical novel and the heroic myth.

In an American novel on the characteristically large scale, over five hundred pages, Parke Godwin revisits the historical Robin Hood in *Sherwood* (1991). The idea of Norman versus Saxon still fascinates, but Godwin is scholar enough to place the drama credibly in the late eleventh century, making Robin a full-blown Saxon, named Edward Aelredson. However, Robin fights with Norman rebels against the king, and so the novel is able to suggest a form of nationalist resistance without class affiliation, much like that dreamed up by Scott, but here, rather as in the Curtiz film, to be associated with America's own concept of honourable rebellion which, in a final note, Godwin associates with 'Boston Common, Bunker Hill or Valley Forge' (1991, p. 526). A second volume is promised, but this relocated Robin seems to offer little to the tradition beyond a forest version of the American national saga of family and sentiment, a harmless enough informative page-turner, but lacking both the vigour and the political edge of the major versions outside the novel.

Live popular theatre, though ceding much of its dominance to film, has not lost touch with the Robin Hood theme, though there is none of the old regularity about its appearance. The pantomime is still performed, though it is not one of the favourites; perhaps that is because the story line is so scanty that it is usually coupled with 'Babes in the Wood'. But Robin Hood musicals have been seen in recent years, across a wide range of styles, though without success in esteem or at the box-office.

Lionel Bart's much publicized follow-up to 'Oliver' and 'Blitz' was a musical based on the outlaw legend and called, with striking bathos, 'Twang!'. Robin was played by James Booth, best known for cockney comedy in 'Carry On' films, while Bernard Bresslaw as Little John and Barbara Windsor as Delphina, a version of Marian, came from the same stable. The reviews of the 1965 production were savage: Jeremy Rundall commented in *Plays and Players* that 'almost everything about it is bad' and the Daily Mail review printed merely the word, 'Ouch!' While it is probable that both music and staging were less than polished, the real problem for the press was that this production carried the farcical repertoire style of the 'Carry On' company into conflict with the sentimental respectability expected in a West End production. Bart's previous triumphs had been deeply patriotic, straight forward musical comedy in mode. 'Twang!' was inherently pantomime, but it lacked both the magic and the romance, and it wandered only between straight farce and ironic treatment of the modern musical (see illustration 22). More formally satirical than traditional theatre could handle, it closed within a week, its aim judged to be completely off target.

But that kind of deeply comic rehandling of the tradition could succeed in less exclusive contexts and could make through its farcical form some telling points – including the need for conventional theatre, and society, to face a little satire. The Bristol Old Vic pantomime of 1984 (written by Dennis Nielson, 1985), behind the highly carnivalesque title 'Robin Hood: The Truth Behind the Green Tights' addressed the events of the year as well as timeless Robin Hood verities. The central figure is 'Albert Ross' a little man, presumably seen as the albatross around the neck of British liberty. He is a coward, and dismisses the myth of Robin as mere gentry self-indulgence: 'Well, he's not like us, is he? Eh? He may profess to represent the views of the common man, the ordinary man in the field, but he's one of them,

Illustration 22   Lionel Bart's 'Twang!: awkward positioning
(Courtesy *Independent* Newspaper; photo Lensmedia.)

isn't he? He's gentry . . . Don't tell me he goes prancing about in that
forest for my sake! It's the green tights he likes, and the singing!'
(1984, p. 3)

But Albert finds courage, especially from the voices of the trees —
a touch of Noyes persists here. The little man is persuaded to join a
kind of greenwood popular front — the Miners' Strike is referred to in
'Will Scargill' being one of the outlaws. Their promise is 'To uphold
people's rights' (p. 45), but this is pantomime not propaganda, and it
carnivalizes the notion of resistance as Albert sings:

> Though I don't mind the singing
> I'm not sure about the tights.
> I know the outlaw's code,
> I always will endorse it,

Thy Merry Cast

ROBIN HOOD	KELLY WRIGHT
MAID MARIAN	KATY PHILLIPS
FRIAR TUCK	HONEY EDWARD
LITTLE JOHNNIE	GEORGE RICHARDSON
SCARLET WILLIE	ZOE SMEETH
KEVAN DUVET	ALICE WARNER
THERESA GREEN	JO BULL
ARNEE	DIANE LEEMING
SHERIFF OF NOTTINGHAM	AMANDA MURPHY
GAY OF GUISBURNE	JENNIE MAILLEY
MRS. OVERALL	AMY FEAR
NARRATORS	VICKY NEWTON
	KATHERINE DUFFIN

Sheriff's Posse

Lady Gladiators

PHOENIX	CHARLOTTE ARIS		
FLAME	JENNY BENTLEY		
SCORPIO	YVETTE MOTTRAM		
LIGHTNING	HELEN NIXON		
PANTHER	DEBBIE NORTHEN		
JET	CAROLYNE YOUNG		

Lord Gladiators

SARACEN	GEORGIE BARRADALE
SHADOW	KIRSTY GROGAN
HAWK	NUALA HAYDEN
WOLF	TERESA HOUGHTON
WARRIOR	JULIE RANDALL
COBRA	JO URQUHART

Fair Peasants

HANNAH GLAZIER
JENNY CLOUGH
HEIDI BARON
CLAIRE BOWDEN
PHILIPPA BALL
CLAIRE BARTON
CLARE HEMPSALL
CLAIRE SHERIFF

POSTMAN - KATHERINE KENNEDY
SHAKESPEARIAN - ROSIE ALABASTER

Swinging Trees

LUCY FERGUSON
NATALIE GOODSON
RUTH CLARE
AMY HEWITT
SUSANNAH VEITCH
SONYA MOOR
EMMA WALMSLEY
AMANDA WARD
CATHERINE DAVIE
SARAH BURROWS
LISA FEAR

Illustration 23   Robin Hood, the school concert
(Courtesy Stamford High School; photo Lensmedia.)

> Rob the rich, give to the poor,
> And always wear your corset. (p. 46)

But this modern play-game does hold on finally to a sense of anti-authoritarian possibility; the last chorus repeats the lesson Albert has learnt that in good and well-organized company anything is possible:

> Never say can't, always say can,
> To make the jump from mouse to man. (p. 64)

The same mixture of critique and comedy was to be found in a little noticed 'Robin Hood' produced in the Ecology Theatre in London's Covent Garden early in 1992. This, very appropriately, stressed the green politics which could be found in the myth, but had other points to make along a continuum of modern cultural studies discourse: Robin was played by a woman, not to show off her legs but to make a feminist point, while leading outlaws were represented as those heroes of international popular culture, George Michael and Arnold Schwarzenegger.

Oscillating between farce and faith, theatrical performances like those two seem close to the antique structures of the Robin Hood myth, and there are less public versions, equally rooted in local community and modern globalized consciousness. At the girls' High School in Stamford, Lincolnshire (home of William Stukeley, Robin Hood's genealogist) the end of year entertainment in 1993 was a Robin Hood performance. The cast-list (see illustration 23) has a spirit of carnival very like the ancient Mummers' Play (see p. 106): the well-known figures are joined by two Hollywood heroes in disguise – Kevan Duvet and Arnee, as well as the schoolyard joke-names Theresa Green and Gay of Gisburne, while from up-to-date downmarket television come the Gladiators.

In the public theatrical domain a more sombrely single-minded innovation of that year was the 1993 production of 'Robin, Prince of Sherwood', with music and lyrics by Rick Fenn and Peter Howarth. The programme carried no credit for the structure of the performance and its conception, but presumably this was in the hands of Bill Kenwright, director and producer. Robin Hood was represented as young, vigorous, and extremely loud-voiced: this is the world of pop music, sports costuming and aerobic choreography. The style is

Lloyd-Webber on the football terraces, and the positioning of Robin is
as if the Michael Praed figure had forgotten all sense of class, communality and mysticism and been thrown back on the resources of eighties
self-absorption. The outlaw leader is billed with aggressive individualism as 'the hero that lives in you all', and he is introduced by a
repetitive, heavily rhythmic chant of 'Call him Robin Hood', with the
stress placed as Americans do on the first syllable of the name.

Theorists have spent much time in recent decades talking about
naming and self-identification as being the point of crisis in a world
dominated by what Fredric Jameson called, in the title of a recent
book *Post Modernism, or The Cultural Logic of Late Capitalism*. In
keeping with such views, the presentation and conceiving of the performance were fully concordant with the garish, noisy, confusing world
of the modern shopping mall and the final statement about Robin
'he's harnessed the will to survive' has just that vague combination of
privacy and bland generality that is at the heart of the new consumerist world order – an irony-free reverse of 'Twang'.

This gallimaufry of crass music and over-simple pomposity was
tolerated in London for eight weeks and lost the half million it cost
(according to the *Sunday Times*, 30.5.93); the Daily Telegraph called
it 'a doomed farrago'; but like the outlaw himself it left the metropolis, and people were paying to see it on tour, for the most part, it
seemed, slightly deafened parents with girls in early adolescence. But
even in such grotesque form the hero's figure still had some power to
appeal. There does indeed appear to be a Robin Hood who lives in us
all, though for many he may not be a matinee idol with a stentorian
voice and a simplistic version of identity politics.

A more dynamic form of the myth in the modern market-place is,
as of old, linked to location. There are several Robin Hood tourist sites
in the Nottingham area – a forest park to visit and two separate
recreations of aspects of the tradition. The best known of these, right
in the heart of Nottingham, is called 'Tales of Robin Hood', a title
that suggests the serial, multiple and fictional character of the myth
at its more immediately accessible.

Inside this compact theme-park lies a potent mixture of fact and
feeling. The 'Tales' offers a good deal of firmly empiricist material –
an exhibition shows just the sort of arrow-head that Robin might have
used, represents the scholarly arguments about identity, provides maps
and histories of Nottingham and district. But in addition to these
outlaw museum studies, the visitor is also permitted another form

of identity, namely self-identification with the myth itself. You are enabled, as the 'Souvenir Guide' says, to 'Ride through medieval Nottingham in our unique adventure cars'. They are small, and the emphasis is highly individualized: you can personally 'Meet its people. Smells its smells. Join its daily life' (1989).

Empiricism and involvement are skilfully combined in an exhibition that re-energizes the myth in terms of modern, educated, individualized – and consumerized – self. Here children can receive an outlawry certificate with their own names on it, buy the green pointed hat that is Robin Hood ritual dress, eat the lollipop that represents the body of the outlaw myth. This modern form of communion, to which you make a purchasing pilgrimage with the family, indicates that a faith of some sort in Robin Hood is still at the centre of modern practices, certainly for the English and, judging by the visitors, for many others, especially from America.

And, most engaging of all, the sense of impromptu flexibility, of rapid outlaw response, survives. In 1990, soon after the Tales opened, it happened that a parked car slipped its handbrake, careered backwards down the hill and crashed through the plate glass window of the exhibition shop. The damage was quickly boarded up and the event absorbed into the myth. Next day large black letters read across the boards (see illustration 24): 'The Sheriff Strikes Back'. The expectation that everyone will understand the underlying narrative is impressive enough, but so is the sense that this can be treated as a collective joke and that it can, with full transgressive confidence, embrace other cultural material: the reference in the wording is obviously to the sequel to Star Wars, then proving very popular.

Not only in Nottingham, not just in Britain and its language, but right around the world, the myth of Robin Hood, the good outlaw, is a matrix of ideas and conflicts that is still a resource for reference and representation in newspapers, radio, television and all forms of more overtly-fictional genres. In our own period the new forms of film and television have been particularly well-suited to develop the outlaw myth, but it seems very durable in other modes too, especially those with an element of theatre, of physical conflict with symbolic depth.

Over time there have been many Robin Hoods, and an increasing number of Maid Marians; the authority against which they make resistance seems to have had as many forms as there are periods and contexts for the elements of the tradition; the meaning of the myth is

Illustration 24   Folklore in Nottingham, 1990
(Photo Lensmedia.)

never stable, and may be quite contradictory even in one period. Bower, before drafting his pro-Catholic heroic fable, may well have read or heard a copy of the fiercely anti-clerical 'Robin Hood and the Monk'. At the production of the restoration *Robin Hood and His Crew of Souldiers* someone might have been selling broadsheets of the firmly rebellious 'Robin Hood's Progress to Nottingham'; after watching the individualist fervour of the musical 'Robin, Prince of Sherwood' you could rent on video the anarchic socialism of Patrick Bergin's 'Robin Hood'.

While there are lines of tradition to be seen across time – the *Gest*, Munday, Scott, Peacock and Tennyson all have had some of the impact their innovative force deserves – it is still very rare for any Robin Hood version to be easily and fully identified in terms of source. There seem to be few dominant influences in the myth at any one time – even though the Norman versus Saxon myth is shaped by Scott and Peacock, there are still many of their immediate successors who ignore it; similarly the crusade connection seems not to have any particular line of authority, it just appeals to those who want an adult military Robin at the start of the story. What comes across from any attempt to relate Robin Hood materials to their sources is that motifs keep being reinvented — like the witch who more than once plays Marian, or the repeated disguises by which someone is saved from hanging. The myth repeats itself because of the simple power of its structures and their recurrent appeal. It is the restricted character of the story which makes it so easy to handle effectively in many popular forms, though so hard to master in the inherently complicated — not necessarily complex — terms of the novel.

In all the texts the only notion that recurs is the sense that Robin resists bad authority. No one incident is compulsory, no one character other than the hero is always present. A spirited central figure and a force of oppression: they form the ground on which the potent myth operates; all else is local, contemporaneous, capable of alteration.

The inherent simplicity of the myth makes it, like other elementary life forms, extremely enduring, massively variable, and in some way annoying and even threatening to those who put their faith in complication and elaboration. For those who write ponderous and allegedly searching biographies, who philosophize at length about the depths of human capacity or lament the manifold essence of personal depravity, the Robin Hood myth bears nothing but frustration. But there is more than that in the myth for those who find meaning and value in structures beyond the private, in direct encounters of communal construction — good against evil, group against individual, oppressed against oppressor, town against forest, nature against culture, king against subject, man against man, even sometimes man against woman — and, increasingly, present against past. And within that politically potent structure there remain the flexibilities of the personal, symbolized in the potential of the hero who is decidedly one thing but can always be another: who is alone, but part of a group; young, but inherently mature; playful, yet able to kill; single, yet always to be partnered; associated with nature, yet always entering the town; set in the past, yet somehow able to recreate the issues of the present.

'Robin Hood in Barnsdale Stood' was the old axiom of both law and common parlance. The statement imagines Robin Hood as static: yet it also implies he will at any moment spring into dynamic action. Such a sudden release of energetic motion is still of compelling interest, and it can even now represent processes that have considerable force for anyone, in any place and time, who finds value in the sense of vigour, mystery and resistance which is still embodied in the name of Robin Hood.

Appendix

References to Robin Hood
up to 1600
(Collected by Lucy Sussex)

1213–16   Robert Hood, servant of the Abbot of Cirencester, killed Ralph. Usually regarded as a coincidence, but cf. other western early references.

1228–32   'Hobbehod' in Yorkshire: an outlaw 'fugitivus' named Robert Hood.

1262   William the son of Robert le Fevere from Enborne in Berkshire on the border of Hampshire (south of Newbury) is indicted for various larcenies and the harbouring of thieves. He flees, is outlawed and his chattels are seized without warrant by the prior of Sandleford. The prior is pardoned by the king for this act and in the receipt for this writ the fugitive is referred to as William Robehod (compare with Hobbehod in 1228 entry).

c.1280   Adam de la Halle's *Jeu de Robin et Marion*

1296   Fletching, Sussex. First appearance of surname 'Robynhod' with Gilbert Robynhod.

1324   Edward II employs a *valet de chambre* called Robyn Hode, who leaves his employment: Joseph Hunter compared this record to events late in the *Gest*.

1325   Katherine Robynhod (possible patronymic) in London coroner's roll.

1332   Robert Robynhod in West Harting, Sussex.

1354   Man called R.H. (outlaw pseudonym?) awaiting trial in prison for offences in Rockingham forest.

*c.*1377   Langland's *Piers Plowman* mentions: 'If I shulde deye bi this day me liste noughte to loke / I can nought perfitly my paternoster as the prest it syngeth / But I can rymes of Robyn hood and Randolph erle of Chestre / Ac neither of owre lorde ne of owre lady / the leste that evere was made.'

1376–9   Gower has names Robin and Marion in *Mirour de l'homme*.

*c.*1380   Chaucer in *Troilus and Criseyde*. Reference to proverb later used re R.H. 'Defamen love, as nothing of him knowe. Thei speken, but thei benten nevere his bowe.'

1381   John Ball, to rebels: 'biddeth Piers Plowman go to his work and chastise wel Hobbe the Robbere'. Suggests Robert/Robin/Hobbe may be colloquially used for thieves (cf. 1262 entry).

1381   Robert Robynhod, Winchelsea, Sussex.

*c.*1392   Adam de la Halle's *Robin and Marion* annually performed at Angers at Whitsuntide.

*c.*1400–25   Lincoln Cathedral ms: 'R.H. in scherewod stod hodud and hathud hosut and schod ffour / And thunti [sic] arowus he bar In hit hondus.'

*c.*1400   Date for the *Gest* accepted by many scholars, but see pp. 46–8.

*c.*1405–10   *Dives and Pauper* refers to those who 'gon levir to heryn a tale or a song of R.H. or of sum rubaudry than to heryn messe or matynes'.

1405–10   Hugh Legat preaches sermon 'For mani, manime seith, spekith of R.H. that schotte never in his bowe.'

1417   Robert Stafford, chaplain of Lindfield in Sussex, becomes robber in Surrey and Sussex, assuming name of 'Friar Tuck'.

1419–20   *Reply of Friar Daw Topias* repeats Legat proverb (see 1405–
            10): 'And many men speken of Robyn Hood and shotte nevere
            in his bowe.'

c.1420   Andrew of Wynton *Orygynale Chronicle of Scotland* assigns R.H.
            and L.J. to Barnsdale and Inglewood *c*.1283: 'Litil Iohun and
            Robert Hude/Waythmen war commendit gud; / In Inglewode
            and Bernnysdaile.' He also refers to one 'Hwde of Edname'
            who helped Alexander Ramsay take Roxburgh in 1342, which
            is regarded as a reference to R.H. in Laing's edition.

c.1422   Cartulary of Monkbretton Priory refers to a stone of R.H.
            near Slephill, Barnsdale.

c.1425   Ms of *Troilus and Criseyde*, marginal gloss identifies R.H. with
            1380 proverb.

1426–7   Earliest reference to R.H. plays, Exeter: *'lusoribus ludentibus
            lusum RH'*. This is ten years after first reference to May play
            there.

1429   Lawsuit, in Court of Common pleas, first appearance of legal
            formula 'Robin Hode in Barnsdale stode' (unless Lincoln Ca-
            thedral ms is a variant of this. See *c*.1400–25).

1432   'Adam, Bell, Clyme, Ocluw, Willyam, Cloudesle, Robyn, hode,
            Inne, Greenwode, Stode, Godeman, was, hee, lytel, Joon,
            Muchette, Millersson, Scathelok, Reynoldyn.' Humorous return
            in parliamentary rolls, Wiltshire.

1438   Ship called 'Robyn Hude' or 'ly Robert Hude' at Aberdeen.

1439   Piers Venables, 'gentilman' of Aston Derby, compared to R.H.
            in a petition to parliament. Venables had rescued a prisoner
            (comparable to rescue of Sir Richard in *Gest*?), with a com-
            pany of men, those named in the petition being described as
            'yomen', and went into the woods 'like as it hadde be R.H.
            and his meyne'. Subsequently they 'kepyn the wodes and
            strange contrays' by 'fought and manassinge to scle'. The
            rescue took place the first Sunday after Christmas.

c.1441   Walter Bower in the continuation to Fordun's *Scotichronicon* assigns R.H. to 1260s, describes how eagerly common people celebrate R.H., L.J., and provides story (the first to be recorded) of Robin's defeat of the 'viscount', after finishing mass in the forest.

1441   Southacre, Norfolk. A group of yeomen and labourers block the road, singing 'We are Robynhodesmen, war, war, war,' and threatening to murder Sir Geoffrey Harsyk (Kings Bench, 1441).

c.1450   'R.H. and the Monk' ballad.

c.1450   Ms of *Troilus and Criseyde* has marginal gloss of R.H. proverb from 1380: 'Thei spekyn of robynhod but thei bente never his bowe.'

c.1450   *Robin and Gandelyn* in Sloane ms.

late C15th   Poem 'Kene men of combur comen belyue/For to mote of myche what more than a lytyll / How Reynall and R.H. runnen at the gleve.' 'Combur' is Cumberland, related to setting of 'Adam Bell' Child no. 116, and to Inglewood, see Andrew of Wyntoun, *c*.1420.

1460–80   In the Physician's College ms of *The Canterbury Tales* in the tale of Sir Thopas, R.H. is substituted for Bevis of Hampton: 'Men speken of romances of prys / Of Horn child and of Ypolys / Of Robynhoode and sir Gy / Of sir Lybeaux and Pleyndamour / But sir Thopas he bereth the flour / Of roial chivalry.'

late C15th   'A Gest of R.H.' referred to, perhaps ironically in *How the Plowman learned his Pater Noster*: 'Eche had two busshels of whete that was gode/They songe goynge home ward a gest of Robyn Hode.'

Late C15th   Burlesque in Scots ms: 'the sow sate on hye bank and harpyd on R.H.'. Another version in Porkington ms from the 1460s.

Late C15th   Lambeth ms: 'He that made this songe ful good / Came of the northe and of the sotherne blode / And somewhat kyne to R.H.'

Late C15th   'R.H. and Guy of Gisborne' ballad.

1471   George Ripley in *Compound of Alchemy* quotes R.H. proverb
              from 1380: 'For many men spekyth with wondreng: Of R.H.
              and of His Bow, whych never shot therin I trow.'

1473   Paston letter re absconding of servant hired to play R.H. and
              St George, who has 'goon into Bernysdale'.

1474   Thame, Oxfordshire. Money gathered by R.H. at Whitsun.

*c.*1475   Plays about R.H. and sheriff and R.H. and friar survive in
              ms.

1475/6+   References to R.H. in village plays, Croscombe, North Som-
              erset.

1485   R.H.'s close in Nottingham, described to 1500.

1486   An account of King Henry VII's progress at York (where he
              saw pageants in his honour) mentions the Barnsdale area 'a
              litill beyonde Robyn Hoddez ston'.

1487–8   Exeter. R.H. play.

1492   Earliest possible date for Worde edition of *Gest*.

1492   R.H. (as Robertus Hod) in Edinburgh May Games.

1496   Thame, Oxfordshire. Money gathered by R.H.

1497   Roger Marshall of Westbury in Staffordshire has to defend
              himself in Star Chamber on charges of leading a riotous as-
              sembly to Willenhall under the name of R.H. It began with
              an arrest in Walsall of two citizens (from Wednesbury and
              Dudley) for assault, which roused Marshall and three others,
              including a priest and a squire (plus 200 followers) to assem-
              ble in Wednesbury and threaten a rescue. They were read the
              riot act, and forbidden to attend the fair at Willenhall, next
              Trinity Sunday. However, Marshall (referred to mysteriously
              as Robert this time, possibly through his association with
              R.H.) and the priest came with 100 armed men, Marshall

calling himself R.H. Also there were 60 armed men from Wolverhampton, led by the 'Abbot of Marram'. At the fair they threatened to assault any Walsall men present.

Marshall denied the charges, stating that this was a normal 'Robin Hood' practice. Note Abbot alongside R.H., and cf. Scottish references, 1508, 1570.

*c.*1498	*'Tempus de Robynhode'* plays, Wells, Somerset.
1498	Edinburgh. End of R.H. and L.J. in May Game.
*c.*1498–9	Reading. Spring festival 'gaderyngs of R.H.' St Lawrence.
1499	Henley on Thames. Council resolves that money collected at R.H. game should be spent on silver censer.
*c.*1500	Welsh song *'Robin Hwd ai kant'* in ms.
*c.*1500	'R.H. and Potter' ballad.
1500	R.H.'s well at Nottingham, also known as St Anne's Well.
1500	L.J. joins R.H. in Edinburgh May-Game.
1500	Date for first Pynson ed. of *Gest* (a few leaves only).
1501	Gavin Douglas in *Palace of Honour* refers to R.H. and Gilbert with the 'quhite hand', in the context of a nonsensical stanza also including Piers Plowman, John the Reeve, Rauf Coilyear and Finn MacCool.
1501	Thame, Oxfordshire. Money gathered by R.H.
1501–3	*Ane Littill Interlud of the Droichis Part of the Play* formerly attributed to William Dunbar, has Wealth the giant say: 'Sen I am Welth cumyn to this wane, / Ye noble merchandis ever ilkane / Address yow furth with bow and flane / In lusty grene lufraye, / And follow furth on Robyn Hude, / With hartis coragous and gud, /And thocht that wretchis wald ga wod, / Of worschipe hald the way.' Unclear whether this is play or poem, but reads like performance piece.

1502   In Robert Fabyan's *Chronicle*, published 1534, this year is noted: 'Also thys yere about Midsomer was taken a felowe, whych had renued many of Robin Hodes pagentes, which named himself Granelef.' This seems like an outlaw pseudonym taken from the *Gest*.

1503   R.H. of Perth paid by King of Scotland.

1503–8   William Dunbar's poem 'Of Sir Thomas Norray', includes verse: 'Was never vyld Robeine vnder bewch / Nor yet Sir Roger of Clekkinslewch / So bauld a bairne as he / Gy of Gysburne, na Allan Bell, / Na Simones sonnes of Quhynfell / At schot war nevir so slie.'

1500–10   Anonymous Scottish poem: 'Thair is no story that I of hier / Of Johne nor Robene Hude / Nor yit of Wallace wicht but weir / That ne thinkes halfe so gude.' In Hyndford ms, compiled around 1588.

1505   R.H. of 'Hendley' (Henley on Thames) visits Reading.

1505   R.H. of Finchamstead also visits Reading.

1506   Date given in STC for Worde ed. of *Gest*.

1506?–09   Goes ed. of *Gest*.

1506–7   Beginning of costume records for R.H., the frere (F.T.), 'the lady' (M.M?), L.J., associated with Morris dancing at Kingston-on-Thames.

1507   Last appearance of R.H. at St Lawrence, Reading.

1508   L.J. and R.H. in May-Game Aberdeen, and later that year on St Nicholas day: 'all personis burges nichbouris and Inhabiaris burges sonnys habill to Rid to decor and honour the towne in that array conveniant tharto sall Rid with Robert huyd and litile Iohne quhilk was callit in yeris bipast Abbot and priour of Bonacord one euery Sanct Nicholas day throw the towne as wse and wont has bene quhen thai war warnit be the said R.H. or L.J. or ony ane of thame.'

1508   Exeter. St John's: expense for renovation of St Edmund's arrow for R.H.

1509–10   Banning of R.H. plays by Exeter Council as public nuisance: 'hensforth ther shall be no riot kept in any parysh by the yong man of the same parish called R.H. but oonly the Churche holyday.'

1509   Alexander Barclay's *Ship of Fools* (version of *Narrenschiff*) has three mentions of R.H.:

> The holy Bybyll, ground of trouth and of lawe,
> Is nowe of many abiect and nought set by,
> Nor godly Scripture is nat worth an hawe;
> But talys ar lovyd grounde of rybawdry,
> And many blynddyd ar so with thyr foly,
> That no Scripture thynke they so true nor gode,
> As is a folysshe yest of R.H. (198)

> And in the mornynge whan they come to the quere,
> The one begynneth a fable or a history,
> The other lenyth theyr erys it to here,
> Taking it in stede of the Invyntory;
> Some other maketh Respons, Antym and Memory,
> And all of fables and jestis of R.H.,
> Or other tryfyls that skantly ar so gode.' (1394)
> [parody of church service]

> Holde me excusyd, forwhy my wyll is gode
> Men to induce unto vertue and goodnes;
> I wryte no iest ne tale of R.H.,
> Nor sowe no sparcles ne sede of vyciousnes;
> Wyse men love vertue, wylde people wantonnes;
> It longeth nat to my scyence nor cunnynge
> For Phylyp the Sparowe the dirige to synge! (1962)

(Note dig at Skelton.) First published by Pynson, first publisher of the *Gest*.

1509   M.M. named for first time at Kingston.

1510   Henry VIII and eleven nobles break into the Queen's chamber dressed like R.H., see p. 110.

1510–15?   Date of Lettersnijder ed. of *Gest*.

1512–25   Henry Percy, fifth earl of Northumberland, has in the house-
           hold records of his two Yorkshire castles money put aside to
           buy livery for R.H.

1513–4   Alexander Barclay 4th Eclogue (free translation of Mantuan):
           'Yet would I gladly heare nowe some mery fit, / Of maide
           Marian, or els of R.H.' Lines are spoken by a shepherd. This
           the fourth time Barclay (most likely a Scot) mentions R.H.
           Also, first literary allusion to M.M.

1513   Tintinhull, Somerset. R.H.'s ale.

1515   Pageant for Henry VIII: 200 yeomen at Shooter's Hill on way
           to Greenwich. R.H. is present 'clothed all in grene' and the
           king goes with him and his men 'into the grene wode, and
           to se how the outlawes lyve, see p. 110.

1515?   Notary ed. of *Gest*.

1517   Aberdeen. R.H. and L.J. in May Games.

1518   Aberdeen. R.H. and L.J. in May Games.

After 1518 Impersonation of R.H. and L.J. by tenants of Prior of
           Worcester.

1519   Worcester, St Helens. R.H. play.

*c.*1520   In catalogue of Oxford bookseller 'Roban Hood' price 2d.

1520   John Rastell *Interlude of Four Elements*. Ignorance sings garbled
           ballad of R.H. 'But yf thou wylt have a song that is good /
           The best that ever was made'. The point is that this is what
           Ignorance considers a good song. The song begins 'R.H. in
           Barnesdale stood' – either a reference to the legal proverb, or
           a variant of the song in the Lincoln ms.

1520   Henley-on-Thames. R.H.'s money in Parish register.

1520   Skelton *Magnifycence* mentions F.T. in what reads like Abbot
           of Unreason context: 'They bare me in hand that I was a spy, /
           And another bade me put out mine eye; / Another would

mine eye were bleared, / Another bade shave half my beard, / And boys to the pillory gan me pluck, / And would have made me Friar Tuck, / To preach out of the pillory hole / Without an antetheme or a stole, [. . .] By my troth had I not paid and prayed, / And made largesse [as I might], / I had not been here with you this night.'

1521	John Major *History of Greater Britain*. Historical source for R.H., set in time of Richard I: feats of R.H. are told all over Britain.
1521	Dundee. R.H. play or May Game.
c.1522–3	Proverb 'Good even, good R.H.' in Skelton's *Why come Ye Nat to Court*.
1525	Croscombe, Somerset. End of R.H. play.
1526–7	Ashburton, Devon. R.H. play involving new tunic made for R.H.
1528	Worcester, St Helens. R.H. play.
1528	Sir Thomas More, in *Heresyes*: 'To handle holie scripture in more homely maner than a song of R.H.'
1528	'. . . to read R.H., and Bevis of Hampton, Hercules, Hector and Troilus, with a thousand histories and fables of love and wantoness, and ribaldry, as filthy as heart can think, to corrupt the minds of youth.' William Tyndale, *The Obedience of a Christian Man*.
1528	Jerome Barlow and William Roye, in anti-Wolsley tract *Rede me and Be nott Wrothe* say the church prevents the 'layeman' from reading 'eny frutfull englisshe boke / wholy scripture concernynge . . . But as for tales of Robyn hode, / with wother iestes nether honest nor goode / They have none impedimente' (ll. 1424–32).
1529	End of costume records, Kingston-on-Thames, Surrey, for R.H. and Morris dancing.

1530   Amersham, money received 'of the lord for R.H.'

1530   Cleeve Prior, Worcestershire. Tenants play with R.H., M.M. in late July.

1531   In Lord High Treasurer of Scotland: 'Item, vj quarteris gray taffatis of Jeynes to be ane part of the Kingis R.H. baner.'

1532   Hythe, Kent. R.H. play.

1533   Sir Thomas More, *Confutacion*: 'If thei had told hym that a tale of R.H. had bene holye scrypture.'

1533   'The Image of Ypocresye', polemical poem in ms Lansdowne 794: 'Away these bibles / For they be but ridles! / And give hem robyn whode / To red howe he stode / In mery grene wode, / when he gathered good / Before noyes ffloode!' Spoken by 'sysmatickes and lowsy lunatickes'!

1534   Latest possible date for Worde ed. of *Gest*.

1534   Dumfries, Scotland, R.H. and L.J. in May Games.

1534   Leicester, R.H. game causes complaints by church officials.

1535–9   Bishop Latimer attacks R.H. games: 'I tarried there half an houer and more, at last the key was founde, and one of the parishe commes to me and sayes. Syr thys is a busye daye with us, we can not heare you, it is R.H.'s daye. The parish are gone a brode to gather for R.H., I praye you let them not. I was fayne there to geve place to R.H., I thought my rochet shoulde have bene regarded, thoughe I were not, but it would not serve, it was fayne to geve place to Robyn hoodesmen.

                It is no laughynge matter my friends, it is a weepyng matter, a heavy matter, under the pretence for gatherynge for R.H., a traytourer, and a thefe, to put out a preacher, to have hys office less estemed, to prefer R.H. before the ministracion of Gods word, and all this hath come of unpreaching prelates. This realm hath been ill provided for, that it hath had such corrupt judgements in it, to prefer R.H. to God's word.'

Sermon given before Edward VI. E.K. Chambers suggested this might have occurred at Melton (1903, p. 180, n. 3).

1535   Ombursley, Worcestershire. Start of R.H. play.

1536   Betley window, showing M.M. and F.T. is painted (possibly prior to this date).

1536   Stratton, Cornwall. Start of R.H. play.

*c.*1536–9   Sir Richard Morison complains to Henry VIII in his manuscript 'A Discourse Touching the Reformation of the Lawes of England': 'In somer comenly upon the holy daies in most places of your realm, ther be playes of R.H., M.M., F.T., wherin besides the lewdenes and rebawdry that ther is opened to the people, disobedience also to your offices, is tought, whilest these good bloodes go about to take from the shiref of Notyngham one that for offendyng the lawes shulde have suffered execution. How moche better is it that those plaies shulde be forbodden and deleted and others dyvysed to set forthe and declare lyvely before the peoples eies the abhomynation and wickednes of the bisshop of Rome, monkes, ffeers, nonnes, and suche like, and to declare and open to them thobedience that your subiects by goddes and mans lawes owe unto your magestie.'

1536   R.H. and L.J. in Dumfries.

1537   R.H. and L.J. in Dumfries.

1537   The play *Thersites* has two mentions of the R.H. characters: 'Where is Robin John and Little Hood? / Approach hither quickly, if ye think it good; / I will teach such outlaws with Christ's curses, / How they take herafter abbots' purses' [allusion to *Gest?*] and: 'I will make thee, ere I go, for to duck, / And thou were as tall a man as FT' [he is fighting a snail]

1538   Last reference to R.H. at Kingston-on-Thames.

1539–40   Ayr. R.H. plays, in May.

*c.*1540   John Leland *Collectanea Itinerary* associates R.H. with Barnsdale and Kirkeslee.

1540   R.H.'s stone near Whitby.

1540–1   Woodbury, Devon. R.H. and L.J. coats bought.

1541–2   Ashburton, Devon. R.H. play with purchase of *'tunicarum pro Roberti Hode cum eis adherentibus'*.

1542   Nicholas Udall's *Apothegmes* (translation of Erasmus' *Apothegmata*) mentions R.H. 'Old wiues foolyshe tales of R.H.' And also: 'he [Diogenes] begoonne to syng suche an other foolyshe song [as Robyn hood, in Barnesdale stood &c.] & sembleed as though he would daunce withall.'

1542/3   Ayr. R.H. play.

1543   End of R.H. play, Stratton, Cornwall (it involved a house as part of set).

1544   R.H.'s Bay referred to.

1545   Perth. R.H. in May-Game.

1545   William Turner in *The Rescuing of the Romish Fox* charges Bishop Gardiner with: 'ye yourself forbad the players of London [as it was told me] to play any mo plays of Christe / but of rh and lJ / and of the Parlament of byrdes and suche other trifles.'

1546   'Tales of R.H. are goode among fooles' and 'Many a man spekith of R.H.' John Heywood, *Dialogue conteinying . . . the Proverbes*.

1546–7   Ayr. R.H. play.

1547   The Duke of Somerset in a letter to Bishop Gardiner: 'The people bieth those foolish ballats of Jack a Lent, So bought they in times past, pardones, and carroles, and Robbin hoodes tales.' Jack a Lent, says Baskerville, was a 'vegetation daemon and scapegoat'.

1547–8   Ayr. R.H. and L.J. play.

1548   R.H. walk in Richmond park, Surrey.

1548	Edward Hall *Union of Lancastre and York* mentions Henry VII's R.H. mayings.
1549	Ayr. R.H. and L.J. in play.
1549	Wedderburn's *Complaint of Scotland* refers to R.H. tales and dances.
1549	Latimer in his sermons comments: 'We might as well spend that time in reading of profane histories, of Cantorburye tales, or a fit of R.H.'
1550	Walter Lynne in his translation of *The true beliefe in Christ and his sacramentes* which he has rendered as: 'that al men, women and chyldren would read it. Not as they have bene here tofore accustomed to reade the fained stories of Robin-hode, Clem of the Cloughe, wyth suche lyke to passe the tyme wythal . . .'
1550	Robert Crowley, in his *Voyce of the Last Trumpet*: 'But if thou canste do any good / In teachyng of an A. B. C. / A primer, or else Robynhode: / Let that be good pastyme for the.' These lines are spoken to a lewd or unlearned priest, apparently not in irony.
*c.*1550?	'R.H. and the Curtal Friar' ballad.
*c.*1550?	'R.H. and the Butcher' ballad.
1550–1	Ayr. L.J. and R.H. play.
1553	Shrewsbury. R.H. play.
1553	Richard Robinson's *Ancient Order of Prince Arthur*: 'Myself remembreth of a childe, in contreye native mine, / A Maygame was of R.H., and of his traine, that time / To traine up young men, stripplings, and eche other younger childe, / In shooting; yearly this with solempne feast was by the guylde / Or brotherhood of townsmen don.'
1553–8	'A Tale of R.H.' or 'The Overthrowe of the Abbyes' (see p. 95) Allegory of the dissolution of the monasteries, with R.H. representing the bishops, Adam Bell the abbots and L.J.

the universities. Includes the lines: 'Talke of Bevis, fighter peerlesse, / Or of Ascleparte the fearlesse; / Talke of lyons and of wonders, / lightnings flashe, or roores of thonders, / fyre and hayle, and stormes of blood, / Or tell a tale of R.H.'

1553–4   Exeter. R.H. ale.

1553–4   Ayr. R.H. play involving gunpowder.

1554–5   First reference to R.H. plays, Chagford, Devon: young men of the parish are paid for the 'howde'.

1555   Peebles. R.H. in May-Game.

1555   Scottish Parliamentary statute banning R.H. and L.J. in May Games.

1555   Robert Braham, in his 'Pistle to the Reader' (actually a preface to Lydgate's *Troy Book*), states that the careful reader who examines Caxton's edition: 'shall rather find his doings worthy to be numbered among the trifling tales and barren luedries of R.H., A Beves of Hampton.'

1555   Chagford. R.H. play: 'Item of Iohn Northcutt And other R.H. ys Company.'

1555–6   Chagford. R.H. play: 'Robard Iopass Iohn frend and other of the howde.'

1556   Melton Mowbray, Leicestershire. '29/8d received of Stephen Shaw that he gathered and his company at R.H.'s play, two years.' An entry of 5/-received from John Hopkins in payment of R.H. money.

1557–8   Ballad 'Of Wakefylde and a Grene' most likely 'R.H. and the Pinder', in Stationer's Register.

1557–8   Chagford. R.H. play: 'Iohn Newcomb Iunior and other of the howddes men.' Another payment mentions 'Roberd lopas Iohn penycott and of other of the howdde ys men'. Coats for the howddes are also bought.

1558–9   Chagford. R.H. play: 'Robert Lapas howdde that yere' is paid, and also 'Iohn Newcomb Iunior & other owddes men'.

1559   Henry Machyn's Diary: 'The xxiiij day of June ther was a May-game, and sant John Sacerys, with a gyant, and drumes and gunes [and the] ix wordes [worthies], with spechys, and a goodly pagant with a quen . . . and dyvers odur, with spechys; and then sant Gorge and the dragon, the mores dansse, and after R.H. and L.J., and M. [M.M.] and F.T., and thay had spechys rond a-bowt London.'

'The xxv day of June the sam May-gam whent unto [the palace?] at Grenwyche, playng a-for the Quen and the consell.'

1559   Proverb R.H.'s mile – a mile several times its usual length. In William Cunningham's *Cosmographical Glasse.*

1559–60   Chagford. Hoodsmen paid.

c.1560   Copland edition of *Gest*, with plays of R.H. and potter and R.H. and friar. Mentioned are R.H., F.T., Lady free (M.M.?) L.J.

1560   Thomas Churchyard, *A Replication onto Camels Objection*: 'Your knowledge is great, / your judgement is good / The most of your study hath / ben of R.H. / And Bevis of Hampton and / Syr Launcelot de Lake / Hath taught you full oft / Your verses to make.' Four lines later he remarks, presumably sarcastically: 'I prayse you no more lest / You thinke I flatter – / I must retourne, to / Thee pith of my matter.'

1560–1   Braunton, Devon. St Brannock's Church pays for meat and drink for R.H. plus company.

1561   Edinburgh riots involving apprentices and craftsmen 'efter the auld wikit maner of R.H.' John Knox gives the date as 1560 [wrongly]: 'For the rascal Multitude were stirred-up to make a *Robin-Hood*, which enormity was of many years left off, and condemned by Statute and Act of Parliament; yet would they not be forbidden, but would disobey and trouble the Town'. Marginalia re this in the 1732 edition (and possibly earlier editions) says: 'A foolish play used in time of

Darkness. Hence we say any foolish thing to be like a play of R.H.' (Note use of word 'play' rather than tale as in English version of the proverb.) Stallybrass (1985) says that a tailor was elected as 'Lord of Inobedience'. The mob forced open the jail, and smashed a gibbet. The magistrates were themselves imprisoned until they published a proclamation pardoning the rioters.

1561–2   Braunton, Devon. St Brannock's Church buys cloth for R.H.'s coat, and at Whitsun pays the company.

1561   Chudleigh, Devon. Coats bought for R.H., L.J., the Vice, and six other players. R.H.'s coat is especially elaborate. Later in the year the money from the gathering is paid into the church coffers.

1562   A. Brown in Scotland paid 5/- for making a proclamation at the Cross for discharging of R.H.

1562   Mary Queen of Scots' statute forbidding R.H. and L.J. in May-Game.

1562–3   'Ballett of R.H.' in Stationer's Register. Suggested by some sources to be the Copland ed. of *Gest*.

1563–4   Chagford. Hoodsmen paid.

1563–4   Braunton, Devon. St Brannock's buys L.J. a coat.

1564   Chagford. Hoodsmen appear three times in church accounts.

1565   Proverb 'R.H.'s pennyworths' Cambridge ms.

c.1565   'Doctor A.B.' in his *Merie tales of the Mad Men of Gotam*: Two characters on their way to Nottingham swear by R.H. and M.M.

1565   Aberdeen. Illegal R.H. and L.J. in May-Game. Letter from Queen Mary on the subject.

1565   Edinburgh. Minstrel Sandy Stevin is convicted of blasphemy after taking part in a mock church service and alleging 'that he would give no more credit to the New Testament then to a tale of R.H., except it were confirmed by the doctors of the church.' Referred to in John Knox's *History*. Thomas Randolph, English ambassador to Scotland, writes to Cecil about this: 'one of the Queen's chappel, a singing man, said, that he believed as well a tale of R.H. as any word written in the Old Testament or New.'

1566   Abingdon, Berks. R.H. play with bower.

1567   Farway, Devon. R.H. chosen.

1567–70   Play, *The Marriage of Wit and Science*: 'Why sir do ye thinke to doe any good, / If ye stande in a corner like Roben hood. / Nay, you must start it and face it out with the best: / Set on a good countenance, make the most of the least; / Whosoever skip in, look to your part, / And while you live, beware of a false heart.'

1568   Alexander Scot 'In May quhen men zeid everichone / With R.H. and L.J. / To bring in bowis and birkin bobbynis.'

1569   Richard Grafton *Chronicle at Large* assigns R.H. as earl to period of Richard I.

1569   Lewis Wager's interlude *The Longer Thou Livest the more Fool Thou Art* has its character Moros repeatedly refer to R.H. He enters singing a nonsense medley of ballads, which includes the lines: 'Robin lende to me thy Bowe, thy Bowe, / Robin the bow, Robin lende to me thy bow a' / Later in the text Moros keeps calling Manhood (actually the Vice Wrath) R.H., as in 'Good Lord what meaneth my man R.H.'

1570   Dumfries. L.J. and R.H. play.

1570   Arbuthnot, Scotland. Choosing of R.H. and Abbot of Unreason by Johne the Commoune-Weal leads to treason charge.

1571–2   Honiton buys 1 lb of gunpowder when R.H. of Colyton comes to town.

1571   Edmund Campion, *History of Ireland* 'Many a good-fellow talkes
                of R.H., that never drew in his Bow.'

1573–4   Woodbury, Devon. R.H. gathering.

1574   R.H. play, Woodbury, with 25 yards of canvas bought to
                make R.H.'s house.

1574–5   St Andrews. Prohibition of R.H. plays.

1575   Hector Boethius (Boece) makes reference to L.J. in his *Scotorum
                Historiae a Prima Gentis Origine*, claiming to have seen his
                enormous bones at Pet in Moray.

1575   Coventry. 'Stories of R.H., Bevis of Hampton, Adam Bell'
                owned by Captain Cox.

*c.*1575–91   Tune of 'Robin Hood' in Giles Lodge's Lute Book (Folger
                Shakespeare Library).

1575   Bride-ale at Kenilworth, described by Robert Laneham – tra-
                ditional morris-dance, with M.M., the fool, six dancers.

1576   Claudius Holyband's phrasebook *The French Littelton* includes
                'Wee leape to the taile of R.H., folow your talke'.

1576–7   Woodbury, Devon. R.H. ale.

1576–7   Honiton. Payment to R.H.

1577   Scottish General Assembly requests prohibition of R.H., King
                of May on sabbath.

1577   Laurence Ramsay *The practice of the Diuell*: 'Suffer all sclaunder,
                against God and his trueth, / And prayse the olde fashion, in
                King Arthurs dayes; / Of Abbaies, of Monasteries, how it is
                great rueth, / To haue them pluckt downe, and so the eldest
                sayes: / And how it was merrie, when R.H.'s playes, / Was in
                euerie Towne, the Morrice and the foole, / The May poll, &
                the Drum, to bring the Calfe from schoole.'

1577   *Misogonus* 'This is a smurkynge wench indeede, this a fare M.M., She is none of thes coy dames'. and also: 'Passion of me! it is R.H., I think, verily!'

1577   Nicholas Breton *The Workes of a Young Wit*: 'Like R.H., I wot not how, / I must goe raunge in woodmens wyse, / Cladde in a Cote of greene or gray, / and gladde to get it if I maye.'

1577   Nicholas Breton in *Floorish Upon Fancie*, describes Fancie's chamber: 'Besides, in pictures too, / And toyes of straung devise / With stories of olde R.H., / And Walter little wise: / Some showes of warre long since, / And Captaines wounded sore, / And souldiers slaine at one conflict / A thousand men and more: / Of hunting of wilde Beasts, / As lions, Bores, and Beares: / To see how one an other oft, / In sunder straungely teares. / Of gallant Cities, Townes: / Of gardens, flowers, and trees.'

Also, from poem 'The Toyes of an Idle Head' in the same book: 'To play at dice is but good sporte, / So it be used in good sorte: / But who delights in cardes and dyse, / Indeede, I cannot count him wise. / For he that playes, till all be gone, / With R.H. and L.J., / May trace the wooddes: for wise men say, / Keepe somewhat till a rayny day.'

1578   Yeovil. R.H. replaced by 'Keeper of the Ale'.

1578   King and Council of Scotland requested to prohibit 'playis, as King of May, R.H. and sick others.'

1579   G. Gilpin, translating Philips van Marnix's *The beehive of the Romish church*. 'In summe, a man doth often spende a pennie or two, to see a play of R.H., or a Morisse daunse, which were a great deale better bestowed [than] uppon these apishe toies of these good Priests, which counterfeite all these matters so handsomlie, that it will do a man as much good to see them, as in frostie weather to goe naked.'

1579   In George Gascoigne's *The Posies* 'Yea R.H.', analogous to Skelton proverb 1522–3.

1579	L. Tomson's translation of Calvin's *Sermon . . . on the epistles to Timothy and Titus*: 'God will not haue us occupied like little children in puppets or hobie-horses, as players and Robin Hodes.'
1579	Edinburgh. Proclamation against R.H. plays.
1580	John Lyle *Euphues and his England* cites 1380 proverb: 'For there it more delighteth them to talk of R.H., then to shoot in his Bow.'
1580	Edmund Assheton demands suppression of 'R.H. and the May games as being lewde sportes, tending to no other end but to stir up our frail natures to wantonness.'
1580	Proverb 'to out shoot R.H.' first in Sydney's *Apologie for Poetrie*: 'And lastly . . . they [anti-poets?] cry out with an open mouth, as if they out shot R.H., that Plato banished them [poets] out of hys Common-wealth.'
1580	Privy Council Scotland: 'Dischargeing all and sindrie his Majesteis liegis of using of R.H. and uthe vane and unlesum gammis.'
1581–2	Woodbury, Devon. Two green coats bought, probably for R.H. and L.J.
1582	'R.H. pennyworths' mentioned in George Whetstone's *Heptameron of Civil Discourses*. An expression probably deriving from 'R.H. and Potter' where R.H. in disguise, sells pots at great discount.
1582	Dalkeith. R.H. in May Game.
1582	Christopher Fetherstone's *Dialogue Agaynst light, lewde, and lasciuious dancing*: 'The abuses which are committed in your may-games are infinite. The first whereof is this, that you doe use to attyre in womans apparrell whom you doe most commonly called *maymarrions*, whereby you infringe that straight commaundement which is given in Deut. xxii. 5, That men must not put on womens apparrell for feare of enormities.'

1583   Cranston (Dalkeith). R.H. and L.J. in May Game.

1584   St Ives, Cornwall. R.H. play.

1584   Richard Wilson's *The Three Ladies of London* play has Sincerity
            say: 'There never was more preaching and less following, the
            people live so amiss. / But what is he that may not on the
            Sabbath-day attend to hear God's word, / But he will rather
            run to bowls, sit at the alehouse, than one hour afford, /
            Telling a tale of R.H., sitting at cards, playing at skittles, or
            some other vain thing, / That I fear God's vengeance on our
            heads it will bring.'

1585   Dirleton, Scotland. The King of Scotland 'passed the time
            with the play or R.H.'

1586   William Camden's *Britannia* described Kirklees as R.H.'s
            burial ground: *'His relictis* Kirkley *quondam virginum
            sacrarum fedem, & Roberti Hoodi decantatissimi praedonis
            tumulum praeterlapsus Calderus* Wakefeldiam *alluit, re pannaria
            inclitam.'*

1587   Thomas Churchyard *The Worthines of Wales*: 'Though we count
            but R.H. a jest, / And Old wives tales, as tolting toyes
            appeare: / Yet Arthur's raigne the world cannot denye.'

1587–8   Marprelate controversy tract *The Just Censure and Reproof of
            Martin Junior* mentions Potter (as in 'R.H. and the Potter'):
            'Anderson, parson of Stepney [in margins "This Chaplain
            robbed the poor men's box at Northampton, played the Pot-
            ter's part in the Morrice Dance, and begot his maid with
            child in Leicester; and these things he did since he was first
            priest"] should make room before him [John Bridges, Dean
            of Sarum, presented here as the Morris fool] with his two-
            handed staff, as he did once before the Morrice dance, at a
            market-town in the edge of Buckingham or Bedford shires,
            where he bore the Potter's part.'

1588   Haddington, Scotland. R.H. plays prohibited.

1588   St Columb Major and St Columb Minor, Cornwall. Plays of
            R.H.

1588   Last reference to R.H. play, Chagford. Hoodsmen sell 'summer rode' but keep R.H.'s silver arrow.

1588   Bridgnorth, Shropshire. R.H. play.

1589   *Hay Any Work for Coper* by Martin Marprelate 'the Summer Lord with his May game, or R.H. with his Morris dance going by the church.'

1589   Thomas Nashe *Return of Pasquill and Marforius* refers to the May-Game with Martin Marprelate as M.M.: 'Martin himselfe is the Maid Marian, trimly dressed-up in a cast gown and a kercher of Dame Lawson's, his face handsomely muffled with a diaper-napkin to cover his beard, and a great nosegay in his hands.'

1589   Haddington, Scotland. R.H. plays prohibited.

1589   Richard Harvey *Plain Percival the Peacemaker* mentions May Games with M.M.: 'a quintessence [beside the Foole and the Maid Marian] of all the picked youth, strained out of a whole endship, footing the Morris about a May-pole'.

1589   Puttenham, *The Arte of English Poesy*. 'Everyman should talke of the things they haue best skill of, and not in that, their knowledge and learning serueth them not to do, as we are wont to say, he speaketh of R.H. that neuer shot in his bow.'

1589   Warner's *Albion's England* refers to R.H. as a 'county' and 'mal-content'. Also speaks of play-game: 'At Paske began our Morris, and ere Penticost our May: / Tho R.H., L.J., F.T. and Marian deftly play.'

1590?   White ed. of *Gest*.

1590   First appearance of proverb re the Pinder of Wakefield: 'Were you as good as George a Greene I would not take the foile at your hands.' Richard Tarlton, *Tarlton's Newes out of Purgatorie*.

1590   Cranston, Scotland. R.H. in May Game.

1591   Scottish General Assembly fulminates against R.H. plays.

1591   John Harington's translation of *Orlando Furioso*: 'As our English proverbe saith, many talke of R.H.' Repetition of 1380 proverb. Also: 'This is a Tale indeed of R.H., Which to beleeue, might show my wits but weak.'

1592   John Stow *Annales of England* assigns R.H. to period of Richard I. Uses Major as source. Refers to F.T. apparently without making the connection. Matilda story appears here also, translated from its source, the Latin 'Chronicle of Dunmow' by Nicholas de Bromfield (sixteenth-century).

1592   Robert Greene *A Quippe for an Upstart Courtier* xi 248–9: 'to make the foole as faire forsooth, as if he were to play M.M. in a May game or Morris-daunce.'

1592–3   Shakespeare's *Two Gentlemen of Verona* allusion to 'the bare scalp of R.H.'s fat friar.'

1593   George Peele *Edward I* has characters play a R.H. May-Game, with some ballad material.

1593   Gabriel Harvey Pierce's *Supererogation*: 'Phy, long Meg of Westminster would haue bene ashamed to disgrace her Sonday bonnet with her Satterday witt. She knew some rules of Decorum: and although she were a lustie bounsing rampe, somewhat like Gallemella, or M.M.'

1594   *A Pastoral Plesant commedie of R.H. and L.J.* in Stationer's Register. Lost.

1594   *Matilda. The Fair and Chaste Daughter of the Lord Robert Fitzwater*, poem by Michael Drayton, the probable source for Munday's M.M. Drayton also writes about Matilda and King John in his *Heroicall Epistles* (1619) and has M.M. in his Poly-Olbion.

1596   Anthony Munday's play *John A Kent and John a Cumber* contains Morris dancers, with the Moor referred to as a 'monstrous Murrian' and M.M.: 'let mayde Marian haue the flurt at him, to set an edge on our stomacks, and let me alone in faith to ierke it after her.' The play concerns Ranulf, Earl of Chester and his daughter, Marian.

*c.*1596–1626   Nicholas Breton's poem [The Nightingale and Phillis]: 'Came Phillis sweete owte of the wood / And in her hand a lute; / Who when she playde but R.H. / Strooke Philomela mute.'

1597   Anthony Holborne's *Citthern Schoole* contains 'My Robin is to the Greenwood gone; or, Bonny Sweet Robin' cf. *Hamlet*, 'For Bonny Sweet Robin is all my joy'.

1597   Carew mss: 'Sundry loose persons, as some of the Mc-Shees . . . and others, became R.H.'s, and slew some of the Undertakers.'

1597   Shakespeare's *Henry IV* refers to R.H. twice. Falstaff tells Mistress Quickly that 'M.M. may be the deputy's wife of the ward to thee'. Also refrain of 'R.H., Scarlet and John' from 'Jolly Pinder of Wakefield' which later appears in the 1609 *Philaster*.

1597   Nicholas Breton *Wit's Trenchmour* [on the wife of an Innkeeper]: 'the helpe of M.M., a good Hostes to draw on gesse.'

1598–9   Anthony Munday. *The Downfall* and *The Death*. These two plays make R.H. Earl of Huntington, see pp. 121–29.

1598   R.H.'s buttes, Brampton, Cumberland.

1598   Ferguson ms 'Mony speaks of good Robin Hood that never drew his bowe'. Reference to proverb.

1599   *A Pleasant Conceited Comedy of George a Green, the Pinner {Pinder} of Wakefield*, (by Robert Greene?) Printed by S. Stafford, see pp. 119–21 for date of writing as 1592(?).

1599   George Silver *Paradoxes of Defence* 'These men speake like such as talke of R.H.'. Reference to proverb.

1599   Thomas Nash *Nashes Lenten Stuffe* has two passages relevant to the R.H. legend, first in a mock dedication: 'Most courteous unlearned louer of poetry, and yet a Poet thy selfe, of no lesse price than H.S., that in honour of M.M. giues sweete Margaret for his Empresse, and puttes the Sowe most saucily uppon some great personage.'

And, from 'In Prayse of the Red herring': 'Citty, towne, cuntry, R.H. and L.J. and who not, are industrious and carefull to squire and safe conduct him in.'

c.1600   William Ballet's ms lute book gives 'My Robin is to the Greenwood gone' as 'R.H. is to the Greenwood gone'.

c.1600   Shakespeare's *As You Like* It refers to R.H. in scene 1; see p. 133.

c.1600   Date of Sloane ms life of R.H.

1600   Kemp's *Nine Daies Wonder* refers to a country girl he danced with at Sudbury in his morris from London to Norwich as a M.M.: 'my merry Maydemarian.' As Kemp was a comedian, the part he would play in a morris would be the Clown, who was paired with the M.M.

1600   Nicholas Breton *Pasquil's Passe, and passeth not*: 'From fine M.M. and her Morris dance, [. . .] The Lord of heau'n and earth deliuer me.' Later in same poem: 'From a delight in hunting after newes, / Or louing idle tales of R.H.'

1600   Nicholas Breton *Pasquils Fooles-Cap*: 'Hee that will treade a *Measure* as he walks / And counterfaite M.M.'s countenance'. In the same poem: 'Hee that doth loue to talke of *R.H.*, / Yet neuer drewe one Arrowe in his Bowe: / And yet doth thinke his skill is wondrous good, / That scare the compasse of a marke doth knowe / When such a *Goose-cappe* doth a shooting goe, / Tell him, that in the aime of *Wisdomes* eye, / Wide handed Wits will euer shoote awry.'

1600   Nicholas Breton *Pasquils Mistresse*: 'If she make curtzy like M.M., / And weare her linnen neuer so well slickt, / And be the flower of the frying pan.'

1600   *Looke About You*, a play featuring R.H., Earl of Huntington, but otherwise little of the R.H. legend. R.H. is involved with Marian, wife of Lord Fauconbridge, in scenes close to bedroom farce, see pp. 131–3.

1600   *R.H.'s Pennyworth's* by W. Haughton. A lost play mentioned
                in Henslowe. A version of 'R.H. and the Potter'?

1600   E. Blount's (?) translation of Tomasso Garzonl's *The Hospitall
                of Incurable Fooles*: 'one while she could be as merry as M.M.'
                [On an old lady who goes mad upon looking into a mirror.]

References

PRIMARY SOURCES: PRINTED

(Note: texts available in F.J. Child's *English and Scottish Popular Ballads* are not listed separately.)

Andrew of Wyntoun 1903–14. *The Orygynale Chronicle*, ed. D. Laing. Edinburgh: Edmonston and Douglas.

Anon *c*.1400. *Gamelyn*, ed. W.W. Skeat in *The Collected Works of Chaucer*, vol. IV, 1894. Oxford: Clarendon.

Anon *c*.1560. *Robin Hood and the Friar*, ed. Mary A. Blackstone, P.L.S. Performance Text no. 3, 1981. Toronto: P.L.S.

Anon 1566. *The Merie Tales of Skelton*. London: Colwell.

Anon undated (later 16th C) 'A Tale of Robin Hood' ('The Overthrow of the Abbeys'). MS Harley, 367, fol. 150, and ed. Gutch, II. 39–44.

Anon *c*.1600. 'Life of Robin Hood', Sloane MS no. 780, British Library and ed. Thoms, II. 124–37 and Gutch I, 379–89.

Anon 1600. *Looke About You*, London: Ferbrand; reprinted 1913. London: Malone Society.

Anon 1661. *Robin Hood and His Crew of Souldiers*. London: Davis.

Anon 1662. *The noble birth and gallant atchievements of that remarkable outlaw Robin Hood*. London: Vere and Gilbertson.

Anon 1712. *The Whole Life and Merry Exploits of Robin Hood, Earl of Huntington*. London: Willis.

Anon 1723. *A Collection of Old Ballads*. London: Roberts.

Anon 1727. *Robin Hood and the Duke of Lancaster*. London: Jones; reprinted in Gutch, and Percival.

Anon 1730. *Robin Hood, An Opera*. London: Watts.

Anon *c*.1750. *The English Archer*. London: Hodges.

Anon 1769. *The Exploits of Renowned Robin Hood*. London: no publisher.

Anon 1777. *The Adventures of Robert Earl of Huntington Vulgarly Called Robin Hood*. Glasgow: Robertson.

Anon 1819. *Robin Hood: A Tale of the Olden Time*. Edinburgh: Oliver and Boyd.

Anon 1822. *Robin Hood and Jack Cade's Daughter.* Edinburgh: Maidstone.

Anon *c.*1840. *A Life of Robin Hood.* Manchester: No publisher.

Anon 1851. *New and Original Grand Christmas Pantomime – Robin Hood.* Manchester: Theatre Royal Press.

Anon 1858. *The Life and Exploits of Robin Hood.* Halifax: Milner and Sowerby.

Anon 1876. *Robert the Bold.* New York: Pott.

Anon 1990. *Tales of Robin Hood, Brochure.* Nottingham: Tales of Robin Hood.

Arnold, Matthew 1869. *Culture and Anarchy.* London: Smith, Elder.

Barclay, Alexander *c.*1510. *The Eclogues,* ed. B. White, 1928. Oxford: Early English Texts Society, o.s. 175.

Barton, Bernard 1828: *A New Year's Even and Other Poems.* London: Hatchard.

Beagle, Peter 1968. *The Last Unicorn.* London: Ballantine.

Benet, William Rose 1930: 'The Death of Robin Hood.' New York, *Saturday Review of Literature,* 15, Nov. p. 1.

Blishen, Edward 1969. *Robin Hood.* London: BBC.

Blyton, Enid 1930. *Tales of Robin Hood.* London: Newnes.

W. Bolland, 1925. *A Manual of Year-Book Studies.* Cambridge University Press.

Bower, Walter 1722. Continuation of Fordun's *Scotichronicon,* ed. T. Hearne. Oxford: Sheldonian Theatre.

Brooke, Frances 1788. *Marian: A Comic Opera.* London: Cadell.

Burnand, Sir Francis *c.*1850. *Robin Hood or The Forester's Fate: An Extravaganza.* London: Lacey.

Burrage, Alfred *c.*1901. *Sweet Liberty of Death.* London: Robin Hood Library, I, 1901.

Camden, William 1607. *Britannia,* two vols London: Bishop; trans. R. Gough, three vols 1809. London: Payne and Robinson.

Carpenter, Richard 1984. *Robin of Sherwood.* London: Puffin.

Chase, Nicholas, 1983. *Locksley.* London: Heinemann.

Child, Francis James, 1857–9. *English and Scottish Ballads,* eight vols Boston: Little Brown.

—— 1869–92. *English and Scottish Popular Ballads,* ten vols Boston: Barker. (Quoted throughout in the five-volume reprint, New York, Dover: 1965.)

Cundall, John see 'Percy, Stephen'.

'Dan' 1974. 'Robin Hood's Schooldays', *The Beano.* London: D.C. Thomson.

Davenport, Robert, 1655. *King John and Matilda: A Tragedy.* London: Pennycuicke.

Davis, Owen 1927. *Robin Hood and the Merry Outlaws of Sherwood Forest.* New York: French.

De Koven, Reginald, 1891. *Maid Marian.* London: Hopwood and Crew.

Drayton, Michael 1594. *Matilda the faire and chaste daughter of Lord R. Fitzwater.* London: Ling and Busby.

—— 1622. *Poly-Olbion,* in *Works,* ed. J.W. Hebel, vol. IV, 1961. Oxford: Blackwell.

Drinkwater, John 1925. *Robin Hood and the Pedlar,* in *Selected Plays,* vol. I. London: Sidgwick and Jackson.

Dumas, Alexandre, the Elder (attrib.) 1872. *Robin Hood, prince des voleurs.* Paris: Levy.

—— 1903. Trans. H. Allinson, *Robin Hood: Prince of Thieves.* London: Methuen.

—— 1873. *Robin Hood le proscrit.* Paris: Levy.

—— 1903. Trans. H. Allinson, *Robin Hood The Outlaw.* London: Methuen.

Edgeworth, Maria 1817. *Harrington*, three vols London: Hunter.

Egan, Pierce, the Younger 1840. *Robin Hood and Little John: or The Merry Men of Sherwood Forest*. London: Forster and Hextall.

Emmett, George 1869. *Robin Hood and the Outlaws of Sherwood Forest*, Young Englishman's Edition. London: Temple.

Evans, Thomas 1777. *Old Ballads, Historical and Narrative, with some of modern date*, four vols London: Evans.

G.F. 1840. Review Article on Pierce Egan's *Robin Hood and Little John*, in *London and Westminster Quarterly*, 33 (1840), pp. 425–91.

'Forest Ranger' *c*.1870. *Little John and Will Scarlett: Outlaws of Sherwood Forest*, in 40 numbers. London: Harrison.

Forster, E.M. 1971. *Maurice*. London: Edward Arnold.

Fraser, Antonia 1957. *Robin Hood*. London: Weidenfeld and Nicholson.

Frischmann, Phillipa and Lane, Philip 1981. *Robin Hood and the Greenwood Gang*. London: Universal.

Godwin, Parke 1991. *Sherwood*. New York: Morrow.

Gough, Richard 1786. *Sepulchral Monuments in Great Britain*, two vols London: Nichols.

Gow, Ronald 1932. *Five Robin Hood Plays, The Nelson Playbooks*, ed. John Hampden. London: Nelson.

Grafton, Richard 1568–9. *A Chronicle at Large and meere History of the affayres of England; and Kings of the Same*. London: Tottle and Toye.

Green, Roger Lancelyn 1956. *The Adventures of Robin Hood*. London: Puffin.

Greenberg, Martin H., ed. 1991. *The Fantastic Adventures of Robin Hood*. New York: Signet 1991.

Greene, Robert (?) 1599. *George A Greene*. London: Stafford; ed. J.C. Collins, *The Plays and Poems of Richard Greene*, vol. II, 1905. Oxford: Clarendon.

Gudgeon, F. 1909. *Robin Hood and his Merry Men*. London: Frowde and Hodder.

Gutch, J.M. ed. 1847. *A Lytelle Gest of Robin Hood with other Auncient and Modern Ballads and Songs Relating to the Celebrated Yeoman*, two vols London: Longman.

Hall, Edward 1809. *The History of England during the Reign of Henry the Fourth and the Succeeding Monarchs to the end of the Reign of Henry the Eighth*, ed. Sir H. Ellis. London: Johnson, Rivington et al.

Hampden, John ed., 1931. *Six Modern Plays, Teaching of English Series*, no. 164. London: Nelson.

Hazlitt, W.C. 1892. *Tales and Legends of National Origin*. London: Swann and Sonnenschein.

Holdstock, Robert 1984. *Mythago Wood*. London: Gollancz.

Holinshed, Raphael 1577. *The Chronicles of England, Scotland and Irelande*, three vols London: Harrison.

Horowitz, Anthony 1986. *Richard Carpenter's Robin of Sherwood: The Hooded Man*. London: Puffin.

Hughes, John 1832. *The Pindar of Wakefield's Legend*. London: Moyes.

Hunt, Leigh 1855. *Stories in Verse*. London: Routledge.

James, G.P.R. 1843. *Forest Days*, three vols London: Saunders and Otley.

Jonson, Ben 1905. *The Sad Shepherd with a Completion by F.G. Waldron*, ed. W.W. Greg, in Material zur Kunde des alteren Englischen Drama, vol. 11. Louvain: Uystpruyst.

Jonson, Ben 1941. *The Sad Shepherd*, ed. C.H. Herford and F. and E. Simpson in *The Works of Ben Jonson*, vol. VII. Oxford: Clarendon.

Keats. John 1970. *The Poems*, ed. M. Allott. London: Longman.

Kilvert, Francis 1938. *Diary*, ed. W. Plomer. London: Cape.

Kings Bench 1441. *Kings Bench* 27 737 Rm 5r. London: HMSO.

Kushner, Ellen 1985. *Outlaws of Sherwood Forest, Choose Your Own Adventure*, 47. New York: Bantam.

Lamb, Charles 1837. *Letters*, ed. T. Talfourd. London: Moxon.

Langland, William 1975. *Piers Plowman: The B Version*, ed. G. Kane and E.T. Donaldson. London: Athlone.

Latimer, Hugh 1869. *Seven Sermons Before Edward VI*, ed. E. Arber. London: Murray.

Leland, John 1770. *Collecteana* in *Itinerary*, third ed. Oxford: Fletcher.

Lewis, Richard, see 'Porrence, Peter'.

Logan, John 1783. *Runnamede*. London: Cadell.

Machyn, Henry 1848. *The Diary of Henry Machyn, Citizen of London*. London: Camden Society, vol. 42.

MacKinley, Robin 1988. *The Outlaws of Sherwood*. New York: Ace.

McNally, Leonard and Shield, William 1784. *The Comic Opera of Robin Hood, or Sherwood Forest*. London: Cadell.

Major, John 1521. *Historia Majoris Britanniae Tam: Agliae quam Scotiae*. Paris: Ex Officia Ascensiana.

—— 1892. *A History of Greater Britain As Well England and Scotland*, trans. and ed. Aeneas J.G. Mackay, *Scottish History Publications*, 10. Edinburgh University Press.

Malory, Sir Thomas 1470–1. *The Works*, ed. E. Vinaver, second ed. 1967. London: Oxford University Press.

Mason, Paul 1987. *Richard Carpenter's Robin of Sherwood Game Book 2: The Sword of The Templar*. London: Puffin.

Matheson, Elizabeth 1914. *Robin Hood and His Merry Men*. London: Oxford University Press.

May, Robin 1985. *Richard Carpenter's Robin of Sherwood and the Hounds of Lucifer*. London: Puffin.

Mendez, Moses 1751. *Robin Hood: A New Musical Entertainment*. London: Cooper.

Miles, Bernard 1979. *Robin Hood: His Life and Legend*. London: Hamlyn.

Miller, Thomas 1838. *Royston Gower*. London: Nicholson.

Munday, Anthony 1601. *The Downfall of Robert Earle of Huntington*. London: Leacke; reprinted Malone Society, 1965.

—— and H. Chettle 1601. *The Death of Robert Earle of Huntington*. London: Leacke; reprinted Malone Society, London, 1967.

—— 1615. *Metropolis Coronata, The Triumph of Ancient Drapery*. London: Purslowe.

Newbolt, Sir Henry 1917. *The Book of the Happy Warrior*. London: Longman.

—— 1925. *The Greenwood, Teaching of English Series*, 40. London: Nelson.

Niccols, Richard 1616. *London's Artillery*. London: Welby.

Nielson, Dennis 1984. *Robin Hood: The Truth Behind the Green Tights*. London: French.

Noyes, Alfred 1911. *Sherwood*. London: Watt.

—— 1926. *Robin Hood*. Edinburgh: Blackwood.

Oakden, E.C. 1925. *Pattern Plays, Teaching of English Series*, no. 20. London: Nelson.

O'Keeffe, J. 1795. *Merry Sherwood or Harlequin Forester*, seventh edition. London: Longman.

Oman, Carola 1939. *Robin Hood: The Prince of Outlaws*. London: Dent.

Oxenford, John 1860. *Robin Hood: An Opera*, with music by G.A. MacFarren. London: Cramer, Beale and Chappel.

Parker, Martin 1632. *A True Tale of Robin Hood*. London: Grove; reprinted Child, 1965, III, no. 154, pp. 227–33.

Paston family 1976. *Paston Letters and Papers of the Fifteenth Century*, ed. Norman Davis, two vols Oxford: Clarendon Press.

Peacock, Thomas Love 1822. *Maid Marian*, ed. George Saintsbury, 1895. London: Macmillan.

Peck, Francis 1735. 'Robin Whood Turned Hermit' MS Additional 28638, British Library; reprinted Gutch, II. 412–15.

Peele, George, 1593. *The Famous Chronicle of Edward I*. London: Jeffes; reprinted Malone Society, 1911.

Percival, Milton, ed. 1916. 'Robin Hood and the Duke of Lancaster,' in *Political Ballads Illustrating the Administration of Sir Robert Walpole*, Oxford Historical and Literary Studies 8. Oxford: Clarendon Press.

'Percy, Stephen' (= John Cundall) 1840. *Robin Hood and his Merry Foresters*. London: Bohn.

Percy, Thomas 1765. *Reliques of Auncient English Poetry*, three vols London: Dodsley.

—— 1867. *The Percy Folio Manuscript*, ed. F.J. Furnivall and J.W. Hales. London: Trubner.

'Porrence, Peter' (= Richard Lewis) 1865. *The Life and Adventures of Robin Hood*. London: no publisher.

Porter, Alan 1944. *The Sad Shepherd: The Unfinished Pastoral Comedy of Ben Jonson Now Completed*. New York: Day.

Pyle, Howard 1883. *The Merry Adventures of Robin Hood of Great Renown in Nottinghamshire*. New York: Scribners.

—— 1979. *The Merry Adventures of Robin Hood*, adapted by Deborah Kestel. New York: Playmore Press.

Quiller-Couch, Sir Arthur T. 1908. *Robin Hood: Old Ballads*. Oxford: Clarendon.

—— 1910. *The Oxford Book of Ballads*. Oxford: Clarendon.

Reynolds, John Hamilton 1928. *Poetry and Prose*. London: Milford.

Ritson, J. 1795. *Robin Hood, A Collection of all the Ancient Poems, Songs and Ballads Now Extant Relative to the Celebrated English Outlaw (To Which are Prefixed Historical Anecdotes of His Life)*, two vols London: Egerton and Johnson.

—— 1832 second ed., two vols London: Pickering.

Robinson, Richard 1583. *The Auncient Order of Prince Arthur*. London: Wolfe.

Robinson, Tony 1989. *Maid Marian and her Merry Men: Robert the Incredible Chicken*. London: BBC Books.

Scott, Sir Walter 1819. *Ivanhoe*, ed. A.N. Wilson, 1986. London: Penguin.

—— 1820. *The Abbot*, ed. A. Lang, Borders Edition, vol. XI, 1892. Edinburgh: Blackwood.

—— 1810. *The Lady of the Lake*, 1942 ed. London: Collins.

Skelton, John 1980. *Majorifycence*, ed. P. Neuss. London.

Southey, Robert and Caroline 1847. *Robin Hood: A Fragment*. Edinburgh: Blackwood.

Squire, J.C. 1928. *Robin Hood: A Farcical Romantic Pastoral*. London: Heinemann.

Staplehurst, Graham 1987. *Richard Carpenter's Robin of Sherwood Game Book 1: The King's Demon*. London: Puffin.

Stocqueler, Joachim, Brooks C.W. and Kearney, C.L. 1846. *Robin Hood and Richard Coeur de Lion*, in *Plays*, 1859. London: Fairbrother.

—— 1849. *Maid Marian or, The Forest Queen*. London: Pierce.

Stokes, J.D. 1986. 'Robin Hood and the Churchwardens in Yeovil,' *Medieval and Renaissance Drama in England* 3, pp. 1–25.

Stow, John 1592. *The Annales of England*. London: Newbery.

Stukeley, William 1743–52. *Palaeographica Britannica*, vol. II. Stamford: Rogers.

Tennyson, Lord Alfred 1891. *The Foresters*, in *Poems and Plays*, Oxford Standard Authors edition, 1965. London: Oxford University Press.

Thoms, William 1858. *A Collection of Early English Prose Romances*. London: Nattali and Bond.

Thoreau, Henry 1863. 'Walking' in *Excursions*. Boston: Tickner and Fields.

Tiddy, R.J.E. 1923. *The Mummers' Play*. Oxford: Clarendon.

Trease. Geoffrey 1934. *Bows Against the Barons*. London: Martin Lawrence.

Vansittart, Peter 1981. *The Death of Robin Hood*. London: Owen.

Waldron, Francis 1783. *The Sad Shepherd, with a Continuation by Francis Waldron*. London: Nichols.

Warner, William 1589. *The First and Second Parts of Albions England*. London: Orwin.

White, T.H. 1938. *The Sword in The Stone*. London: Collins.

Williams, Jay 1956. *The Good Yeoman*. London: Macdonald.

Wordsworth, William 1954. *Collected Works*, ed. E. de Selincourt. London: Oxford University Press.

—— 1850. *The Prelude*, ed. E. de Selincourt, 1926. London: Oxford University Press.

Wu, William F. 1990. *Robert Silverberg's Time Tours: The Robin Hood Ambush*. New York: Harper.

PRIMARY SOURCES: FILMED

Note: listed in chronological order.

Robin Hood and His Merry Men. Clarendon 1909.

Robin Hood – Outlawed. British and Colonial 1912.

In the Days of Robin Hood. Producer unknown. 1912.

Robin Hood. Eclair 1913.

Robin Hood. Thanhouser 1913.

Robin Hood. United Artists 1922.

The Adventures of Robin Hood. Warner 1938.

Robin Hood Makes Good (animation). Warner 1939.

The Bandit of Sherwood Forest. Columbia 1946.

The Prince of Thieves. Columbia/Katzman 1948.

Rabbit Hood (animation). Warner 1949.
Rogues of Sherwood Forest. Columbia 1950.
Tales of Robin Hood. Roach 1951.
The Story of Robin Hood and His Merrie Men. Disney 1952.
Adventures of Robin Hood (TV): Sapphire 1956–60.
Men of Sherwood Forest. Hammer 1957.
Son of Robin Hood. 20th Century Fox 1958.
Robin Hood Daffy. Warner 1959.
Sword of Sherwood Forest. Hammer 1961.
A Challenge for Robin Hood. Hammer 1962.
Robin and the Seven Hoods. Warner 1964.
Robin Hood (animation). Apia TV films 1971.
Wolfshead. Hammer 1973.
Robin Hood (animation). Disney 1973.
Robin and Marion. Columbia/Raster 1976.
Arrows of Robin Hood. Sovfilm 1978.
The Adventures of Robin Hood (animation). ASD 1981.
Robin Hood: A High Spirited Tale of Adventure. Muppets 1981.
The Zany Adventures of Robin Hood. Austin 1984.
Robin of Sherwood (TV). Goldcrest 1984–6.
Maid Marian (TV). BBC 1988–9.
Fellow Traveller. BBC/HBO 1989.
Robin Hood: Prince of Thieves. Morgan Creek 1991.
Robin Hood. 20th Century Fox/Working Title 1991.
Robin Hood: Men in Tights. Columbia 1993.

SECONDARY SOURCES

Anderson, Benedict 1983. *Imagined Communities*. London: Verso.
Baldi, Sergio 1949. *Studi Sulla Poesa Popolare D'Inghilterra e di Scozia*. Rome: Edizioni di Storia E Letteratura.
Barnard, John 1989. 'Keats's "Robin Hood", John Hamilton Reynolds and the "Old Poets",' *Proceedings of the British Academy*, 75, pp. 181–200.
Barry, Edmond 1832. *Thèse de littérature sur les vicissitudes et les transformations du cycle populaire de Robin Hood*. Paris: Rignoux.
Barton, Anne 1984. *Ben Jonson: Dramatist*. Cambridge University Press.
Behlmer, Rudy 1965. 'Robin Hood on the Screen', *Films in Review*, 16, pp. 91–102.
Bellamy, John C. 1985. *Robin Hood: An Historical Inquiry*. London: Croom Helm.
Bell's Life 1859. Melbourne: Bell.
Bessinger, Jess B. Jr 1974. 'The *Gest of Robin Hood* Revisited,' in *The Learned and the Lewed*, ed. L.D. Benson. Harvard University Press, pp. 355–69.
—— 1966. 'Robin Hood: Folklore and Historiography, 1377–1500,' *Tennessee Studies in Literature*, 11, pp. 61–9.

Bevington, David 1968. *Tudor Drama and Politics*. Harvard University Press.

Bhabha, Homi (ed.) 1989. *Nation and Narration*. London: Routledge.

Bristol, Michael 1985. *Carnival and Theater: Plebeian Culture and the Structure of Authority in Renaissance England*. London: Methuen.

Bromwich, Rachel 1978. *Trioedd Ynys Prydein*, second ed. Cardiff: University of Wales Press.

Bronson, Bertrand 1959–72. *The Traditional Tunes of the Child Ballads*, four vols Princeton: Princeton University Press.

Buckley, Jerome 1960. *The Growth of a Poet*. Harvard University Press.

Butler, Marilyn 1979. *Peacock Displayed*. London: Routledge.

—— 1981. *Romantics, Revolutionaries and Reactionaries: English Literature and Its Background*, 1760–1830. London: Oxford University Press.

—— 1992. 'Introduction' to Maria Edgeworth, *Castle Rackrent*. London: Penguin.

Callenbach, Ernest 1969–70. 'Comparative Anatomy of Folk-Myth Films: Robin Hood and Antonio das Mortes,' *Film Quarterly*, 23, pp. 42–7.

Cecil, Algernon 1915. *Life of Robert Cecil, First Earl of Salisbury*. London: Murray.

Chambers, E.K. 1903. *The Medieval Stage*, two vols Oxford: Clarendon.

—— 1923. *The Elizabethan Stage*. Oxford: Clarendon.

—— 1933. *The English Folk Play*. Oxford: Clarendon.

—— 1945. *English Literature at the Close of the Middle Ages (Oxford History of English Literature)*, vol. II pt. 2. Oxford: Clarendon.

Chase, Malcolm and Whyman, Mark 1991. *Heartbreak Hill*. Cleveland: Borough Council.

Clawson, William H. 1909. *The Gest of Robin Hood*. University of Toronto Library.

Collins, John Churton 1905. See under Greene, Robert 1599 in Primary Sources.

Cooper, Helen 1977. *Pastoral: Medieval into Renaissance*. Ipswich: Brewer.

Coss, Paul R. 1985. 'Aspects of Cultural Diffusion in Medieval England: The Early Romances, Local Society and Robin Hood,' in *Past and Present*, 108, pp. 35–79.

Crook, David 1984. 'Some Further Evidence Concerning the Dating of the Origins of the Legend of Robin Hood,' in *English Historical Review*, 99, pp. 530–4.

Dawson, Christopher 1970. *His Fine Wit*. London: Routledge.

'D.H.' (= Richard Gough) 1793. Note on Earl of Huntington, *Gentleman's Magazine*, March, p. 226.

Dickstein, Morris 1971. *Keats and His Poetry: A Study in Development*. Chicago University Press.

Dictionary of National Biography 1885–1900, ed. Sir Leslie Stephen and Sir Sidney Lee. London: Smith, Elder.

Disher, M.W. 1925. *Clowns and Pantomimes*. London: Constable.

Dobson, R.B. and Taylor, John 1976. *Rymes of Robin Hood: An Introduction to the English Outlaw*. London: Heinemann.

Doyle, Brian 1989. *English and Englishness*. London: Routledge.

Eidson, J.O. 1964. 'Tennyson, *The Foresters* and the American Stage,' *Philological Quarterly*, 43, pp. 549–57.

Ellis, Bob 1991. 'Roughcut', *Encore*, 2–15 August, p. 10.

Fowler, David C. 1968. *A Literary History of the Popular Ballad*. Durham: Duke University Press.

Gable, J.H. 1939. *A Bibliography of Robin Hood*. Lincoln: *University of Nebraska Studies in Language and Criticism* no. 17.

Gagey, E.M. 1937. *Ballad Opera*. New York: Blom.

Gough, Richard, see 'D.H.'

Graves, Robert 1948. *The White Goddess*. London: Faber.

Gray, Douglas 1984. 'The Robin Hood Poems', *Poetica* 18, pp. 1–39.

Hales, J.W. and Snell, F. 1910. 'Robin Hood' in *Encyclopedia Britannica*, 11th ed., pp. 420–1. London: Cambridge University Press.

Halliwell, Leslie 1990. *Halliwell's Film Guide*, seventh ed. London: Paladin.

Hanawalt, Barbara A. 1992 'Ballads and Bandits: Fourteen Century Outlaws and the Robin Hood Poems,' in *Chaucer's England: Literature in Historical Context, Medieval Studies at Minnesota*, 4, pp. 154–75.

Hancock, Ralph and Fairbanks, Letitia 1953. *Douglas Fairbanks: The Fourth Musketeer*. New York: Holt.

Hark, Ina Rae 1976. 'The Visual Politics of *The Adventures of Robin Hood*,' *Journal of Popular Fiction*, 5, pp. 3–17.

Harris, Percy Valentine 1972. *The Truth About Robin Hood*, seventh ed. Mansfield: Linneys.

Harvey, I.M.W. 1991. *Jack Cade's Rebellion*. Oxford: Clarendon.

Hayes, Thomas W. 1992. *The Birth of Popular Culture: Ben Jonson, Maid Marian and Robin Hood*. Pittsburgh: Duquesne University Press.

Hill, Christopher 1965. 'The Norman Yoke' in *Puritanism and Revolution*, pp. 50–112. London: Secker & Warburg.

Hilton, Rodney ed. 1976. *Peasants, Knights and Heretics*. Cambridge University Press.

Hoare, Adrian and Anne 1985. *On the Trail of Robert Kett*. Wymondham: The Wymondham Society.

Hobsbawm, E.J. 1985. *Bandits*, second ed. London: Penguin.

Hogan, C.B. 1968. *The London Stage, 1660–1800, Pt. 5, vol. 2, 1776–1800*, Carbondale: Southern Illinois University Press.

Holt, J.C. 1982. *Robin Hood* (revised ed. 1990). London: Thames and Hudson.

Hunter, Joseph 1852. 'The Great Hero of the Ancient Minstrelsy of England: Robin Hood, his period, real character etc. investigated,' *Critical and Historical Tracts*, IV, pp. 28–38. London: Smith.

Jones, Kathleen 1988. *A Glorious Fame: The Life of Margaret Cavendish, Duchess of Newcastle, 1623–73*. London: Bloomsbury.

Keen, Maurice 1961. *The Outlaws of Medieval England*. London: Routledge.

Kevelson, Roberta 1977. *Inlaws/Outlaws: A Semiotics of Systematic Interaction: 'Robin Hood' and the 'King's Law'*. Bloomington: Indiana University Press.

Kinnard, Roy and Vitone, R.J. 1986. *The American Films of Michael Curtiz*. London: Scarecrow.

Knight, Stephen 1993. 'Robin Hood and the Royal Restoration,' *Critical Survey*, 5, pp. 298–312.

Lardner Jr., Ring 1991. 'Life Under a Cloud' *Age*, Melbourne, 22 March, 1991, p. 14.

Maddicott, J.R. 1978. 'The Birth and Setting of the Ballads of Robin Hood,' in *English Historical Review*, 93, pp. 276–99.

Mangan, John 1991. 'Sherwood is Her Wood,' *Age*, Melbourne, March 21, p. 10.

Martin, Robert B. 1980. *The Unquiet Heart*. Oxford: Clarendon.

Matthews, David 1980. *Michael Tippett: An Introduction*. London: Faber.

Matthews, John 1993. *Robin Hood: Green Lord of the Wildwood*. Glastonbury: Gothic Image.

Miles, Bernard, 1984. 'C Leopatra: her latest lover – Lindsay and the theatre,' in *Culture and History: Essays Presented to Jack Lindsay*, ed. Bernard Smith, pp. 225–8. Sydney: Haleard Leamonger.

Mill, A.E. 1927. *Medieval Plays in Scotland*. Edinburgh: Blackwood.

Murray, Margaret 1931. *The God of the Witches*. London: Faber.

Nelson, M.A. 1973. *The Robin Hood Tradition in the English Renaissance*. Salzburg: *Salzburg Studies in English Literature, Elizabethan Studies* 14.

Nesbitt, Elizabeth 1966. *Howard Pyle*. London: Bodley Head.

Newbolt, Sir Henry 1925. 'Peacock, Scott and Robin Hood,' *Dalhousie Review*, 4, pp. 411–32.

Nicoll, Allardyce 1965. *A History of English Drama 1600–1900*, vol. II, *Early Eighteenth Century Drama*. Cambridge University Press.

—— 1966. *A History of English Drama, 1600–1900*, vol. III, *Late Eighteenth Century Drama, 1750–1800*. Cambridge University Press.

Owen, L.V.D. 1936. 'Robin Hood in the Light of Research,' in *The Times, Trade and Engineering Supplement*, 38, no. 864, p. xxix.

Pearsall, D.A. (ed.) 1962. *The Floure and the Leafe and The Assembly of Ladies*. London: Nelson.

Pinto, V. de Sola and Rodway, Allan 1957. *The Common Muse*. London: Chatto and Windus.

Prideaux, W.F. 1886. 'Who Was Robin Hood,' *Notes and Queries*, 7th Series, II, pp. 421–4.

Raglan, Lord 1949. *The Hero*. London: Watts.

Richards, Jeffrey 1977. *Swordsmen of the Screen: From Douglas Fairbanks to Michael York*. London: Routledge.

Rubin, Abba 1984. *The English Jew in English Literature 1660–1830*. Westport: Greenwood.

Schickel, Richard 1976. *Douglas Fairbanks – The First Celebrity*. London: Elm Tree.

Scott, Clement V. and Howard, Cecil 1891. *The Life and Reminiscences of E.L. Blanchard*. London: Hutchinson.

Shippey, Tom 1991. 'Japes in the Greenwood,' in *Times Literary Supplement*, 2 August, p. 16.

Simeone, W.E. 1951. 'The May Games and the Robin Hood Legend,' *Journal of American Folklore*, 64, pp. 265–74.

Spence, Lewis 1928. 'Robin Hood in Scotland,' *Chambers Journal*, 18, pp. 94–6.

—— 1948. *The Fairy Tradition in Britain*. London: Rider.

Stallybrass, Peter 1985. 'Drunk with the Cup of Liberty': Robin Hood, the Carnivalesque and the Rhetoric of Violence in Early Modern England,' *Semiotica*, 54, pp. 113–45.

Steadman, J.M. Jr 1919. 'The Dramatization of the Robin Hood Ballads' *Modern Philology*, 17, pp. 9–23.

Tardif, Richard 1983. 'The "Mistery" of Robin Hood: A New Social Context for the Texts,' in *Words and Worlds: Studies in the Social Role of Verbal Culture*, ed. Stephen Knight and S.N. Mukherjee, pp. 130–45. Sydney Association for Studies in Society and Culture.

Tennyson, Hallam 1897. *A Memoir of Lord Tennyson*, two vols London: Macmillan.

Thierry, August 1825. *Histoire de la conquête de l'Angleterre par les Normands*. Paris: Firmin Didot.

Thorndike, A.H. 1902. 'The Relationship of As You Like it to the Robin Hood Plays'; in *Journal of English and Germanic Philology*, 4, pp. 59–69.

Ungerer, S. 1961. 'An Unrecorded Elizabethan Performance of Titus Andronicus,' in *Shakespeare Survey*, 14, pp. 102–9.

Vinaver, Eugene 1971. *The Rise of Romance*. Oxford: Clarendon.

Wickham, Glynne 1963. *Early English Stages, 1300–1600*, vol. 2. London: Routledge.

—— 1981. *Early English Stages, 1300–1600*, vol 3. London: Routledge.

Wiles, David 1981. *The Early Plays of Robin Hood*. Cambridge: Brewer.

Williams, Raymond 1973. *The Country and the City*. London: Chatto and Windus.

Winwood, Sir Ralph 1725. *Memoir of Lord Burleigh* in Edmund Sawyer ed. *Memorials of Affairs of State in the Reigns of Queen Elizabeth and King James*, three vols London: Ward.

Index

Note: Proper names, places, major thematic issues and texts with references to the myth have been indexed alphabetically. In order to provide a synoptic view of the ballads, their titles have been indexed under Robin Hood Ballads, and an entry on characters of importance is found under Robin Hood Characters.